Advance Praise

"Cohen's book not only captures the essential parts of Peter Drucker's management principles, he offers tangible advice on how to effectively use them as a management consultant. This is a thorough and well-researched book from a man who worked so closely with Drucker that it reads as if Drucker wrote this himself. This is sure to become the go to book for anyone interested in business consulting."
F. Lee Reynolds, Senior Manager - Studio Tour, Universal Studios, Hollywood

"Peter Drucker is gone. Fortunately his student, Bill Cohen, carries on Drucker's work. *Consulting Drucker* is not just good advice for those who are professional consultants. It reveals aspects of Drucker's work that are rarely discussed and not closely analysed. How was Drucker able to be so successful as a consultant, working alone, in so many different environments? His consulting work included industries and many countries from governments and the military to even individual entrepreneurs and religious organizations. This book has the answers, answers that all managers need and can profit from."
Bill Bartmann, author of *Bouncing Back* and other books; President and Founder, CFS, CFS2, Inc. and Financial Samaritan.com, assisted 4.5 million debtor clients in rebuilding their lives.

"Peter Drucker once explained his greatest strength as a consultant was to be ignorant and asked a few questions. It sounds simple but difficult to apply. Now you can learn and practice Drucker's legendary consulting methodology through *Consulting Drucker* written by Dr. Cohen, the first and favorite PhD graduate of Drucker. His first hand observation from Drucker with simple but effective techniques is very fascinating and insightful. You just cannot miss this invaluable book."
Julia Wang, President, Peter F. Drucker Academy, Hong Kong

"Business consultants come in three flavours. The first is familiar with Peter Drucker the author. The second loves Drucker, occasionally quoting him to clients. The third understands Drucker, applying his ideas multiple times a day. I have yet to meet a business consultant who has not heard of Peter Drucker. General Cohen, one of Professor Drucker's first students and a veteran business consultant and business academic, here describes and explains Drucker's early beginnings, his routines, and his lasting intellectual contributions. By reading this book, you'll save countless hours deciphering his work, and your clients will benefit immediately."
Nevin Kamath, JD, former Director, The Consulting Institute, CIAM and former Senior Consultant, McKinsey & Company, President and Founder, Kamath & Company

"I acquired an EMBA from Claremont Graduate School, Drucker School of Management where I had the privilege of experiencing Peter Ducker's lectures and discussions first hand. I have known Bill Cohen for over three decades and had the privilege of professionally sharing his account of Peter Ducker's management and leadership frameworks in the military, industrial and healthcare sectors. Dr. Cohen's recent expanded account *Consulting Drucker* is insightful, astute and accurate."
Albert M. Randall, MD, Colonel, USAF, Ret. Board of Directors Corona Regional Medical Center

Advance Praise
From
Previous Books

From *A Class with Drucker*

"A fresh look at the timeless wisdom of Peter Drucker. This riveting book reveals previously unpublished ideas that Drucker shared with his students and offers a glimpse into what it was like to know the man himself."
Edward T. Reilly, President and CEO,
American Management Association

"A Class with Drucker is more than a book – it is a great gift, bringing Peter Drucker and his classroom alive for all of us who never had the privilege of a class with Drucker ... Bill Cohen's journey with Drucker adds a new dimension to our understanding and appreciation and keeps the Drucker legacy vibrant and alive for future generations."
Frances Hesselbein, Chairman and Founding President,
Leader to Leader Institute

"Bill Cohen brings that laboratory of learning alive to those of us who didn't have the pleasure, privilege or opportunity to sit at the feet of the master in Peter's classroom. One can feel the energy, the humour, the discipline, the interaction, the edge, the energy, the simplicity and the relevance of Peter's practice of teaching. This is a gift Bill has produced as a way of returning the favour and blessing of Peter's friendship and caring for Bill over more 30 years."
Ira Jackson, Dean, Peter F. Drucker and Masatoshi Ito Graduate School of Management, Claremont Graduate University

"Drucker said it best when he said that marketing and innovation are the most important business functions because they generate new customers. So, believe me, anything he said about marketing is worth reading. There's no better thinker."
Jack Trout, President, Trout & Partners Ltd., and co-author of *Positioning*

"Every successful organization must be about "creating and keeping customers." This book is about the essence of marketing. It reflects Bill Cohen's unique ability to understand and communicate Peter Drucker's thoughts and ideas about this subject with the added touch of how to implement them in a dynamic and changing world."
C. William Pollard, Chairman Emeritus, The ServiceMaster Company

"Perhaps the only real flaw in Peter Drucker's work is that there is so incredibly much of it – some 10,000 book pages, plus countless articles from newspapers, magazines and scholarly journals. How can you possibly begin to pull out just what you're looking for? Thankfully, we now have *Drucker on Marketing* in which Bill Cohen has synthesized and analysed and brought to life the single subject that, in many respects, lies at the heart of all of Drucker's writing: how to create a customer. This is a major contribution."
Rick Wartzman, Executive Director, Drucker Institute and columnist for Forbes.com

"Easy reading, good logic, and a novel approach. It will deservedly attract a wide range of readers."
James Wood, Chairman and CEO,
The Great Atlanta and Pacific Tea Company, Inc.

From *The Art of the Strategist*

"This book is a 'must read' for anyone responsible for leading an organization. It is so engrossing that it is almost impossible to put down, but more importantly it is a sure recipe for success. I am gifting a copy to the management of all of my portfolio companies."
Harvey Knell, CEO, KCM Management, Inc.,
former President and CEO, Grace Homes Centers West

"Outstanding! An indispensable guide for strategists and decision makers. Master the ten principles in this book and you will master your competition."
Michael A. Mische, CEO, Synergy Industries,
former Principal, KPMG Peat Marwick
and author of *Strategic Renewal*

"Everyone who reads this book will wish that they had done what it recommends a long time ago."
Ambassador **Ronald F. Lehman, II**, PhD, former Director
of the U.S. Arms Control and Disarmament Agency and
Assistant Secretary of Defense for International Security Policy

Published by
LID Publishing Inc.
524 Broadway, 11th Floor, Suite 08-120,
New York, NY 10012, US

The Record Hall, Studio 204,
16-16a Baldwins Gardens,
London EC1N 7RJ, UK

info@lidpublishing.com
www.lidpublishing.com

A member of:

BPR
Business Publishers Roundtable

www.businesspublishersroundtable.com

© William A. Cohen, PhD, 2018
© LID Publishing Inc., 2018
Reprinted in 2019

Printed in the United States
ISBN: 978-1-911498-67-4

Cover and page design: Caroline Li & Matthew Renaudin

CONSULTING
DRUCKER

PRINCIPLES AND LESSONS
FROM THE WORLD'S LEADING
MANAGEMENT CONSULTANT

WILLIAM A. COHEN, PHD

MADRID | MEXICO CITY | LONDON
NEW YORK | BUENOS AIRES
BOGOTA | SHANGHAI | NEW DELHI

Dedication

I'd like to dedicate this book to the following individuals:

Dean Paul Albrecht who along with Peter Drucker developed the PhD Programme to which I am proud to have been the first graduate.

Minglo Shao who had both the determination, ability, and generosity to found both the Peter Drucker Academy of China and the non-profit California Institute of Advanced Management (CIAM) and to serve as its chairman.

My colleagues, administrators, professors, and board members at CIAM who through their courage and hard work have performed above and beyond the call of duty and succeeded under adversity in building a school teaching Drucker's principles and while implementing new concepts and elements available nowhere else.

CIAM's students and graduates who by their success are proving the value of Peter Drucker's concepts.

Finally to two people who not only impacted on this book, but on its author:

My wife, Dr Nurit Cohen, who through 48 years of wars, challenges, defeats, and victories on several continents has never wavered in her support.

And of course, Peter Drucker himself who saw something in me during a time of great trial that I did not see in myself.

Table of Contents

Foreword

I would like to offer my deepest gratitude to Dr William Cohen for his kind invitation to write the prologue for his new book, for his friendship through the years, and for the honour of serving as a member of the board of the *California Institute of Advanced Management (CIAM)*. I would also like to acknowledge his unwavering entrepreneurial spirit, particularly in the face of the many challenges he overcame to found CIAM in 2011. I mention CIAM because this institution is based on the principles and values of Peter F. Drucker, which form the pillars of this book.

William Cohen, a friend and colleague of mine, was directly inspired by Peter Drucker. A member of the first generation of Drucker PhDs from the *Peter F. Drucker and Masatoshi Ito Graduate School of Management of Claremont Graduate University*, we learn a lot about Drucker through the eyes of Cohen.

Both of these men, William Cohen and Peter Drucker, have in common a powerful vision, energy, and drive, necessary qualities to make big things happen. Indeed, we are very fortunate to have the opportunity to continue Drucker's ideas and dreams, enabling them to grow and multiply on a larger scale. Through this book, Dr Cohen shares with us Drucker's ideology and philosophy. He honours and recalls Drucker's consulting principles, while remembering his achievements and recounting his anecdotes, which are readily applicable in both our business and personal lives. In the process, we learn the instruments and skills to empower organizations and companies to build the foundational pillars required to generate economic, social, and environmental value.

I am a great admirer of both men. Dr Cohen's work draws me closer to Drucker's extraordinary lessons and principles, which are so easy to read and understand but often so difficult to implement in our day-to-day lives. All of these principles have proved invaluable for the many people who have inspired young professionals for decades among companies all over the world.

But who is Peter Drucker? Many know him as "the man who invented management". Drucker directly influenced a remarkable number of leaders from a wide range of organizations across all sectors of society, including General Electric, IBM, Intel, Procter & Gamble, Girl Scouts of the USA, The Salvation Army, [The American] Red Cross, and United Farm Workers, as well as several presidential administrations.

Throughout his work, Drucker called for a healthy balance between short-term needs and long-term sustainability; between profitability and other obligations; between the specific mission of individual organizations and the common good; and between freedom and responsibility. This book offers a practical application and explanation of the methodology that Drucker used in his work as a consultant to his clients.

It's all about learning from our mistakes – how to make things different – to get the desired results. When you want the right answer, you must learn to ask the right question. With his clients, Drucker asked direct questions about each of his client's responsibilities and problems (this was his modus operandi, he just asked questions). These questions led to additional questions, which eventually led the client to determine what needed to be done. Drucker then laid out options about how to accomplish this work, and got the client's agreement to proceed.

That's why he used to say, "keep doing what made you currently successful in the past, and you will eventually fail." Applied correctly, Drucker's genius will save you thousands of wasted hours and much frustration. In that way, you will create new ideas for success, and offer better advice to your clients, subordinates, bosses, and fellow executives to help them achieve success. In this book, you will find these principles, concepts, and experiences from hundreds of Drucker's clients, along with others who practise his principles.

Drucker viewed himself as a scientist who investigates human actions and environments. That's why he used to call his work-client relationships "laboratories". He offers a very different, unique perspective of what consulting should be, and those ideals and principles are reflected in this book, along with his work. His methodology is distinct from the conventional; that is what makes it really special and interesting to study, to understand,

and to apply to new era enterprises. This book provides the tools that will enable readers to get more deeply in touch with Drucker's principles in a an easier didactic way, learning about how to conduct professional consulting for startups, small businesses, corporations, and non-profits.

Thanks to Dr Cohen's work, effort, and knowledge of Peter Drucker's life and philosophy, he not only allows us to gain a clearer view and understanding, but also keeps alive Drucker's dream – guiding us throughout his legacy.

"Without action, nothing gets done."
– Peter Drucker

Dr Francisco Suárez Hernández

About Dr Francisco Suárez Hernández

Francisco Suárez Hernández is the vice president of corporate affairs of Coca Cola FEMSA. FEMSA is one of the largest corporations in Mexico, the largest beverage company in Latin America and the largest Coca Cola Bottling Company in the world.

Introduction

My Meeting Peter Drucker, the Father of Modern Management

By Philip Kotler

Though we met and I visited Drucker in his home and remained in contact with him and with Frances Hesselbein, I was not in on any of his consulting sessions in his home with Doris in Claremont. I do remember Peter stressing that the most important tool of inquiry is asking the right questions. Peter's Five Questions about a business are the best set of starting questions. In talking with Peter about the problems of some companies, he preferred taking a long term and strategic view of a company and how its business will or should respond to new demographic, technological, economic, social and political forces. He did not care to talk about a tactical problem facing a company. He was influenced by Schumpeter's concept of capitalism as "creative destruction". Peter saw all companies facing discontinuities (later called disruptions by Clayton Christensen) and he urged companies to imagine what discontinuities they might have to deal with.

I wrote up my personal experiences with Peter in Bill's earlier book, *Drucker on Marketing*, and it will be expanded when I publish *My Adventures in Marketing*. Bill thinks that my story says much about Drucker's character and values, certainly of primary importance for any consultant. Because of this and as a tribute to Peter, I have given Bill permission to include it in *Consulting Drucker.*

It all started with a phone call. From the other end of the phone, I heard a man speaking in English with a German accent. As I listened carefully, he said, "This is Peter Drucker." I was astonished and tried to keep calm. This was because I had closely read his books that are rich in insight and I had great respect for him although I never met him. A call from Peter Drucker meant more to me than if our US President called. He asked "Would you come to Claremont [in California] and talk with me about various things?" I hopped aboard the first airplane the following morning. It was in the second half of the 1980s.

Peter is not only the father of modern management. He also is a major pioneer in the discipline of modern marketing. For more than 40 years, Peter had been explaining to managers that the centre of the company was its customers. Everything in the company should revolve around meeting and satisfying the needs of its customers. Creating customer value is the purpose of marketing.

I was influenced by four questions that Peter posed to companies:
- What is the primary business of your company?
- Who is your customer?
- What does your customer find value in?
- What should you make your primary business?

Later, of course, he added a fifth, coming from initially "What are you going to do about it?" which became "What is your plan?"

Each time Peter came face to face with one of the CEOs of a company such as P&G or Intel, he asked these questions. And CEOs testified that they achieved many insights in trying to answer Peter's questions. I put similar questions to many companies I consult.

Peter's books and remarks are full of appropriate sayings about marketing and customers. I would like to mention some of them along with what they imply.

For example, he said: "The purpose of a business is to create a customer." This statement was in direct opposition to the view of most managers in those days that the purpose of a business is to create profit. For Peter, this view of managers is an empty theory that lacks the important idea of how to create profit. It is to create customers. To create customers, a company has to provide higher value (benefits minus costs) than its competitors. The only source of profit is customers.

Peter also said: "Business has only two basic functions – innovation and marketing; all the rest are costs." While being fully aware that all business functions are necessary and make a contribution, he singled out these two functions. Innovation means that companies cannot stand still when technologies and consumers' tastes are changing. And marketing needs to be strong if customers are to learn about the product and to know its features and price and locations. A company cannot be successful if it is strong only in innovation or in marketing but not in both.

He also clarified the difference between marketing and sales. He stunned managers by saying that "the purpose of marketing is to make selling unnecessary". He thought that it was important to understand customers' needs deeply and create products that customers line up to buy without any sales prompting.

Peter criticized companies that first designed a product such as a car and only afterwards tried to decide who it is for and what to say about it. It makes more sense for the company to start with a full concept of the customer target and the product's purpose and then design the car to meet and satisfy that customer target.

Back to Peter's phone call and my flight to meet Peter Drucker in Claremont, California. Peter picked me up at the airport, and we went straight to Claremont Graduate University, where he taught. He was a professor of art as well as of management. The university gave Peter a private gallery where he stored his collection of Japanese folding screens and hanging scrolls.

Peter opened and unfolded one hanging scroll after another. Appreciating them, we talked about each work of art. The hours passed quickly. We discussed the fact that Japanese people have a different way to interpret and evaluate art. They like "sabi" a quiet quality that a work of art might have. They like "wabi" a feeling that the work of art had earned a history and experience. Japan's sense of beauty is quite different from Western standards. Peter and I then left the gallery and lunched at a nearby restaurant.

Peter then invited me to his home. I met Peter's wife Doris, who is trained as a physicist and who was a wonderful tennis player and then in her nineties. She greeted me with a smile. I was surprised by the modesty of their home. I was even more surprised to think that Peter had entertained top executives coming from many world-famous companies in their not-so-large living room. There was probably no need for Peter and Doris to show off.

On the evening of that day, Peter took me to a recording studio near his home. Peter was doing research on NPOs (nonprofit organizations) as I was. In the quiet recording studio, he asked me to speak about, how marketing can help leaders of nonprofit organizations improve their performance.

Peter's questions ranged over various topics and were stimulating. His questions about museums and orchestras provoked me to undertake more research into these cultural institutions. Peter summarized our Claremont discussion about nonprofit organizations in his book *Managing the Nonprofit Organization* published in 1990.

When the Peter F. Drucker Foundation for Nonprofit Management was established in 1990, I was invited to become a member of its advisory board. The foundation was set up to help NPOs learn from other NPOs and from managers and scholars to improve their NPO. I attended several annual meetings of the board and made presentations on how nonprofit organizations can develop exciting, creative solutions to social problems.

Peter and I exchanged letters from time to time. What impressed me was that Peter always wrote letters by hand. He used neither a typewriter nor a personal computer to do so. Of course, he may have used these appliances on other occasions, but he never used them for his private letters to me.

For a period, The Drucker Foundation operated under the name of the Leader to Leader Institute. More recently, Frances Hesselbein's board asked her to give the foundation her own name. I know that she did this under pressure. Peter was at first also unwilling to set up a foundation with his name and finally agreed on the condition that his name be removed some years later. His modest character showed itself in such gestures.

Each time I met with Peter, I was stimulated by his overwhelming knowledge of history and his prescient insights into the future. I cannot imagine how he acquired his vast knowledge in such a wide variety of fields.

I think of Peter as a rare Renaissance man who is one of the most remarkable persons that I have had the pleasure to know.

Philip Kotler,
My Adventures in Marketing

About Philip Kotler

Philip Kotler is currently the S. C. Johnson Distinguished Professor of International Marketing at the Kellogg School of Management at Northwestern University. He is the author of over 58 marketing books, including *Marketing Management, Principles of Marketing, Kotler on Marketing: How to Create, Win, and Dominate Markets*, and *Marketing: From Products to Customers to the Human Spirit.*

Professor Kotler is the recipient of numerous awards including 23 honorary degrees and other honours. He was the first person to receive the "Leader in Marketing Thought" award from American Marketing Association. In a survey of 1,000 executives conducted in 25 countries about the Most Influential Business Writers/ Management Gurus by *The Financial Times*, Kotler ranked fourth after Peter Drucker, Bill Gates, and Jack Welch.

Chapter 1

The World's Greatest Independent Consultant

Whem Peter Drucker was my professor – and even later when an unexpected friendship developed – I never thought that I'd write about his principles and concepts, or anything about him. I didn't want to be mentored by him in the traditional sense either. I can't really say why. It may have been my own stubbornness or some desire to "make it on my own" without the help of anyone else. Even after I managed to achieve a modicum of notoriety from my own work, I frequently (almost subconsciously) quoted Drucker in my speeches, taught Drucker in the classroom, and applied his ideas frequently. But I avoided what I considered taking advantage of having been his student, and later his friend.

My First Book about Drucker

It was in 2007, two years after his death, when for the first time I finally sat down to write specifically about what I had learned from Drucker. This in-depth introspection resulted in *A Class with Drucker* (AMACOM, 2008) and gave me tremendous insight as I realized, perhaps for the first time, how much I owed Drucker intellectually, and the tremendous impact his ideas had had on my own thinking.

He once wrote to the head of the search committee at a major university that had proposed to hire me, writing that he, along with other faculties, had learned from me at least as much as they had been able to teach me. I'm not sure if this was entirely complimentary, as it might have referred more to my stubbornness and inability to learn what he attempted to teach, rather than any special information or insights that he and other faculties had gained from having to put up with me in their classes.

I did not consider myself a superior student in any way. Peter's partner in developing one of the first – if not the first – PhD programme for working executives was his dean, Paul Albrecht. Paul's wife, Bernice, and my wife, Nurit, had hit it off and Bernice had been literally talking "out of school". After a party at my house, Nurit told me, "Paul says you are brilliant, but lazy." I answered immediately that either she or Bernice must have misunderstood what Paul had actually said. I told her it was far more likely that he had said the exact opposite: that I worked very hard, but was rather dull-witted.

It was not until I started writing this earlier book (*A Class with Drucker*), that I realized the enormous extent of Peter's intellectual gifts to me personally. My first book on Drucker was followed by several others: *Drucker on Leadership* (Jossey-Bass, 2010), *Drucker on Marketing* (McGraw-Hill, 2013) and *The Practical Drucker* (AMACOM, 2014).

These invariably resulted in a number of interviews and what seemed like endless questions. There was much still unknown and misunderstood about this towering management genius and how he was able to do what he did and what he had actually recommended to his consulting clients that brought success to them and fame to himself. In attempting to answer these questions, it is important to understand that Peter Drucker was not only a great management teacher. While he is known as the "father of modern management", he was also the most celebrated independent management consultant – ever. Yet little was publicized about this aspect of his contributions – his consulting and how it was conducted. Nor, in this context, even what he recommended and what he did not. As he himself maintained to all who would listen, virtually all his ideas came from his consulting. He said that his clients and their organizations were his laboratories, conjuring up images of Drucker at work in a white coat with the smell of pungent chemical compounds or the sparks of electrical activity in the background—not too far afield from the famous *Frankenstein* movie scene. Despite the attraction and mystery of this imagery, the consulting aspect of his legacy is little explored. But the history of Drucker's work as a consultant is not the point of this book. It is application that Drucker sought again and again, and the application of Drucker's consulting practices is what this book is about.

How to Make It Big as a Consultant

How to Make It Big as a Consultant (AMACOM) is the only book I've written on the subject of consulting. It went through four editions (1985, 1991, 2001, and 2009) and was published in many languages. It was also named as "Best Business Book of the Year" in 1985 by the *Library Journal*. That book did not exclude Drucker. In fact, the latest edition includes numerous references to him. However, it did not specifically seek to apply his principles or consulting methodologies. Yet Drucker was at his most extraordinary in the consultant's role. Jack Welch, called "Manager of the Century" by *Fortune* magazine in 1999,[1] is one of the best-known CEOs to acknowledge Drucker contributions to his success.

Drucker Swings into Action as a Consultant

Legendary General Electric CEO Jack Welch sat down with management consultant Drucker shortly after Welch became CEO of GE in 1981. Drucker posed only two questions, but they changed the course of GE's future. Those two questions were worth billions of dollars over the course of Welch's tenure as CEO. The first question was: "If GE weren't already in a business, would you enter it today?" Then Drucker followed up with, "And if the answer is no, what are you going to do about it?" Welch decided that if GE couldn't be number one or number two in a market, the business would have to be fixed, sold, or closed.[2] His actions afterward earned Welch the unflattering title of "Neutron Jack" for eliminating employees while leaving the buildings standing. However, as confirmed by Welch, that strategy – based on his consultation with Drucker and the questions Drucker asked – were the core secrets of his fantastic success at General Electric during his tenure. This included increasing GE's stock value 4,000% during his tenure.

Drucker not only consulted for large corporations as an independent. He consulted for small businesses, non-profits, and governments all over the world, the military, and many churches. However, unlike others, he had no giant consulting firm or an extensive staff. He was a sole practitioner in the true sense of the word, and even as a worldwide celebrated expert in continual demand, he answered his own phone. Call Drucker's home telephone and you'd hear a voice in a Viennese accent answer intoning, "This is Peter Drucker." Drucker answered his own telephone and his consulting office was in his home.

He did not always accept consulting assignments, either. He wrote about advising one organization, which had sought his advice on leadership, that they should consult ancient wisdom and read *Xenophon*, a 2,000-year-old text that he said was "the first systematic book on leadership, and still the best". Nor did he always charge for his services. Minglo Shao, a wealthy Chinese entrepreneur and owner of numerous businesses worldwide and co-founder of the California Institute of Advanced Management (of which I had the honour to be founding president, and now president emeritus), flew to Claremont, California, several times a year to consult with Drucker. But despite numerous offers from Shao, Drucker refused to accept a penny for his advice. He wanted only for Shao to use the knowledge he gave him to help China as it began to develop democratically and entrepreneurially.

Many of my own techniques and concepts originated with ideas from Peter Drucker. I just didn't realize it myself until I sat down with my notes from my time as his student and reflected on what he taught. The debt I personally owe Peter – and Peter is what he asked all his students to call him – for pushing me in the right direction and showering me with his wisdom, ideas, and friendship is significant. This is most emphatically true of everything we taught at the special graduate school specifically founded as a non-profit to offer an affordable MBA based on Drucker's concepts.

How Drucker Got His Start as a Management Consultant

Drucker didn't plan to become a consultant. I know this because he told his students that his first experience in consulting started not long after arriving in this country. Previously, Drucker had been a newspaper correspondent and journalist, as well as an economic analyst for a bank and an insurance company. However, having a doctorate (though not in management, but in international and public law), Drucker's intellectual gifts were mobilized for World War II in 1942.

He was told that he was to work as a "management consultant". He said that he had no idea what a management consultant was. Drucker even checked a dictionary, but the term couldn't be found. He said he went to the library and the bookstore. "Today," he told us, "you will find shelves of titles on management. In those days, there was almost nothing. The few books didn't include the term, much less explain it." He asked several colleagues and had no better luck. They didn't know what a management consultant was either.

On the appointed time and date Drucker proceeded to the colonel to whom he'd been assigned, wondering all the while exactly what he was getting into. As he told the story, I imagined a serious-faced receptionist asking him to wait and an unsmiling sergeant arriving, probably armed, to escort him to the colonel. This must have been a little intimidating for a young immigrant in the US, who not too many years earlier had fled from Nazi Germany, where much of the population was adorned in one uniform or another.

He was led into the office by yet another stern-faced assistant. The colonel glanced at Peter's orders and invited him to be seated. He asked Drucker to tell him about himself. He questioned Drucker at some length about his background and education. But though they seemed to talk on and on, Drucker did not learn what the colonel's office was responsible for, nor was he given any understanding as to what he would be doing for the colonel as a management consultant. It seemed as if they were talking round and round with no purpose.

Drucker was more than a little uncomfortable dealing with the colonel. He hoped that he would soon get to the point and explain exactly what kind of work Peter would be involved in. He grew increasingly frustrated. Finally, Drucker could take it no longer. "Please, sir, can you tell me what a management consultant does?" he asked respectfully.

The colonel glared at him for what seemed like minutes, but was probably only a few seconds, and responded: "Young man, don't be impertinent."

"By which," Drucker told us, "I knew that he didn't know what a management consultant did either."

But Drucker knew that the person who had made this assignment would know what was expected of a management consultant. And from reading about Arthur Conan Doyle's character, Sherlock Holmes, while he was living in England, he knew what a "consulting detective" did. Equipped with that knowledge and the assumption that the colonel did not know anything about management consulting, Drucker started to ask the colonel direct questions about his responsibilities and problems. In some ways this was the foundation of Drucker's unique modus operandi in all his work, including consulting: he asked questions. These questions led to additional questions, and eventually the colonel himself reasoned what he wanted done. Drucker then laid out some options about how this work should be accomplished, and got the colonel's agreement to proceed. The colonel was not only well satisfied, he was clearly relieved. He accepted Drucker's proposals in their entirety. This proved to be Drucker's first successful consulting engagement. So, Peter Drucker was not only the father of modern management; but he may have also been the father of modern independent management consulting as well, at least with this colonel.

Later he told me that the man in the office, (or was it cubical?) next to his was Marvin Bower, who later became managing director of McKinsey & Company in its years of major growth. *The New York Times* called McKinsey & Company "the most prestigious consulting firm", with 9,000 consultants worldwide. Drucker had direct connections to consulting from the beginning, even if at first he didn't know it.

Drucker's Peculiar Advice about Almost Everything

You may think it strange, but Drucker didn't believe in business ethics. He urged his clients to be ethical. However, he made it clear that what was ethical and what was not differed among cultures and that there was no such thing as "business ethics" – only ethics. "Procuring prostitutes for visiting executives didn't make you unethical," he said. "It did, however, make you a pimp."[5]

He once told the story of a large Japanese company that wanted to open a plant in America. After an investigation of many locations in several different states, a suitable site was located. So important was this operation that a special ceremony was scheduled that included the governor, many senior state officials, and the CEO from Japan.

The Japanese CEO spoke fairly good English; however, to ensure that everything would be understood correctly, the company hired an American Nisei, or second-generation woman of Japanese descent, to translate his speech into English.

With dignity and in measured tones, the Japanese CEO began to speak, noting the great honour it was for his company to be able to locate their new plant in this particular state in the United States, with mutual benefits to his company and the state's citizens. He also discussed the benefits to the local economy and to Japanese-American friendship. Then, nodding in the direction of the governor and other state officials, he said "Furthermore, Mr Governor and senior officials, please understand that we know our duty. When the time comes that you retire from your honoured positions, my corporation will not forget and will repay you for the efforts that you have expended in our behalf in giving us this opportunity".

The Japanese-American interpreter was horrified. Instantly she made a decision to omit these remarks in her English translation. The Japanese CEO, who understood enough English to realize what she had done but little of the American culture to understand why, continued his speech as if nothing had happened. Later, when the two were alone, the executive asked the interpreter, "How could you exclude my ethical reassurances to the governor and officials? Why did you leave this important part out of my speech?" Only then could she explain, to his amazement, that what is ethical – even a duty – in Japan is considered unethical and corrupt in the United States.[6]

Consulting and the California Institute of Advanced Management

In 2010, I cofounded and was appointed president of the nonprofit California Institute of Advanced Management (CIAM). CIAM is a graduate university granting a single degree: an MBA in Executive Management and Entrepreneurship. However, we developed an interchangeable online programme and a doctorate as well, and in all cases, CIAM applies Drucker's mandate of learning through application. For example, students learn how to apply theory by doing actual consulting in every one of the 12 courses required – from accounting to marketing and general management. Teams of four students, and one course done solo, by an individual student provide consulting for small businesses, non-profit organizations, large corporations, and the government. These consulting engagements are all done without charge.

We also began consulting remotely using electronic visual and audio contact. We did this first in Canada, Israel and Mexico. When CIAM held its second graduation, Dr Francisco Suarez flew 1,500 miles, from Monterrey, Mexico, to speak in El Monte, near Los Angeles. At the time, Dr Suarez was director of sustainability at FEMSA. FEMSA is one of the largest corporations in Mexico, the largest beverage company in Latin America, and the largest Coca-Cola bottling companies in the world. One of FEMSA's television advertisements for Dos Equis beer features "the Most Interesting Man in the World" nodding solemnly at the end and saying, "I don't always drink beer, but when I do, I drink Dos Equis. Stay thirsty, my friends." If you've seen that ad, that's FEMSA.

Dr Suarez is now a vice president. A team of four CIAM students had completed a consultancy for his organization several months earlier. All this was accomplished with weekly meetings electronically. Another team of four has completed a long-distant consulting engagement for an organization in Israel, 7,563 miles away, even as the client was under potential attack from rockets from the Gaza Strip during the 2014 war. In addition, another team recently concluded a presentation electronically in Lebanon. Remote consulting with clients in Africa, China, and other parts of the world are planned.

All this is under CIAM's Consulting Institute, which was then headed by a man whom, like Drucker, has a Juris Doctor (JD), a professional doctorate in law from Harvard, and was also a former McKinsey & Company consultant. Our students and professors all had experience with Drucker's concepts of consulting. Today, CIAM is under the able leadership of former VP Jennie Ta, who carries on the traditions of incorporating Drucker's methods in both teaching and consulting.

How to Use and Master Drucker's Techniques and Concepts

This book is based on the consulting of Peter Drucker, but also builds on his ideas and methods, for as Drucker himself said, "Keep doing what made you successful currently and in the past, and you will eventually fail." Applied correctly, Drucker's genius will save you thousands of wasted hours and much frustration. You will not only avoid countless blunders and create new ideas for success, but it will enable you to offer better advice to clients, subordinates, bosses, and fellow executives, which will lead them toward success. The principles, concepts, and experiences of hundreds of Drucker's clients, and others practising his principles, are all here. The aim is to understand Drucker's thinking, why he thought this way and, moreover, to apply his unique ideas in your own business as a practising manager or consultant.

As Drucker taught and, I believe, would have approved, *Consulting Drucker* is not theoretical – it is practical. You will understand his way of thinking and the tools he used to build perhaps the most successful independent consulting practice ever, and the principles and concepts that helped hundreds of his clients achieve great success. As Drucker wrote and exhorted those of us who were lucky enough to have been his students: "Without action, nothing gets done." The action part is essential, and that part is up to you. You have to take Drucker's ideas and apply them to your own issues. From this, there are no limits to what you can do. So let's get started!

[1] Time-Warner, *Fortune* magazine, "GE's Jack Welch Selected Manager of the Century," 1 November 1999, accessed at http://www.timewarner.com/newsroom/press-releases/1999/11/01/fortune-selects-henry-ford-businessman-of-the-century, 22 November 2015.

[2] John A. Byrne, "The Man Who Invented Management," *Business Week*, 28 November 2005, accessed at http://www.bloomberg.com/bw/stories/2005-11-27/the-man-who-invented-management, 22 November 2015.

[3] Dan Rather interview, "Jack Welch: I Fell in Love," *60 Minutes*, 24 March 2005, accessed at http://www.cbsnews.com/news/jack-welch-i-fell-in-love/, 22 November 2015.

[4] Peter F. Drucker, *The Practice of Management* (New York: Harper & Row Publishers, 1954), p.194.

[5] Peter F. Drucker, *Management: Tasks, Responsibilities, Practices* (New York: Harper & Row Publishers, 1973), p. 367

[6] This story was given in class. This version is from William A. Cohen, *How to Make It Big as a Consultant*, 4th edition (New York: AMACOM, 2009), pp.168-169.

Chapter 2

The Drucker Consulting Difference

D rucker's management consulting approach differed greatly from other giants in the field and, in fact, from just about any other management consultant. These differences included the basic organization of his consulting practice; his services; what he demanded of clients; his focus on thinking through to solutions rather than more rigid, structured approaches; an emphasis on questioning clients rather than providing answers; an emphasis on managerial gut decisions over only use of numbers and quantitative methods; his use of historical analysis; and so much more.

Applying Drucker's Methods Requires Understanding

To understand and practise Drucker's methods, it is first necessary to understand his education and how he came into a consulting career, and the fact that it was integrated into his teaching and writing activities. According to him, consulting was not his profession. In fact, according to Drucker, neither were writing or teaching. He might have paused to consider the accuracy of the descriptive title of chapter one, The World's Greatest Independent Consultant, and with great reluctance might even have agreed to its being essentially true. But he probably would have reminded me that he was neither a consultant, a professor, nor even a management author, but a "social ecologist".

What Is a Social Ecologist?

One dictionary defines an ecologist as "someone who investigates the interactions among organisms and their environments".[1] If we look up "social", we see that this has to do with "of or relating to people or society in general".[2] Add the two together and we see that Drucker saw himself as one who studies and investigates human interactions and their environments.

There is one more word we need to add to the definition of what Drucker felt was his profession: "scientist." He usually did not use this word in the basic definition of his activities, but it was certainly implied. A scientist is "a person who is engaged in and has expert knowledge of a science, usually, most frequently, a biological or physical science".[3] Keep this in mind as we examine the differences in Drucker's consulting. Drucker saw himself as a scientist who investigates human actions and environments.

Drucker's Strange Non-consulting Organization

Years ago, a writer wondered about the fact that of all the world-famous, "brand name" consultants, Drucker alone did not establish a major consulting organization supporting or expanding his activities. There was and is no "Drucker Consulting Group" or "Drucker and Associates," or "Drucker LLP or LTD".

McKinsey and Company, the largest consulting firm in the world, with 9,000 consultants worldwide, was founded by a former University of Chicago accounting professor, James O. McKinsey, in 1926. Its biggest growth was under Martin Bower, who, as explained in the previous chapter, occupied a cubicle next to Drucker's during their work as US government management consultants during World War II. Bower and Drucker were friends, but Drucker did not follow Bower's lead to build a worldwide consulting organization. Call Drucker's telephone number and you didn't get a receptionist or a secretary unless you dialled his university. In his consulting practice, he had neither. Drucker lived until 2005, a technologically modern time. However, he never had a website, either. If you wanted Drucker, you were either his student, a client, or looked him up in the phone book. He may have actually turned more potential clients away than he accepted. But remember, Drucker was not primarily a consultant. He was primarily a scientist and a social ecologist, even though many (including me) think that he was the world's greatest independent consultant.

And Drucker thought of himself as a scientist, even if he did not use the word to describe himself. He painted a word picture of working in his "laboratory", which he said was like a business or corporation. And if he wasn't wearing a white coat, his imagery may have encouraged your mind to dress him in one anyway. It did mine.

This mind-set explains a lot. Since Drucker clearly thought of himself as a scientist, like many scientists, he never coveted great wealth. Instead of billing his clients $10,000 a day, in later years he requested that they donate $10,000 a day to his foundation. He lived in a modest house in Claremont, California. He drove a relatively inexpensive car. He mowed his own lawn. He did not wear $1,000 suits or expensive watches and his shoes were not high fashion either. He acted exactly the way he lived.

Once, while mowing his lawn, Drucker was confronted by a young community organizer who wanted him to sign a petition for some long-forgotten cause. Doris, Drucker's wife, ran out of the house and rescued him. "Peter isn't signing anything," she said and took the pen away. This was reported by the city mayor in 2009 – he was once that young political volunteer. He told this story as he renamed the street adjacent to Drucker's office at Claremont Graduate University "Drucker Way" four years after Peter's death.

How Drucker Became a Consultant Helped Form the Drucker Difference

It is worthwhile reviewing how Drucker became a consultant. He prepared himself well, but it was not a conscious preparation. I'll explain that in a later chapter, because his methods can be adopted successfully by any who set their sights on becoming an independent management consultant in the mould of Drucker, or frankly, any other mould. Meanwhile, recall that according to the story he had told us in class, until Drucker's World War II assignment as a management consultant, he didn't even know what a management consultant was. After the war, Drucker began to teach, but not at any of the nation's famous business schools – not at Harvard, not at Wharton, and not at the University of Chicago. Drucker began his teaching career at two girls' schools, Bennington and Sarah St. Lawrence. He didn't teach business or management; he taught politics and philosophy. It wasn't until his book, *Concept of the Corporation*, was published in 1946, based on his experiences at General Motors, that Drucker began to offer extensive paid management consulting to many organizations.

Drucker's book was a masterpiece, but controversial. Although legend has it that he had full access to everything at GM and that he actually attended meetings with famed General Motors president Alfred P. Sloan, little original evidence has been found at GM that support these claims. Some say that this is because Sloan and others didn't like the book, and therefore not only ignored his work but even concealed evidence that Drucker had any significant role in analysing GM's operations. In later years, after Drucker became known as the father of modern management, GM itself adopted this story. Nevertheless, Drucker's book included a very favourable review of GM's management, as Drucker was very impressed with GM's organization and operations. Without a doubt, the book acted as a marketing vehicle and Drucker was approached for various consulting services by many other organizations.

Those who have become independent management consultants do so through a variety of portals. Some start with established consulting organizations, or as managers in various business organizations, and then go out on their own. Some are forced into independent consulting because they have been laid off from their jobs and need the income. Others begin in academia and are hired because of their areas of expertise. There is another category, and this is the one in which Drucker falls. They write an article or a book that attracts the attention of an organization and are contacted about the work. I came into consulting through this portal. This is also probably how Drucker became involved with GM. He had written several books by then and was teaching history, and he was also writing for popular magazines such as *The Saturday Evening Post* and others. Drucker's book written before *The Concept of the Corporation* was *The Future of Industrial Man*, published in 1942. It's possible that Donaldson Brown, then a senior GM executive, had read the book, investigated the author, and inquired about Drucker's availability and interest. It was Brown who recruited Drucker to perform the GM management audit, which led to Drucker's writing *The Concept.*[4] Once he became a management professor at New York

University after writing it, the requests for his consulting services probably increased significantly.

Whatever portal brought Drucker to consulting has little to do with the quality of his consulting, but it may well affect both the level and type of consulting performed, as well as various decisions about how and what services he provided. It is important to note that *The Concept of the Corporation* was not a "how to do consulting" book. It was descriptive in nature regarding much about GM's multidivisional structure and also suggested some new ideas, decentralization being one, and a re-examination of some of GM's long-standing policies in all.

According to legend, Alfred Sloan was so upset about the book that he "simply treated it as if it did not exist, never mentioning it, and never allowing it to be mentioned in his presence".[5] In any case, this particular portal led to a ton of consulting for Drucker, speaking before corporations and many other organizations. This is a strong lesson for anyone wishing to follow in Drucker's footsteps. It also set the stage for Drucker's consulting practice for the next 60 years: he would consult on what to do.

Drucker Was Concerned with What to Do, Not How to Do It

As a social ecologist, Drucker was concerned with what to do, not the step-by-step instructions of how to do it. For this reason, he never wrote a book about his consulting. I'm not surprised. Books about consulting, if they are not descriptive of the industry, invariably concern the details of how to accomplish some aspect of the consulting profession, be it technology, sales, presentations, or client relationships. This would not have been the higher level of what to do, which is what the scientist Drucker dealt with. Believe me, I should know. My book, *How to Make It Big as a Consultant* (AMACOM) has sold about 100,000 copies from four US and many foreign editions since it was first published in 1985. However, if I had advised would-be consultants to answer their own phones and accept fees only for a foundation, I doubt if the book would have made it past the first edition or even been accepted for publication.

Drucker's writing about what to do, with almost never explaining how to carry out his ideas, has been both a curse and a blessing for myself and a good many of his consulting clients as well. It meant that I had to become something of a detective to determine how Drucker came to his conclusions and also to translate this information into the action that Drucker constantly urged his clients to undertake. Some of this understanding took years. For example, it wasn't until after Peter's death that I understood what he was talking about when he said that marketing and sales were not only not complementary, but could actually be adversarial. This will be explained later, as it is an essential consideration in consulting for either sales or marketing, or anything else. In any case, these mysteries constituted the curse I spoke of. The blessing was that when I finally deciphered his thinking, it was like finding hidden gold. I also began to suspect that maybe that was exactly his intent. To make clients, readers, and students think rather than merely be fed answers that they were simply to execute.

I recall one client telling me: "This led us to examine the issue more closely and to come up with our own ways of implementing a solution. His questions led us to excellent solutions, which he had forced us to generate through our own thinking and discussions. However, it took some getting used to. I don't remember Peter ever presenting us with fancy overhead presentations or quantified reports."

The Most Difficult Aspect of Being a Drucker Client
I heard once that the manner in which he provided consulting was the most difficult thing about being a Drucker client. One Drucker client that I spoke with expressed it this way: "We had been accustomed to hiring consultants to whom we told what we wanted done or asked them to solve a specified problem. They then went off and returned after some time with mounds of data and reports. Before PowerPoint, they presented their detailed solutions and recommendations on stacks of overheads. We were instructed exactly what we were to do to execute the recommendations. And if we didn't understand it, they were happy to explain themselves in more detail and answer our questions.

Drucker, on the other hand, did none of that. He would begin by asking us questions that we were expected to answer. If the engagement was an all-day event, he might lecture on various topics, which seemed to have nothing to do with our problem. In the process we had to think through logically to arrive at solutions we would have otherwise completely overlooked."

The Chinese philanthropist Minglo Shao, who contributed the money that founded the very unusual non-profit graduate school based on Drucker's teachings, for which I have the honour to be president, told me that every year he would visit Drucker at his home and Drucker would ask him questions about various issues regarding the developments of his many businesses and foundations. However, though he asked questions and may have spoken in generalities about *what* to do, he never once told Minglo how to do it – including the Peter Drucker Academy of China, which Minglo founded. This is probably the only school in the world – other than my alma matter, the Drucker School at Claremont where Peter taught – that has the legal authority to use the Drucker name. To date it has been taught in 32 cities in China, plus Hong Kong, and has 60,000 graduates of various courses and programs.

Drucker's Methodology of Conducting the Consulting Engagement

Drucker did not conduct his engagement the way any other consultant did. And there are few consultants that I know to whom I would recommend it, because to follow it exactly you would need the stature of a Drucker in management, and while I know plenty of outstanding managers and management scholars, none would claim to be Drucker. Almost 20 years ago, Jack Beatty, then an editor of *The Atlantic Monthly*, who had edited several of Drucker's articles, conducted an excellent investigation of how Drucker saw things and acted on these insights. This resulted in the book, *The World According to Peter Drucker*. In interviewing many of Drucker's consulting clients, he found that whether it was a one-on-one or a full room of senior company executives, Drucker lectured without graphics and seemingly touched on just about everything but the problem for which he had been engaged. After as much as a full day of lectures, he would return the main issue to his audience from an entirely new perspective, still unsolved. However, it was this new perspective that enabled the client to solve the issue with minimum direction from Drucker. According to Beatty, Drucker's methodology was a form of teaching.[6]

This last statement struck a responsive chord with me. Many times I had seen Drucker respond to a question from a student or one he himself had proposed and then proceed into an hourlong lecture with many twists and turns, which seemed at best to be only tangentially important to the initial question posed. However, after an hour monologue, he would suddenly tie it all together and come up with an amazing and frequently unexpected solution to whatever issue had been raised. Only if you went back and reviewed your notes of his ad hoc lecture could you understand how it all fit together, and I could well imagine him conducting his consulting in this fashion.

It was also speculated that this process enabled Drucker himself to integrate everything that came into his own reasoning. And in this way he was able to return to the initial problem in such a way as to give to the client an entirely different slant on the issue.

This method could be surprisingly effective. Dudley Hafner, former president of the American Heart Association, told Beatty that Drucker caused the association to reorganize their entire field operation and redefine themselves as an information organization.[7]

The Brain Is for Thinking – Use It!

Although Drucker was well aware of the use of many innovative methodologies developed over the years for analysing business situations and determining strategies, he made almost no use of them, emphasizing instead thinking through every situation on its own merits. He never taught "portfolio analysis" with the famous quadrants of cash cows, shooting stars, problem children, or dogs, as developed by the Boston Consulting Group (BCG) or the GE/ McKinsey nine-cell version, or any other management or business strategy by rote methods. He was one of the first to point out that the main inputs in the BCG matrix would encourage organizations to grow by acquisition without the needed attention to whether or not the acquiring corporation added valued in managing the assets of the acquired business. At the same time, many corporations were growing and were extremely profitable by concentrating their resources on products or businesses where they could grow in profit even while their size remained stable. Eventually, many of the huge, growing conglomerates based on acquisition failed, and Drucker was proven correct. Not that Drucker opposed acquisition or bigness per se. He was all for acquisition if the acquiring organization had something to offer the acquired, and also if other owned businesses were dropped so that resources would be available to make the new acquisition viable.

Drucker's Caution in Applying "Breakthrough" Ideas

Drucker was well aware of new ideas promoted as breakthroughs, but he was extremely cautious in applying them across the board and without much thought; that is, without thinking through each situation individually.

Although his association with and learning of management methods in Japan were much appreciated, and his clients in Japan were quick to adopt Drucker's methods as well, he did not instantly jump on the bandwagon of "Japanese Management". When it caught on in the US in the early 1980s, it eventually evolved into the Total Quality Management revolution, which spread across the world like wildfire. It's worth noting that the basic aspects of this style of management – such as ownership and decentralization, and especially leadership – had long been promoted by Drucker already. However, he was highly suspicious of all methods of "management by fad" and found that they were frequently misinterpreted from what the developer had intended.

Organizations joined the participatory management fad based

on Douglas McGregor's research and his concept of Theory X verses Theory Y, that is, directive versus participatory management. Drucker pointed out that McGregor was merely noting that Theory Y – management with significant participation of the managed – was simply an alternative to the more directive style practised almost exclusively up to that time. He underlined what most adopters missed: that McGregor himself had written that his intent was to describe an alternative management style that could achieve better results under certain circumstances. Drucker suggested that research should be done to uncover exactly what these circumstances were, that participatory management was not the universal answer in all situations, and that the directive form of management should be abandoned in all instances.

Even Drucker's friend and strong supporter, Warren Bennis, a distinguished management expert in his own right, failed to heed Drucker's cautionary advice not to adopt Theory Y's participatory management as the answer for all management problems in all organizations. Bennis, at the time president of the University of Buffalo, embraced and adopted almost complete participatory management in a totally unsuitable environment. According to Drucker, "the result was tremendous excitement, but also a total failure."[8] This was one of Bennis' few major mistakes, either as manager or as leader theorist. It probably had one major benefit: it encouraged Bennis to eventually return to his career as a leadership theorist, author, and teacher. He wrote many books and before he died he won many honours in this area and founded the Leadership Institute at the University of Southern California. About his experience in misapplying Theory Y he wrote: "In the end, I wasn't very good at being a president."[9]

Drucker's Emphasis on Feelings over Numbers in Decision Making

Drucker insisted on measuring just about everything, but the results were to be considered informational only. He avoided decision making by numbers, whereby the decision was made for the manager by merely inputting certain data considered crucial to a software program, turning on a computer, and having the answer magically appear. He pointed out that one could gather data on thousands of businesses, including primary factors, even the weather and some elements thought to be relatively insignificant, and finally the results attained. You could then design the software based on your extensive data. You might claim that by inputting your own situational data, you might be able to predict the project results with some high per cent of accuracy, say 92.5%. That's significant, but may be of little help in a particular situation.

Drucker maintained that this was still inferior to using your brain, thinking through everything and making your own "gut" decision based on available information, your experience, and knowledge of the nature of your own personnel and organization. He noted that knowledge or instinct of one vital factor might well be decisive and that the computer would never pick it up. He reminded his students and his clients that though a certain program might give accurate outcome results 92.5% of the time, for the other 7.5% of the time the results were 100% inaccurate. In other words, if failure or success was the outcome you sought to predict, and if the end result was part of that 7.5% area, your answer was 100% in error. He recommended managerial gut decisions after considering all the information that could be obtained. Drucker told his clients to make "gut" decisions, but these gut decisions were to be made with the brain. The brain was a better device than a computer and provides its own internal "software" for decision making.

As a result, Drucker taught management and performed as a management consultant by doing both while considering management as a liberal art. According to classical antiquity, "liberal art" included those subjects or skills that were considered "worthy of a free person" in order to take an active part in civic life. The core included participating in public debate, defending oneself in court, serving on juries, and maybe even most importantly, military service.[10] Although most didn't know it, Drucker was an avid student of military history and military methods.

Drucker incorporated interdisciplinary lessons from language, history, sociology, psychology, philosophy, culture, religion, and more into his consulting. However, he also took the ancient injunction about military service to heart and although he never spoke or taught about so-called "marketing or business warfare", his consulting advice and writings are filled with military examples. Promoting Frances Hesselbein's 2004 book, *Be Know Do*, based on the US Army Leadership Manual, Drucker wrote: "The army trains and develops more leaders than all other institutions put together – and with a lower casualty rate."[11]

This is the "Drucker Difference in Consulting", and we will see how Drucker applied all of this in practice in the coming chapters.

---

[1] No author listed, *Cambridge Dictionaries Online*, accessed at http://dictionary. cambridge.org/us/dictionary/american-english/ecologist, 1 March 2015.

[2] No author listed. *Merriam-Webster*, accessed at http://www.merriam-webster.com/ dictionary/social, 2 March 2015.

[3] Ibid, accessed at http://www.merriam-webster.com/dictionary/scientist, 2 March 2015.

[4] No author listed, "Peter Drucker," *Wikipedia*, accessed at http://en.wikipedia.org/wiki/ Peter_Drucker, 2 March 2015.

[5] Drucker, Peter F., *Adventures of a Bystander*, (New York: HarperCollins, 1978, 1979, 1991) p. 288.

[6] Beatty, Jack, *The World According to Peter Drucker*, (New York: Free Press, 1998) p.182.

[7] Ibid.

[8] Drucker, Peter F. *Management, Tasks, Responsibilities, Practices* (New York: Harper & Row: New York, 1973, 1974). p. 235.

[9] Bennis, Warren, quoted in "Warren Bennis 1925-2014: An Appreciation," *Thinkers 50*, accessed at http://www.thinkers50.com/blog/warren-bennis-1925-2014-appreciation/ 1 March 2015.

[10] No author listed. "Liberal Arts Education," *Wikipedia*, accessed at http://en.wikipedia. org/wiki/Liberal_arts_education , 2 March 2015.

[11] Hesselbein, Frances and Eric K. Shinseki, *Be-Know-Do*, (San Francisco: Jossey Bass, 2004), back cover.

Chapter 3

What We Can Learn from How Drucker Developed as a Management Consultant

There is a mistaken notion that those who succeed in many activities are somehow gifted and begin with no preparation, right at the top of their game. This isn't true for anyone in any activity that I can think of, and as this chapter demonstrates, it wasn't true for Drucker, either. That's not to say that we can't see things that clearly helped and cut down on both Drucker's preparation time for success and the time it took for him to go from "Good to Great," to borrow Jim Collins' terminology from his bestselling book. However, even with the right preparation, we shouldn't expect instant success that immediately puts us at the top in consulting, or in anything else we undertake. There are inevitable setbacks that we will encounter, just as Drucker did… and we'll determine how to overcome them just as he did, too.

Did Drucker Always Plan to Become a Management Consultant?

I read an article once by an author whom I have long since forgotten. He claimed to have come over to the United States from England on the same boat as Drucker in 1937. He said that he and Drucker talked extensively and that Drucker told him that he intended to build a career and achieve great wealth as a management writer and management consultant and that it was all well planned ahead of time. I doubt it. For one thing, it doesn't sound like Drucker. He didn't talk about himself that way and share what he was going to do or what he had done. Moreover, Drucker's first book, *The End of Economic Man*, had just been written in 1937, but was as yet unpublished. For all he knew, it might have "bombed". Books do that from time to time. Some of mine have, and some of Drucker's did, too. Also, Drucker's first book had little to do with either business or management. And of course, Drucker had no idea what a management consultant was at that point in his life, anyway. We learned that in chapter one.

What Drucker did want to do was teach. That's what he had wanted to do all along. If he had any ideas about writing, it was probably political writing, something along the lines of *The End of Economic Man* while he pursued a career as a Herr Professor in academia. Still, life had already begun to prepare him for consulting, as it does all of us in different ways. It's just that we don't stop to think about this preparation or to organize the consulting resources that we have already acquired or can get if we need them. And that's one of the reasons for this chapter: so you can recognize what you already have that will be useful in the consulting you do and use these resources to help you to reach success, if that is your desire.

Drucker's Early Serendipitous Preparation for Consulting

Serendipitous preparation for consulting is background we may acquire, but never intended to use for the purpose of consulting or anything else. In other words, we got it by accident.

The word "serendipity" came to us courtesy of an 18th century English author by the name of Horace Walpole. Walpole had discovered a number of unknown facts about various topics by accident through his writing. He had randomly looked through old books and come across some surprising insights. Achieving some success with this procedure, he adopted it as a formal process of discovery and coined the term "serendipity" to describe it. The word itself came from a fairy tale he had once read using this method entitled, *The Three Princesses of Serendip*. The princesses made all kinds of discoveries by accident. But "Serendip" wasn't a nonsense word. It's the ancient name of Sri Lanka, from whence the princesses in the story emanated.[1] Congratulations! You too have now uncovered a relatively unknown fact through serendipity.

The first step in Drucker's serendipitous preparation for consulting was his father's insistence on his young son's serious participation in adult conversation, including with guests to the Drucker household. Drucker hadn't even entered adolescence when he was pushed in this direction. According to Drucker, these guests even included men of the calibre of Sigmund Freud. Drucker wrote that his father referred to Freud as "the most important man in Europe" and that he met Freud when he was eight or nine years old.[2] Here Drucker's childhood memories may have been imperfect, but it matters not. If a preteen is introduced to an adult and is even allowed to converse with grownups routinely, that has a later effect in self-confidence, the ability to speak in public, and certainly to converse with a variety of individuals of importance, be it Freud or any other adult. If this were truly Freud that he remembered, this would have made quite an impression on Drucker and his friends as they grew to adulthood.

Now, lest you think "too late, too late – I knew my parents did something wrong in my upbringing," and you weren't fortunate enough to have your father introduce you to Freud or a prominent figure like this at an early age, don't worry about it. I don't know about your parents, but mine invariably mumbled something about "children being seen, not heard" and I never dared to interject a comment or question in an adult conversation. I don't think that I was introduced to someone like Freud or allowed to have serious discourse with any adult until I was well into my teens, or maybe even later. But Drucker did have this serendipitous advantage.

Drucker Misses a Chance at College, But Gets a Serious Education

Drucker's parents wanted him to attend college, but this was post-World War I, and Austria had been on the losing side. With jobs difficult to find in Vienna, he persuaded his parents to allow him to sojourn to Hamburg, Germany, where he succeeded in obtaining an apprenticeship in a cotton trading company. At the same time he enrolled in night school at the University of Hamburg and earned a law degree.

This was his first experience with what is today termed one method of "executive education", whereby one gets an advanced degree while working. This was something he later believed was critical for the development of a manager, and which he considered more important than the undergraduate degree, which he felt was more useful for socialization. He also began a regimen of voracious reading, devouring books both fiction and non-fiction on a variety of subjects. This too provided good preparation and general knowledge for his future career as a consultant. It also sparked his interest in history and what could be gleaned from it, which, according to Drucker, could and must be applied to the present and future.

Once asked what management books Drucker read, his widow, Doris, replied, "None, but he did scan them." According to Doris, Drucker read mainly the newspapers and a lot of history books. His readers can see the results in his writings in which he documents historical happenings from a variety of fields on every page, not only to support his concepts and conclusions but, one suspects, to help reach them. He retained his ability to use history to illustrate his points in the classroom, and while not always 100% accurate in his recollections, he was 100% interesting. Toward the end of his apprenticeship, he was able to find at least part-time work as a journalist, probably due as much to his reading as his legal education.

Completing his apprenticeship, he gained admittance to the University of Frankfurt as a doctoral student and continued his journalistic work at the same time. As his students, we once asked him in the classroom why he chose to get a doctorate in international law, since he told us that he never intended to practise law and had little interest in it. "Because it was the easiest, quickest doctorate I could get," he replied without hesitation. Drucker never minced words. After earning his doctorate, he began correspondence with an uncle at the University of Cologne in the hope of obtaining a teaching position there. However, before he obtained a positive response, Hitler came to power in Germany in 1933.

Hitler Causes Drucker to Drop Everything
Drucker left for England almost immediately. Although Drucker was of Jewish descent on both sides of his family, both families had converted and Peter was raised as a Christian. This was

fairly common in Austria since the mid-1850s, after the Jews were emancipated. As Drucker sometimes noted, there were many professional officers in the Austrian Army who were Jews, including some of high rank. In fact, in the 1860s the chief of staff of the Austrian Army, General Alfred von Henikstein, was a baptized Jew.[3]

Drucker's decision to depart for England at once is significant in analysing both his preparation for becoming a consultant and his ability to analyse situations, come to conclusions, and act without hesitation. Most, if not the majority of ethnic Jews in Germany – whether converts to Christianity or not – did not depart Nazi Germany on such short notice. Drucker left before any anti-Semitic laws could be put into place and even before Hindenburg, Germany's president, died and Hitler assumed the leading role. He left at the best possible time. In short order, would-be Jewish emigrants faced far more than the challenges of a new language, a new job, and leaving their homelands for the unknown. It became increasingly difficult to leave, and finally it became impossible. Drucker looked at the situation realistically, saw the likely consequences – and using a technique he developed and that I'll explain later because it's very useful for a consultant – he made the difficult decision and left immediately to get as far away from Hitler as he could, just as rapidly as possible. He took no chances, recognizing that since Hitler was a fellow Austrian, Austria was not even a possibility.

Drucker's Activities in England and His First Book

Drucker could not have had an easy time of it in England as a foreigner, especially a Germanic foreigner during the Great Depression. His dreams of becoming a professor at the University of Cologne, in fact of becoming a professor anywhere, were gone, at least temporarily. His English must have been imperfect. He could not practise law. He got a job with an insurance company, but in what capacity we don't know. Later he said that he became senior economist at a private bank. We can speculate that, in either case, both these jobs were significantly below what his doctorate endorsed and what the abilities that he ultimately demonstrated would have commanded in Germany or Austria. But he was not yet Peter Drucker, the world famous management theorist, much less the social ecologist scientist that he ultimately claimed as his profession. He was a 24-year-old alien who had almost no work experience and spoke with a heavy Viennese accent. The heavy accent, by the way, he was never able to completely shake.

However, Drucker had been a journalist, and he knew that if he could write well enough to be published in German, he could eventually learn English well enough to be published in English. Why not? Others had. That's the kind of question you might ask yourself from time to time. He knew that "if he could take it, he could make it". Moreover, he took stock of what else he had. Not only did he have a good education, but he had seen fascism first-hand. He spent the next four years putting all this together and laboriously learning the fine points of English writing as he wrote his first book on the origins of totalitarianism and analysing the totalitarian state, with additional insights from his first-hand experiences. As he saw war approaching in 1937 because of Hitler's actions, he again made a decision to get as far away from the approaching storm as he could. He and Doris Schmitz, who also had previously moved to England to escape Hitler, packed up and immigrated to the United States. He had first met Doris at the University of Frankfurt, she too being the daughter of non-practising Jews, and they had married in England despite Doris' mother depreciating her intended, the future "father of modern management," as "that happy-go-lucky Austrian, Peter Drucker."

Drucker's book was published almost two years later on the eve of war, as both English and Americans sought answers as to whether some accommodation might be made with Hitler and a war averted. Some, including Winston Churchill, read Drucker's book and were happy to recommend it. It was sheer serendipity that Churchill became prime minister not long afterward, but I'd bet money that Churchill didn't just buy a book at the airport.

Someone, probably the publisher, or Drucker himself, sent Churchill the manuscript, which he was happy to endorse. At the time, only a little over 20 years after the end of World War I, many were tired of war and "wanted peace in our time." Hitler promised that his annexing and destruction of the country of Czechoslovakia was his last territorial demand in Europe. Many who were highly educated convinced themselves that all Hitler wanted was justice for Germans and disagreed strongly with Churchill, who was sounding the alarm that England needed to hop to and prepare for war. Drucker had no such blinders on and wrote accordingly. So Churchill welcomed Drucker and his book with open arms.

However, the publishing of this bestseller did not assure a university teaching position at a prestigious school in the US, where Drucker lived when the book was published. The best that Drucker could do at that time was to teach undergraduate courses at two girls schools: first a part-time position teaching economics at Sarah Lawrence College in New York, and then a full-time position teaching at Bennington in Vermont, where he taught undergraduate philosophy. Drucker continued to develop and use his writing abilities in English, even writing for popular US magazines on a variety of topics to supplement what must have been a meagre income as a junior professor at what was then far below a top-tiered graduate school.

The Influence of World War II and Marvin Bower

You read about Drucker's mobilization as a management consultant in chapter one. Marvin Bower and Drucker occupied nearby cubicles when both were drafted for service by the US government in World War II. They became friends. Today, Marvin Bower is known as the "father of modern management consulting" and you can't miss Bower's influence in Drucker's consulting.

Bower eventually became a director at McKinsey & Company. As noted earlier, the famous consulting company of McKinsey & Company was founded by University of Chicago accounting professor James O. McKinsey. (To acknowledge any possible bias, the University of Chicago is my own MBA alma mater.) Marvin Bower became director of McKinsey after World War II, in 1950. He had begun creating McKinsey's driving principles and making them part of McKinsey's culture earlier, long before the war. These included putting clients' interests above McKinsey revenues, not discussing clients' affairs, always telling the truth to clients regardless of the consequences, and only performing consulting work that was truly necessary, regardless of the demands of a client.

Under Bower's tenure, McKinsey sales grew rapidly, and it expanded its offices both in the US and overseas. However, sales declined after Bower's retirement some years later, but it is telling that the culture he founded lives on more than 50 years later. The company not only recovered from its temporary decline, but eventually forged a reputation as the most prestigious of all consulting firms. Today, McKinsey & Company has more than 20,000 consultants and more than 120 offices worldwide.[4, 5]

The close office locations of Bower and Drucker allowed their relationship to deepen to a friendship. This was easy to understand; their professional backgrounds were somewhat similar, as both were lawyers by education. However, having first signed on with McKinsey in 1933, Bower had been a consultant for some years before he "joined the army", whereas Drucker, on the other hand, didn't even know what a management consultant was when he started his wartime consulting work. Moreover, Bower had not graduated from just any law school, but from the most prestigious law school in the country, the Harvard Law School, and after that, the most prestigious business school in the country, the Harvard Business School. Finally, he was six years older than Drucker. It is very likely that he was the dominant one in the relationship and that Drucker was heavily influenced by Bower's ideas about consulting, and there's some confirmation of this.

Years later in his career, Drucker described how he was approached by a large organization about giving a speech on the latest developments in leadership. At the time, Drucker was commanding $20,000 for a one-hour presentation. However, he considered the latest developments in leadership – servant leadership – to be totally superfluous, and a speech on the so-called "latest developments" unnecessary and a waste of time. Following Bower's concepts, he rejected the assignment with the admonition: "There is nothing new about leadership that was not already known by the ancients two thousand years ago" and advised his surprised potential clients to read a particular ancient text by Xenophon. This was certainly in line with Bower's principles that he inculcated at McKinsey and no doubt passed on to Peter.

Marvin Bower had also created a sensation in 1963, an era in which other consultants were making a fortune by going public and selling their shares back to corporations at huge multiples of earnings on retirement. Bower did something unheard of that no one else had done previously: he sold his shares back to McKinsey at book value, foregoing millions of dollars in the process. According to one writer, "in doing what he did, he demonstrated precisely the kind of allegiance to the cause he expected of anyone wishing to be successful at McKinsey. He sent the message that working for McKinsey was like joining a special order of men willing to put the higher cause of the firm ahead of self-interest."[6]

When Drucker became internationally famous and was highly successful and wealthy, he still maintained his residence in a modest home on a modest block in Claremont, California. He did not wear expensive suits, nor did he drive a fancy car. Like Bower, he seemed to be sending a message that though he might be world-famous as a scientist and social ecologist, he was in a special order of men (and women) willing to put the interests of his students, his profession, his clients, and society well ahead of self-interest. Though he may have charged $20,000 an hour for a keynote speech, the money was taken as a donation and given to a foundation he had founded.

As final evidence of Bower's influence, Drucker was 94 years old and still at the height of his fame less than two years before his death. He knew best-selling management authors from around the world: Tom Peters, Jim Collins, Charles Handy, Phil Kotler, Rosabeth Moss Kanter, Theodore Leavitt, and the list goes on and on. His close friend and best-selling author, Warren Bennis, was a professor at the University of Southern California only a few miles away from Drucker's home in Claremont.

These authors had all written numerous books, frequently multiple bestsellers and were all world-famous. Any one of them might have jumped at the chance and been eager to take the time to spend with Drucker to write his biography. And as his advanced age began to affect his writing, Drucker worked with a collaborator and second author for several of his books, a fellow professor at Claremont Graduate School where he taught, Joe Maciariello.

But despite many available and willing authors, Drucker choose a new and relatively unknown author to write his biography: Elizabeth Haas Edersheim, who had written a single book, a biography entitled *McKinsey's Marvin Bower*. Drucker initiated the contact and Edersheim visited Drucker periodically to do research on the book. However, she did not drive just a couple blocks or even a few miles, but rather flew from New York for these working interviews, which lasted about 16 months. The effort resulted in *The Definitive Drucker* (McGraw-Hill, 2007), published after Drucker's death. It was not a biography, but about how Drucker saw the past development and the future of management at the end of his long career.

The origin of all this is traceable to the time when Drucker served as a military management consultant with Bower during World War II. Clearly, at least some of Drucker's ideas about the practice of consulting came through the influence of Bower.

Drucker's Big Break

Meanwhile, Drucker wrote another book, *The Future of Industrial Man*, which was published in the US in 1942. This and other writings brought him to the attention of Donaldson Brown, a senior executive at one of the best-known companies in America, General Motors (GM). According to one story, Brown became interested in Drucker due to their common interest in authority. Apparently through Brown's influence,

Drucker was hired for what some have called "a two-year audit" of GM in 1943. His work resulted in his book, *Concept of the Corporation*, which was published in 1946 and was immensely popular. It easily became a business bestseller. In many other cases, when academics write a bestselling book, offers for speaking, more book contracts, and of course consulting come rolling in. The temptation is great, and writing and speaking sufficiently rewarding, that it is not unusual for the former university professor to give up teaching and research to devote himself full time to these associated activities. As Drucker wrote, even Albert Einstein, perhaps the greatest theoretical physicist, gave it all up to become, in Drucker's words, a "professional famous person". Drucker, however, did not do this. Instead, he used his new fame to secure a position as professor of management at New York University, but continued his writing, speaking, and of course, consulting.

The book, *Concept of the Corporation*, was not intended as a tell-all of everything that was wrong about big business or GM. On the contrary, Drucker considered GM practices to be worthy of emulation by others. He did, however, publish ideas for even greater improvement at GM, for practices already considered far out, such as decentralization. This got him in trouble with legendary GM CEO Alfred P. Sloan, who, as explained in chapter two, was said to be so upset about Drucker's recommendations that he retaliated by ignoring the book and acting as if it did not exist. Was Sloan overly sensitive or Drucker overly aggressive? Who knows? What we do know is that Drucker might have followed the advice of his mentor, Marvin Bower, and not written the book at all or at least not commented on the activities of a client. Maybe Drucker got off easy on this one.

[1] No author listed, "What is the Origin of the Word 'Serendipity'?" *Oxford Dictionaries*, accessed at http://blog.oxforddictionaries.com/2012/03/what-is-the-origin-of-serendipity, 20 March 2015.

[2] Peter F. Drucker, *Adventures of a Bystander*, (New York: HarperCollins, 1978, 1979, 1991), p. 84.

[3] No author listed, "Alfred von Henikstein," *Wikipedia*, accessed at https://en.wikipedia.org/wiki/Alfred_von_Henikstein, 23 November 2015.

[4] No author listed, "History of Our Firm," *McKinsey & Company*, accessed at http://www.mckinsey.com/about_us/who_we_are/history_of_our_firm, 19 March 2015.

[5] No author listed, "McKinsey & Company," *Wikipedia*, accessed at http://en.wikipedia.org/wiki/McKinsey_%26_Company, 28 November 2017.

[6] No author listed, "Marvin Bower," *Wikipedia*, accessed at http://en.wikipedia.org/wiki/Marvin_Bower, 19 March 2015.

Chapter 4

How Drucker Established a Top-rated Consulting Practice

I don't think there is a question in anyone's mind that Drucker built a highly unusual yet top-rated consulting practice. His consulting services were in demand, and he received requests almost every week without advertising. He frequently rejected potential business, either because he felt his services weren't really necessary, the job could be better done by someone else, or he was just too busy to undertake it. I don't think that he ever was in a situation where it was financially necessary to accept work or that he felt it necessary to agree to an engagement from a sales point of view. The value in understanding Drucker's achievements in the building of his consulting practice is not just of general interest. Understanding this can enable almost anyone to adapt his ideas in other consulting practices, to make use of a consultant's services, or to adapt Drucker's advice in running organizations and accomplishing tasks. To understand how Drucker was able to achieve high value and results for his clients, we need to first examine both how and why consultants become consultants in the first place.

Why Do Consultants Become Consultants?

American Civil War General William Tecumseh Sherman succeeding Ulysses Grant as commander of the western theatre during the American Civil War once said: "I have heard of men peculiarly endowed with the traits necessary to be a general, but I have never met one." This is equally true of management consultants and their reasons for entering the profession. A few years back, the dean of a major business school reported that a survey showed the preponderance of its students wanted to be management consultants.

There is admittedly a certain glamour in being a consultant. Moreover, considered as a business, independent consulting has to be one of the more attractive ways of earning a living. It offers certain advantages not available in any other profession. Consider working hours. You probably have a time of the day when you work best. Most people do. Some people work better early in the morning, others late in the evening, and there are probably a lucky few who work equally well throughout a 24-hour period. Drucker, too, worked according to when he was the most productive and could establish the best results for his clients.

Zeroing in on Preferences

Knowing Drucker and how he paid special attention to individual preferences and advantages in knowledge work performance, I'm sure that he would suggest that consultants should identify their optimally most productive period to work.

Other preferences were equally important, he maintained. He advised all managers to identify their bosses' preferred method of receiving information. He followed his own advice whenever possible in working with his clients. Some preferred to get his recommendations in writing, he noted, while others preferred to receive information verbally. He also said that it was extremely important for new employees to discover which it was. He recommended that one investigate and discover this as soon as possible when employed by a new boss because the results achieved in effective work was heavily dependent on this single factor alone. Of course, this applies to a newly-employed consultant, as well. Unfortunately, the boss or the client could rarely provide this information; more often than not, they wouldn't even know if they were asked. This could only be ascertained by observation and experience.

My observations and experience in dealing with Drucker as his student was that he preferred communications in writing, although he could easily and did communicate face-to-face verbally and sometimes even on his own initiative with equal effectiveness. So he may have been one of the lucky few that could do both.

The hours in the day he preferred to work were another matter. I suspect that it was during the day and not late at night. In independent consulting, it doesn't make any difference, because except for any unique requirements of the particular consulting engagement, you can select your own hours depending on when you work best. You can take off work when you feel like it, if no client interaction is required.

I sometimes called Peter on the phone and we might talk for about an hour or more, which caused me to feel very guilty, as I just wanted a quick question answered and didn't want to waste his valuable time. However, when I mentioned this, he would say something about thinking through an issue with a client or working hard on some writing project and distance himself from the issue briefly. He said he was glad I called because he really needed and appreciated the break. The point is, regarding independent consulting, taking a break and the time to discuss management, war strategy, or education (we discussed all three and other subjects at various times) was Drucker's decision, and not someone above him that he had to please – with the exception, of course, of his wife Doris.

It goes without saying that there are due dates, deadlines, and meetings with clients or others that must be accomplished for the good of the practice, and I'm sure Drucker considered this also when I, or anyone else, happened to call without previously making an appointment and interrupted him. However, few other professional occupations grant you so much latitude. In independent consulting, you are the boss and the decision maker in almost everything concerning how you practise your profession. As I once overheard a consultant tell a client, and this was not Drucker, "We're going to do this my way, or we're not going to do it at all." That's seems to me a little harsh; after all, one does succeed better as a management consultant with a good bedside manner, just as a practising physician does.

Drucker didn't accept every consulting assignment for a variety of reasons. I'm not talking about his schedule being booked or unable to take on an assignment due to ill health. That happens to all of us from time to time. As I mentioned in the last chapter, I remember once that he rejected an assignment because he felt that what the client wanted was already available and should have been known to him. So, Drucker told the client what he should have known. He even may have recommended a book where the client could find the information, whether it was one of his own books or not. These were all Drucker's decisions, not those of any manager (except maybe when it concerned his wife Doris).

The Advantage of Control over Your Life

Like Drucker, as an independent consultant you can decide which assignments to accept and to reject those that you feel should not be accepted. You are not only a consultant, you're an independent consultant; you are the boss! And this may be no small thing. To examine this advantage further, ask yourself, are you in a job in which you don't like your boss? Must you work with people whom you just do not care to be around? As an independent consultant, here again the decision is yours. You decide whom you wish to work for and not work for, as well as the people you do and do not work with. Whether you do or do not work for a particular client or others who may help you with a project is entirely up to you.

This control over your work life is valuable in many ways. Unless you accept too much work, it usually results in reduced stress. I read somewhere that individuals who have control over their work and work-life balance tend to live much longer and have fewer illnesses than those who are most subject to the control of another or job demands over which they have little say. Drucker lived until just two weeks short of his 96th birthday. I don't know whether being an independent consultant had anything to do with this or not, but his long life, and long work life, are certainly facts.

The Question of Compensation

As an independent consultant, even income is in many ways much more under your control. Are you dissatisfied with your current income? Do you feel you are paid inadequately?

Have you had a freeze on your compensation due to a recession, or even told that your salary would be reduced? In independent consulting you set your own fees; you decide how much you're worth and in that sense how much you want to make. If you are worth more right now or your business has suddenly expanded, you can immediately give yourself a raise. You don't need to wait for a salary committee to determine if you should be paid more. At any time that you feel that you are underpaid, you have the power to remedy this fact immediately. And if Drucker felt like it, he gave his services away gratis without asking for anything in return. Many consultants like to be in a position to do that.

Location, Location, Location

Do you prefer to work at home? In independent consulting you can earn a very high income working from your own home without worrying about parking, driving, or the expense of an outside office. In fact, the office in your own home will probably be tax-deductible. Drucker certainly did this. Drucker worked out of his home – except for visits to clients, teaching and lecturing – during his entire career. That's an important lesson for anyone who thinks a prestigious address, an office with panelled walls, complete with a waiting room and expensive leather chairs, and more are needed. Even after all these years, it's hard to believe that Drucker had no secretary, even before the computer age, and he had no receptionist and answered his own phone. Also, and I'm certainly not recommending this, but I don't think Drucker ever used a computer.

Risky Business

Finally, are you concerned about taking risks associated with your own full-time consulting practice? Yes, there are risks. Drucker even taught his clients how to deal with the risks in their businesses, as we'll see in a later chapter. In fact, you can minimize risk by following some of Drucker's practices. There's no need to risk your time, career, or a large monetary investment. You can start in consulting part-time and ease your way in. That's what Drucker did, and others have done the same, working part time after their full-time jobs, at nights, and on weekends. You won't need to quit your full-time job until you are ready and even already successful. Essentially, and maybe unintentionally, that's precisely what Drucker did.

The Importance of Goals and More Serendipity

In our analysis of why individuals become independent consultants, we cannot overlook the importance of goals. Drucker made a great deal of money as a consultant. Yet he chose not to adopt the lifestyle of the "rich and famous", and at some point decided that hefty consulting fees should go into a foundation he supported rather than into his pocket. And as I reported before, he would charge nothing if he were so inclined. These acts are all good evidence that great wealth was not the primary goal driving his consulting work. There are clearly many reasons to go into consulting other than attaining wealth. Later in life, he explained that except when there was a real need for money – such as during a recession when one might be unemployed and work is hard to find – all workers are volunteers because if they don't like what they are doing, they can easily go elsewhere.

I believe this absolutely. I discussed one of our director's trips abroad for my graduate school, with the intent of some sort of mutual programme for undergraduates at their schools and the MBA at ours. This director receives no compensation, although we do allow relatives of all our administrators and faculty to enrol in our programme at no cost. I congratulated him on a successful trip and told him we could start paying him soon. This individual, a highly decorated retired Air Force colonel said, "Bill, don't worry about it. I don't need the money. When you are having fun in a job, that's pay enough." So perhaps Drucker was correct. I'm going to pay the director eventually, but I thanked him for saying, "Don't worry about it," because I did.

Part-time Consulting

However, some volunteers and some consultants come to independent consulting to supplement earnings from other sources. In one sense, this was what happened with Drucker. He was earning money as a freelance writer and as a part-time professor at Sarah Lawrence College in New York. His writings on politics and society culminated in his book, *The Future of Industrial Man*, and brought him first to Bennington College in Vermont as a full-time professor of politics and philosophy in 1942 and the following year to General Motors to do a top-level management audit. This was a major two-year consulting assignment, which led to his book, *Concept of the Corporation*, to more consulting, and to his academic appointment in management at New York University in 1950. One can see how independent consulting supplemented his writing and professorial income up to this time.

Part-time Consulting by Students

If you think students don't make good part-time consultants, you would be wrong. Our students at the California institute of Advanced Management learn and are required to perform consulting in teams of four, and once solo, for companies large and small, in every course. They do this primarily to demonstrate the application of the theory they have learned. They gather testimonials for their work from satisfied clients as if they are going out of style.

All our clients are entitled to a second engagement after six months, free of charge. Recently we completed a second engagement for an unusual client. It was an old, but small and successful, international consulting firm, with about a dozen or so consultant-employees who all held graduate degrees. The client told me, "Your MBA students are excellent consultants. Can I hire your students for pay?" I thanked him, but declined. I thought that the possibility of a conflict of interest was too much. However, we did cut a deal that our MBA graduates could be hired for pay and we wouldn't take a cent.

When to Transition from Part Time to Full Time

At the point that the part-time consultant makes as much or more money than in his or her "day job", one of two totally different options are available. The lure of consulting may completely draw the part-time independent consultant into full-time consulting activities such that academia or the previous profession is completely abandoned, or consulting may continue as a financially supporting activity. The latter is what occurred in Drucker's case. Drucker built a renowned, top-rated consulting practice, but no matter how large it grew – and it did grow very large – or how famous his consulting became, it was still only one facet of Drucker's central profession, which he called being a social ecologist.

One More Consultant's Tale

I should throw in my own story here, which occurred before I met Drucker. I left the Air Force for a time to work abroad in my wife's country of birth, Israel. When I returned, I took a job as head of research and development for a small company, Sierra Engineering Company in Sierra Madre, California. However, while in Israel I had written an article published in the US about a product I had become involved with before I left the Air Force and went to Israel: personal body armour for aircrews. Unknowingly the article caught the interest of a vice president of an aerospace company, Garrett AiResearch, which was located in the Los Angeles area. AiResearch built turbochargers and turboprops as well as other defence-related products. It eventually merged, was acquired, merged again, and in about 1999 acquired the Honeywell name.

Several years before I met him, when his company was still Garrett AiResearch, this vice president had been in charge of a programme to replace the US Army's protective steel helmet – used in World War II, Korea, and Vietnam – with a titanium helmet. Titanium was lighter, stronger, and more protective, but of course more expensive. He had been promoted to vice president, but somewhere along the way his pet project had been abandoned, even though he felt it still had potential.

Then he read my article in *Ordnance* and thought he had found the right man to conduct some research and recommend either to continue the project or to let it die. He wrote and asked if I were interested. He used my address in Israel that he had obtained from the editor of *Ordnance Magazine*. Unfortunately, I had left Israel and returned some months earlier to, of all places, Los Angeles, exactly where his company was located. However, the story doesn't end that quickly.

His letter was forwarded to my in-laws, who lived in a different city in Israel. Mail could not be forwarded abroad in those days. My in-laws spoke, read, and wrote only Hebrew and everyone corresponded internationally only on very lightweight, special air-mail paper. Larger paper packages, which this was, went by ship and took about six to seven weeks to arrive. You could send packages by air, which is what this vice president at AiResearch had done in the first instance, but in those days that cost a fortune. Israel was still a developing country back in the early 1970s, and my in-laws couldn't afford to waste money. So they held on to the letter, hoping that sooner or later my wife and I would return from the US to visit.

And I did, but without my wife, and under very unexpected circumstances. In 1973, Syria and Egypt launched a surprise attack against Israel in what is known today as the Yom Kippur War. When living in Israel and under Israeli law, I served in the Israeli armed forces and because of my prior military experience was commissioned in the Israeli Air Force as a major. I returned to Israel because of the war. After the armistice, I was given a couple days off and decided to visit my in-laws, where I was handed the letter, which had been written several months earlier. I contacted the writer on my return and he engaged me to do some research as a consultant. It was my first consulting job. My motivation was a combination of supplementing my income (as a research and development director of aviation life-support products) and satisfying my curiosity about consulting and what it was all about.

It was not as an extensive project as Drucker had with GM

for his first project, and it only lasted a few months. I discovered that the army's new Kevlar helmet, the one in use today, was under development and was lighter, more protective, and above all less expensive than the titanium helmet that I had examined. So my recommendation was to abandon the project, and it was abandoned. This definitely whet my interest in consulting, and I was now an experienced, if not a very experienced, consultant. It also was a lesson that any mail still arriving in Israel and addressed to me should be airmailed to me and I would pay the airfare. It is also a lesson for all who want to begin independent consulting today. The connection with Drucker's serendipitous entrance and my own was clear: writing books or magazine articles was an indirect but powerful method of marketing consulting services.

What Makes an Outstanding Consultant?

Simply being a consultant and being an outstanding consultant are two different things. After observing Drucker for more than 30 years, as well as speaking with many highly respected consultants around the country, I identified seven areas that make the difference. They are adapted from my book, *How to Make It Big as a Consultant* (AMACOM, 4th edition, 2009). Drucker exemplified every single one of these seven areas.

The Ability to Interact with All Participants in a Consulting Engagement

It's not so much what you say, but how you say it. Doctors with great medical knowledge but poor bedside manners often find that their patients prefer to go to doctors with much less experience or ability. Therefore, developing a pleasant "bedside manner" while maintaining your integrity gives your clients and others confidence in what you say and do. This can be as important as your technical knowledge. Drucker deemed the courteous treatment of others – especially clients – essential, and though he might respectfully disagree with them, and even chose to turn down work, he always showed others courtesy.

The Ability to Diagnose Problems Correctly

To stay with the doctor analogy, we know that a doctor has access to all sorts of medicines to help cure a patient. But if the physician makes an incorrect diagnosis, the medicine may:

- Not help the patient and, in the consulting context, be a waste of time, money, and resources
- Hurt the patient more. Drucker emphasized the Hippocrates injunction to physicians for those in management: "above all, do no harm"

Your ability to diagnose a problem correctly in a consulting situation is extremely important. Otherwise, your actions may hurt the organization rather than help it. Prescribing the right medicine, that is, giving the correct advice, is one of the most significant criteria of an outstanding consultant. I have seen consultants get carried away with the use of their own sophisticated methodologies such that they forget about the central issue they're supposed to investigate, solve, or resolve. As a result, they get their clients and themselves in trouble by failing to prescribe the correct cure, although they displayed their expertise wonderfully.

The Ability to Find Solutions that Work

Of course, having diagnosed a problem, you are expected to recommend the proper actions to correct the situation. Drucker's methods for dealing with problems can be found throughout this book. Perhaps his most innovative strategy was to ask his clients questions of a type that led to their uncovering potential solutions themselves. This unique methodology in itself set Drucker apart from other consultants who emphasized their own mostly quantitative, analytical methods. I will refer to this again.

Technical Expertise and Knowledge

Perhaps you expected this would be the most important skill for a good consultant, and it is true that technical expertise in any field is important.

Expertise comes from education, experience, and the personal skills you have developed. It may be in any one of a number of areas, and it may develop in a variety of ways.

G. Gordon Liddy, known primarily for his association with the Watergate break-in, commanded a hefty six-figure income as a security consultant after he was released from prison. This has little to do with his going to prison, of course, except maybe for the publicity surrounding the Watergate break-in. Still, I know of a few overly ambitious consultants who would probably be willing to spend a couple years in jail if it meant emerging with the ability to pull down a six-figure income. But my point is that even a somewhat shady background doesn't preclude a consultant's ability to earn top fees and use his perception of technical expertise and knowledge.

Moreover, Drucker claimed that he brought not so much his knowledge and experience to solving problems as his ignorance, confirming that it was the methodology he used for solving problems that was of primary importance.

Not that this methodology was necessarily so highly sophisticated, but rather that it was window-dressing for the results desired.

Good Communication Skills

Charles Garvin, from the well-known Boston Consulting Group (BCG), did extensive consulting in the area of business strategy, beginning in the early 1960s. With 30 years' experience, Garvin identified three major attributes that every good consultant needs. It may surprise you, but he found that the number-one attribute was superior communication abilities. Analytical skills were second, and the ability to work under pressure was third. To emphasize this last point, a good friend of mine was once a principle at McKinsey & Company, the largest and probably the most prestigious consulting firm in the world. He described working late at night and on weekends, and flying around the country to see clients so often that on one occasion the pressure was too much. On the way to the airport, he absolutely broke down and cried, to such an extent that he had to pull over to the side of the road and get control of himself before proceeding. That doesn't sound like much fun!

Strong Marketing and Selling Abilities

Regardless of the technical area you are interested in, whether a functional area in business or something entirely different, you must learn to be a good marketer and a good salesperson. The two are not the same. Marketing is at a higher strategic level, while selling is tactical. Marketing has more to do with having the right product to sell to the right market, whereas selling has to do with persuading others to purchase something that you have. Not only do consultants sell an intangible product, they also must sell themselves. Drucker said that if marketing were done perfectly, selling would be unnecessary.

Managerial Skills

Last, but not the least in importance, is the ability to manage an organization or a practice and to oversee projects. In my mind, an outstanding consultant must also be a good manager. As with other skills, the ability to manage can be learned. But it is far from automatic. This is one huge reason that Drucker emphasized education. He believed that theory was fine, but nothing got done until you translated theory into hard work. At the California Institute of Advanced Management, we built an entire system around this in something that we call IATEP™. This stands for immediately applied theory for enhanced performance, which is described in more detail later in this book.

To sum it up, Drucker built a highly successful consulting practice not only by doing things right, but also by doing the right things. He was both a manager and a leader. Sure, he had some lucky breaks. But he didn't squander them.

Chapter 5

Marketing Drucker's or Anyone Else's Consulting Practice

Drucker taught that marketing was one of two essential functions for any business. As Drucker moved into closer consideration of non-profits and other types of organizations, he extended this concept to all organizations. In Drucker's view, marketing should pervade everything in the organization, any organization. To illustrate just how far Drucker's ideas have expanded marketing's role over the years, President Truman once chided the US Marine Corps for overly promoting itself to the public. Flash ahead 50 years, and not only were all US military organizations practising some aspect of promotion, but the Marine Corps was lauded for its success in this function. I have heard combat-support functions openly refer to the war fighter users of their "products", products such as training, as their "customers".

This chapter contains what Drucker advised clients to ensure marketing's proper emphasis. However, although Drucker counselled clients about marketing's pre-eminence and how to do it properly, some question exists as to whether he marketed his own consulting practice as he advised others. In fact, did he market his consulting practice at all, and if so, how? This chapter will answer both of these questions as well.

Basic Drucker Marketing

To begin, Drucker said that all business had two basic functions: innovation and marketing. Any business – and as he also interpreted this, any organization – must ensure the practice of both. Some would say that innovation is also an element of marketing, since at the tactical level innovation is an important ingredient of success in both product and service. At the strategic level this could mean an important differential advantage in positioning against competitors to win customers.

I have been closely associated many times with organizations that specialized in consulting for small businesses and business start-ups. In fact, one major differential advantage of the MBA graduate school that I now head is that students are required do pro-bono consulting in teams of four or individually in every course they take. This is required in order for them to experience and demonstrate their ability to apply the theories taught in the classroom to actual clients. Many of their clients are small or new businesses. It would be difficult to overestimate the number of owners and entrepreneurs who somehow thought that the simple act of creating or entering into a business would automatically result in customers. When asked, "what is the differential advantage between what you offer and that of your established competitors?", a blank stare was a too-frequent response. It is as if they want to say, "I'm providing customers with the opportunity to buy my product or service. Isn't that enough?" In their minds, the mere fact of offering these goods or services was sufficient. Customers? Why, they'll come automatically, according to this thinking.

These individuals forget that a customer, or prospect, must have some reason to buy the product or service other than the mere existence of the supplier. Usually others are already established in supplying the same product or service. Even if the product or service is a cutting-edge innovation, prospects for it are still spending their hard-earned cash elsewhere. To persuade them to switch from their current suppliers or to start buying something never before purchased is neither automatic nor accomplished without considerable effort. Prospects need to know what this new supplier has that others do not, and if the price is worth trying it or switching from where their money is currently spent.

Nineteenth century essayist and poet, Ralph Waldo Emerson, outlined the need for this basic requirement in words that have come down to us as: "Build a better mousetrap, and the world will beat a path to your door."[1] Though he failed to add that with only the innovation – and without marketing – this was unlikely to happen, no matter how much value was added to the new mousetrap. This calls forth the need for marketing. But what about "Drucker Marketing" and what was its added value? "Drucker Marketing" consists of several major principles, with a number of corollaries. His primary principles, along with the corollaries are:

- The primacy of marketing over all other business functions
- A critical distinction between sales and marketing to the extent that, theoretically, perfect marketing would make selling unnecessary
- The possibility that these two different efforts, marketing and selling, are not only not complementary, but in fact adversarial
- A focus on the customer and what the customer values as opposed to what we may speculate are the customer's desires and evaluation of our offering
- Marketing as a pervasive theme throughout the organization in every department

The Primacy of Marketing over All Other Business Functions

Drucker believed that marketing wasn't just a business function, but that it needed to be considered the *primary* business function. That's not to say that he didn't know that other functions – finance, accounting, engineering, production, you name it – were not important, and or even more critical to an organization in different phases of its development or in different situations. But by his analysis, marketing was the single most important function, because without successful marketing a business, no matter how efficient or effective at these other functions, would be unsustainable and eventually fail.

The Important Distinction between Sales and Marketing

Drucker was one of the first business scholars to recognize that sales and marketing were distinctly different functions, even with different objectives. Marketing is focused on the customer and having what the customer wants. So the marketer needs to find out what the customer wants and to develop, produce, or stock it so that he has something that a prospect already wants. That is the objective: focus on the customer to have something that a prospect wants. Selling is focused on the product or service in stock and persuading the customer to make a purchase from this stock.

This distinction is so important that Drucker wrote an article for an academic journal. This is something my research failed to uncover Drucker doing at any other time or for any other topic: Academic journals are rarely, if ever, read by practitioners. They tend to be highly quantitative and are probably more cited in yet other academic publications, such as other journals read almost entirely by academics, and textbooks read (or not read, as the case may be) by students. Contrast this with practitioners who may actually read to apply the information contained in the article directly, as one finds, for example, in the *Harvard Business Review* or a professional book such as the one you are holding. With this exception, Drucker had little interest in writing for academic journals; some fellow academics despised his work and writings.

Not Reading Drucker

I believe it was on his 80th birthday that the *Los Angeles Times* asked well-known management authors from around the country to write a short essay about what they had learned from Peter Drucker. He received many accolades from the best, including Tom Peters, whose co-authorship of *In Search of Excellence* set off a flurry of books and examinations of American companies that were successful and doing things right, and Mary Beth Moss Kantor of Harvard, whose books and editorship of the *Harvard Business Review* were well known.

One well-known academic who responded had written a bestselling book based on research and began a fad that swept the country for several years on Japanese management. His response was something to the effect that he couldn't answer the question, as he didn't read Drucker, since Drucker didn't write for the "scientific" journals. Well, Drucker did so— once. He wrote what is known in these circles as a "think" piece asserting the important difference between sales and marketing for *The Journal of Marketing*, one of the top academic journals in the discipline in the 1950s and early in Drucker's academic career and even now, 10 years after Drucker's death.

In his article, Drucker applied his own biting humour about the popular trend for presidents of corporations renaming their vice presidents of sales as vice presidents of marketing. Yet their duties and responsibilities remained unchanged. That, according to them, solved the problem. Wrote Drucker: "If you stop calling a man an undertaker and start calling him a mortician, his job does not change one iota. He still digs graves to bury the departed."[2]

Theoretically, Perfect Marketing Would Make Selling Unnecessary

Now Drucker was speaking in theory only, but his point is easily illustrated. Since marketing is about having the perfect product or service desired by the prospect, if you have it and it's known, happy consumers would probably spread the word without you having to do a great deal of presenting the product to prospects and convincing them to buy it, both important steps in selling. Let's say you invent a pill that will cure any illness or disease. You optimize it for a particular market such that it has no negative side effects, is easy to consume, and can be purchased at an affordable price considering the market you are targeting. You might need a little advertising and public relations to get started, but once on the way, selling would be pretty much unnecessary. Impossible? For 70 years The Hershey Company did no advertising for its famous candy bar. According to an ad executive, it didn't need to: "This was a brand that was an American staple, had been passed down for generations, and that people could remember enjoying as a kid."[3] The Hershey people had a product that was desired and could get it to distributors – all marketing, not selling, functions. No selling was required!

The Possibility that Marketing and .
Are Not Complementary, but Advers₍

Drucker deviated significantly from established ma
in even the limitations of marketing and selling conne₍
most marketing textbooks and you'll note that selling
a supporting sub-function of marketing along with adv
promotion, distribution, and public relations. Most catego   .₍
as one of the promotional variables. But Peter maintained that not
only was the function of selling not complementary to marketing,
but that it could be adversarial.

Believe me, I struggled for some years thinking about how selling and marketing could be adversarial, but I never asked him to
explain how he came up with that rather revolutionary thought.
One day, I had a sudden insight and I knew exactly what Drucker
was talking about. Let's assume that marketing is not done perfectly. In fact, let's go all the way – it's the wrong market for the
product being sold. Maybe it has other problems with price or
design, as well. However, you have extraordinary salespeople. They
are so unique and talented that through extraordinary effort and
use of their selling expertise, these wonderful sales wizards are able
to accomplish the impossible and create a modest profit selling
this faulty product to the wrong market.

Is this proof that selling is a complementary function, and
not at all adversarial? Not necessarily. Consider the extraordinary
effort of these salespeople. Much more product could be sold if
the target market was correct or the product better designed or
offered at the right price. Consider the profits created and how
much greater the profits would be under these better circumstances, when marketing had been done correctly. Moreover,
the modest success of these outstanding salespeople might be
misleading. How much better would it have been if they had
failed miserably? Perhaps then this wrong product, price, and
market would have been abandoned and a new and much better
market sought and discovered, and sold to. Are you beginning
to understand Drucker's thinking? Under the circumstances
of these salespeople creating a marginal profit, not only would

selling not have been complementary to good marketing, but more importantly, it would have been adversarial to the firm's profits and best interests as well.

The Focus on the Customer and What the Customer Values

No matter how smart we are, we don't decide what the customer wants and values. Sometimes this can result in additional sales that we never suspected were possible. My friend Joe Cossman introduced the flexible garden hose with holes to the gardening market as an alternative to the water sprinkler, and he sold a bundle. Practically everyone that owned a lawn or garden bought at least one when they were introduced. They were more popular than the ultra light expanding hose that had been introduced in the previous few years.

Cossman, a marketing genius, tracked all the wholesale orders of his product. One day, his analysis revealed that farmer supply and feed stores had begun to order his product in increasing numbers. Since homeowners seemed to fall outside the regular customers of feed stores, he contacted the stores to inquire about the reason for the unexpected interest. He discovered that farmers raising chickens had found that his garden hose with holes made an excellent (and less expensive) air conditioner for lowering the temperature of chicken coups during the hot summer months.

Cossman discovered an additional, but unsuspected, market. Drucker was not surprised at this; it was frequently the case. What did surprise him was when he found how frequently the marketers got even the basics wrong. He decided that the problem was that the suppliers made assumptions about what the prospect wanted that were incorrect. Yet it was always the customer who defined the product or service, not the supplier.

Consider DuPont's experience with a product they named Kevlar. DuPont introduced Kevlar in the early 1970s. Kevlar was a super-cloth with fibres five times the tensile strength of steel. The engineers thought it would make an excellent substitution for the steel reinforcement in heavy-duty tyres. It did, but it made an even better fragmentation protective body armour, and when impregnated for rigidity to protect against blunt trauma, could be used as the basic component in protective helmets worn by battlefield combatants. Thus did the US Army's "steel pot" of World War II fame disappear from the battlefield to be replaced by an impregnated super-cloth originally intended for vehicle tyres by its innovator.

Drucker was also shocked to discover that some marketers didn't like it when someone used a product other than how it was intended. Inventor Alfred Einhorn became so distressed when dentists began using his anaesthetic drug, Novocain, that he travelled up and down Germany, trying to get them to stop, angrily insisting that his invention was intended for use by medical doctors, not dentists. R.H. Macys tried to stop their appliance sales because by the established norms of the time, appliance sales were supposed to be significantly lower in a department store, where the emphasis previously was strictly on clothes. Unlike Cossman, these innovators tried to make sales, causing what they perceived as an abnormality to stop, even though it was in their own and their customers' best interests to exploit the unplanned and unexpected increase in sales, which ultimately proved to be much larger markets than their original intended market.

Drucker wrote a warning that marketers introducing new products or services should begin with the assumption that their products or services might find uses and markets never imagined when the product was designed and first introduced.

Marketing as a Pervasive Theme throughout the Organization

Some years ago, my wife and I visited Turkey. When we inquired about assistance in purchasing a sample of Turkey's world-famous rugs, the hotel personnel recommended several manufacturing companies and advised us to purchase from one of them rather than from a street store or in the Grand Bazaar, where hundreds of vendors exhibited their wares of Turkish rugs. There was a big difference. The highest price for a rug on the street was about $2,000. The hotel staff told us that a top-quality rug would go for at least twice that. We knew that the hotel probably received a commission from the rug companies recommended, but still the hotel's reputation was on the line and it seemed a much better source of purchase. In addition, the hotel said that the company would probably give us a tour of its factory. That had to be worth something. Accordingly, the hotel made a call, and a limousine came to take us to the rug factory for a tour. Marketing actually began with the manufacturer's rep – in this case, the hotel. However, it continued in the limo.

The driver spoke perfect English. He explained that we would be shown the entire process of rug manufacture, and in the case of the silk rugs, from the caterpillars on up. During the drive he explained that rug quality varied greatly and that this company wanted potential buyers to be educated so that they knew the difference between quality rugs and the cheap rugs frequently sold on the Turkish streets. He took us to a sub-plant where the process began. A junior manager stopped the process at every phase so that we understood what was being done and why. His English wasn't perfect, but it was good enough that we understood everything he said and he could answer our questions. We progressed from station to station, from the raw material to weaving.

Even as we moved from station to station and encountered someone who did not speak English, the supervisor explained each function and why different tasks were important and necessary for a superior product. The manager who acted as our guide also translated whenever required. We were told that some manufacturers skipped certain steps, which might save money but would cost the owner in the long run. A quality control engineer who was educated in the states explained how they controlled quality, how each item was inspected and why some were rejected. They all seemed happy to explain their contribution to the rug-making.

From this facility, our limousine driver took us to another facility, where the rugs were stored. Again we were taken from station to station and the different types of rugs, weaves, and colouring were patiently explained. At the end of the tour, we were taken to a large showroom and introduced to the salesman. He showed us samples and asked about the size, material, design, and colouring of the kind of rug we wanted. He wrote down this information. The most expensive types were pure silk, the least expensive wool, and the blends in between. These were reasonably expensive rugs. We had intended to buy only one rug of moderate size and spend a maximum of $4,000. And though we usually don't carry that much money around, we had investigated prices before we left the hotel and had this in cash. We were led to a comfortable couch and were served tea and light refreshments by friendly employees while the salesman chatted with us.

After a few minutes, two workmen began to bring in rugs of the types we had requested. There were about a dozen. We liked two silk rugs, but could not decide between them. The asking price was about $6,500 each. My wife and I had considerable experience in buying products all over the world, but I knew we would have to negotiate. We thought we could probably get one rug for about $5,000. This was more than we intended to spend, but thought that probably it was the best we could do. We told the salesman which rugs we were interested in. He said something to the workmen and they carried the others rugs out.

I smiled and opened with an offer of $4,000 for one of the rugs. He smiled back, but shook his head "no" and knocked off only $500 from $6,500, taking rug's price down to $6000. We haggled some more, and after several additional cycles of pricing eventually got down to about $5,500. Then I had an idea. I told my wife my idea and asked her in Hebrew (she's an Israeli) if we could afford it. She liked the idea and said that we could.

I asked the salesman, "What if we bought both rugs? How much would he charge us?"

He thought for a moment and said, "$10,000".

I said, "Look, we'll give you $7,500 right now for both rugs."

"I can't make a deal like that," he responded. "Only the general manager has that authority, but if you are serious about buying both rugs, I'll see if he's available."

Minutes later a well-dressed, middle-aged man stepped into the room.

"How will you pay for the rugs, Mr Cohen?" he asked.

"$4,000 cash, $3,500 cheque or credit card," I answered. We closed the deal, drank tea, and chatted. On the way back to the hotel, the driver asked if we had made a purchase and he resold the company's reputation and quality.

The lesson here is that marketing of one sort or another occurred from start to finish, beginning at the hotel. Did we get a good deal? Probably, but others have done better. After all, this was the Middle East. But consider this: we intended to spend $4,000 tops. We spent more than twice that. We were told by the hotel that prices would be much higher than on the street or in the Grand Bazaar, so we were prepared. However, we wouldn't have even spent the $4,000 without being absolutely convinced of the quality and reputation of the manufacturer. We were on vacation and would consider occasionally spending more money than we would normally, but $4,000 was a lot of money, especially when the asking price on the street or in the Grand Bazaar was much less. Marketing was pervasive within every department of that organization and it paid off in a large sale that would not otherwise have been obtained.

Did Drucker Take His Own Medicine?

Drucker first had a background in writing and worked as a journalist. He developed his writing abilities further, first in German, and then in English. When we consider if Drucker used the methods of Drucker Marketing in his consulting practice, we have to first remember that Drucker originally came into consulting through his writing articles and books, a major consulting contract with General Motors, and another book and more articles. So he didn't sell his services to build his practice. Clients came to him through his writing. And this is a perfect entry. I got into consulting the same way. It certainly fits the principle of Drucker Marketing, which asserts that marketing is primary over other business functions, including selling. Moreover, it almost automatically ensured that Drucker had a product that prospects desired and valued. If they didn't, he would not have been published in either books or magazines. Moreover, every part of "the Drucker business" was involved in this marketing effort—from his books and articles in *Harvard Business Review* to tapes, videos, seminars, and workshops.

But don't misunderstand. I'm not saying that Drucker intentionally followed any marketing strategy in building his practice, but it worked out that way nevertheless. Moreover, intentionally or not, Drucker manoeuvred his practice into the "Hershey Syndrome". He no longer even had to write to get clients. I'm sure he received offers into his nineties, although he had long since retired from an active consulting role. Like Hershey: "This was a brand that was an American staple, had been passed down for generations, and that people could remember enjoying as a kid." Well, perhaps a little exaggeration in the last few words, but you get what I mean.

I view Drucker's consulting practice as confirmation of the marketing principles inherent in "Drucker Marketing", a term that he never himself used to describe what he recommended in marketing anything.

---

[1] Emerson's actual words were, apparently: "If a man has good corn or wood, or boards, or pigs, to sell, or can make better chairs or knives, crucibles or church organs, than anybody else, you will find a broad hard-beaten road to his house, though it be in the woods." Even the misquote is misquoted today. Originally it was: "If a man can write a better book, preach a better sermon, or make a better mousetrap than his neighbor." No author listed. "Build a Better Mousetrap, and the World Will Beat a Path to Your Door," *Wikipedia*, accessed at http://en.wikipedia.org/wiki/Build_a_better_mousetrap,_and_the_world_will_beat_a_path_to_your_door, 26 April 2015.

[2] Cohen, William A., "The Grandfather of Marketing," *M&SB*, November 2014, accessed at http://www.marketingandsalesbooks.com/en/contribution/114/the-grandfather-of-marketing?c=4, 24 November 24, 2015.

[3] John Luciew, "Hollywood Gets Hershey's Marketing History Mostly Right In 'Mad Men' Finale," accessed at http://www.pennlive.com/midstate/index.ssf/2013/06/hollywood_gets_hersheys_market.html, 7 May 2015.

Chapter 6

Drucker's Ethical and Integrity Bedrock

To Drucker, ethics and integrity were the bedrock of all business and personal practices. However, he recognized that there were differences in cultures and many challenges in operating from this bedrock. So he brought all his talents to bear and investigated all manner of ethics and integrity. He easily could have written a book solely on this one topic. He told clients from all organizations that they could make lots of mistakes and still get through in fine shape, so long as they obeyed the single injunction to maintain their integrity. He told clients that there was no such thing as "business ethics", but that without integrity they would not succeed. The clients who obeyed his injunction to resolve the apparent conflict between ethics and integrity in their private and business lives tended to be more successful than those who paid lip service to Drucker's recommendations. He is rightly credited with the comment that he repeated both in class and in his writings, which drew a line and distinguished between ethics and integrity from morality and the law. Whether hiring call girls to entertain customers was ethical or not was the wrong question. According to Drucker, this was not a question of ethics, but rather aesthetics. To wit, "Do I want to see a pimp when I look at myself in the mirror while shaving?"[1]

Drucker's "Lies" and the Licence to Shade Statements for Emphasis

Doris Drucker died at the age of 103 in 2014. Before she died, I heard Doris say many times: "I was blessed with having a husband who, in addition to being clever, was a man of substance, with strong values and high ethics."

Through his stories and examples, Drucker taught his students, readers, audiences, and consulting clients what he had learned only after intensive study, analysis, and thinking. However, he was sometimes criticized for the examples he used to illustrate his conclusions. Stories that he told occasionally misstated facts in illustrating his concepts. This was true, and if challenged, he did not deny the charge. His response invariably was, "I'm not a historian; I'm trying to make a point."

I have heard Drucker attacked by those who disagreed with his conclusions or the management solutions he recommended. For example, they criticized Management by Objectives, a methodology Drucker promoted and claimed was a fairer and more accurate means of evaluating managers, as well as ensuring that executives were focused on the organization's current goals and objectives. Moreover, his detractors even questioned if his very practical solutions were really based on scientific research. However, I have never heard of his being attacked for a lack of ethics or integrity. He might have been occasionally careless with the accuracy of his examples, but never with his integrity. He did not lie, cheat, or steal, nor did he tolerate those who did. He was one of the most ethical individuals I have ever met – whether in consulting, his business dealings, or his private life. I believe that his ethics played a major role in his consulting practice and should be modelled and followed as Drucker did himself. Not many people would turn down a major speaking contract worth thousands of dollars with an admonishment that there was nothing that the ancients didn't know about leadership and that this wisdom was available in books written two thousand years ago.

Drucker's Ethics vs. Those Commonly Stated

Yet Drucker's ethics were not always the "ethics" that people readily label as such. He despised the term "business ethics" and said that there was no such thing. There was only ethics, period. If a consultant wishes to follow in Drucker's ethical footsteps, and I certainly recommend this, it is important to understand his thinking and what was behind it. Only with this understanding can we proceed to apply Drucker's thinking on ethics as a guide in our own practice and in dealing with clients.

Ethical Decisions May Be More Complex Than You Think

Ethical challenges are pervasive and significant. Clients pay for the consulting. Do they have a right to tell you to omit, deemphasize, or "spin" conclusions in your report and recommendations? Where does the difference between positive thinking about the future of a product, service, or business differ from the facts sufficiently enough to make the consultant's statements a lie? Even legal requirements usually do not permit an advertiser to claim that it makes "the best hamburger on Earth", though most realize that such a statement, impossible to prove, is at best a goal and not a demonstrable fact. But there are limits, ethical as well as legal. When does a "white lie" told to protect someone's feelings become an unacceptable "bald-faced lie"? These questions just scratch the surface of those that a consultant frequently faces.

What Are We Talking About?

The concepts of integrity, ethics, morality, obedience to the law, and even honour are closely related, but they are not the same. Drucker spoke about the need for integrity. He raised issues regarding business ethics. It is important to distinguish among these and other connected concepts. I know that I've overly simplified these here, but it is necessary for an understanding of Drucker's views. Ethics is a code of values. Integrity speaks to adherence to this code of values. Morality is the quality of this adherence. Drucker defined honour as demonstrable integrity and honesty, adding also that an honourable man stood by his principles.[2]

Drucker's writing contained evidence of considerable concern with these concepts. What makes them particularly difficult to understand is that the unique interpretation of each concept determines what is right and good, and what is not. Drucker was acutely aware of the 17th century physicist, mathematician, and philosopher Blaise Pascal's pronouncement that "there are truths on this side of the Pyrenees, which are falsehoods on the other".[3] Drucker recognized that what one culture might find acceptable or even a requirement for ethical behaviour might be totally different for another and even considered unethical. An example he used in class was the custom for corporations in Japan to reward underpaid government officials after their retirement if the corporations had benefitted from the actions of these officials when they were in office. In the US, this was considered unethical and corrupt. In Japan this was both ethical and the right thing to do. He told the story in class which I have frequently repeated illustrating this problem and told in chapter one.

Drucker explained why the actions of the Japanese CEO in that story would be considered an ethical duty and neither unethical nor unlawful in Japan. "In Japan," Drucker told us, "government officials are paid very little. They could live on what they receive in retirement only with great difficulty. It is therefore expected that when they retire, companies that have benefited from their actions during their tenure will assist them, financially and otherwise. Since they could barely get by on their retirement pay, this is considered the only right and ethical thing to do." Drucker concluded that the Japanese CEO acted correctly; since this was unethical and moreover illegal in the US, the American standards would be followed.

Yet Drucker did not agree with so-called "situational ethics" and warned against them. In other words, one did not behave one way in private life and another way in business or professional life. He also believed social responsibility to be a part of an individual's or organization's ethical behaviour. But here again he gave examples of corporations that, seeking to do good, had caused harm to customers, the organization, and to society. He cautioned that, under certain conditions, what would normally be considered a corporation's social responsibility should *not* be undertaken and was probably considered unethical behaviour. Drucker's positions on ethics and integrity might be argued, but they must be understood, for they form the basis of his ideas in dealing with clients and in the application of all his management concepts for consulting.

The Distinction between What Is Legal and What Is Ethical

Drucker made an important distinction: law may have very little to do with ethics or integrity. He made it clear that law and ethics are not the same and gave us two examples. Until the 1860s, slavery was legal in the United States. Moreover, in the Dred Scott Decision of the late 1850s, the Supreme Court ruled that no African-Americans, not even free African-Americans, could ever become citizens of the United States. According to the law, the Declaration of Independence did not apply to them, nor did the US Constitution offer them any protection. So, if you maintain that the law and ethics are the same, you would have to say that if anyone in any way attempted to subvert the law to award constitutional rights to African-Americans in those days, he would not only be in violation of the law but he would have been unethical. However, clearly it was the laws that were unethical, not the violators.

His second example concerned Hitler's Germany. Under Hitler, Germany passed the Nuremberg Laws, which denied German Jews the rights of German citizenship and passed other restrictions on them. As a German citizen, if you attempted to circumvent these laws or violate them directly or failed to report Jews who violated these laws to the authorities, you would be sent to prison or worse, because you were in violation of the law. These actions might include marrying a Jew, officiating at such a marriage, assisting a Jew in the practice of his profession, or failing to report any violation of the laws that were restrictive in other ways, from teaching in schools to the practice of the professions. These were the law of the land. Clearly the violators of these laws were not unethical.

Again, it was the laws that were unethical. Still, we can expect to be punished if we fail to obey a law whether it is a good law or a bad one, but it has nothing to do with ethics.

Drucker on Extortion or Bribery

Drucker noted that bribery was hardly desirable from the viewpoint of the victim, from whom a bribe was extorted. However, the payment of bribes overseas had recently been made illegal in the United States by an act of Congress, The Foreign Corrupt Practices Act in 1977. Soon after, an American company, Lockheed Aircraft, was charged with bribery. Senior Lockheed executives had paid bribes to members of the Japanese government when money was demanded in exchange for subsidizing the purchase of the L-1011 passenger jet for All Nippon Airways. As a result, Lockheed chairman Daniel Haughton and vice chairman and president Carl Kotchian were forced to resign from their posts in disgrace in early 1976.[4] Yet these executives gained nothing personally from the sales of the L-1011 in any way. Why then did these two Lockheed executives commit such a stupid act? In the years 1972-1973, 25,000 Lockheed employees had faced a significant threat of unemployment after cutbacks in the US government order of military aircraft and missiles. Because of delays due to difficulty with the foreign supplier of the L-1011's engines, airlines had cancelled L-1011 orders.

If a major contract to buy the L-1011 could not be obtained, many jobs at Lockheed would be lost. The two executives gained not a cent in monetary or any other advantage from their act of bribery; this was committed solely to help workers keep their jobs and, one could say, in the interests of social responsibility. Furthermore, stock price analysts determined that had Lockheed simply abandoned the L-1011 instead of paying the bribe, company earnings, stock price, bonuses, and stock options for the two Lockheed executives involved would have substantially increased.

Everyone knew that because of the engine delays the L-1011 aircraft was a financial loser and could no longer make money. In fact, the project never made any money despite these and other sales. Drucker was very clear on this: he thought it stupid to pay bribes. He thought that the L-1011 project should have simply been abandoned out of good management decisions. But was this a violation of the law or of business ethics?[5] Drucker noted again that the two Lockheed executives had nothing to gain and everything to lose by agreeing to pay bribes. They were victims. One doesn't punish the victims of a robbery or any other crime. Why in bribery?

Most countries have laws against bribery. Yet it is a fact that bribery, as we define it, is routine and expected in some of these countries. Many would perceive that the promise, or at least the understanding, of the Japanese CEO mentioned in Drucker's earlier example is that his company would reward government officials who helped his company while they were in office to be a form of bribery. But everyone in Japan understands the difference. Other countries that expect "baksheesh" as the traditional way of doing business in their country ignore any laws that may have been enacted as "window-dressing" for countries not having this as part of their own culture, such as the US. One marketing executive from a major Western exporter of aircraft told me how the company routinely paid bribes to secure business and that, in one case, they had to pay twice when the official they paid the first time had been deposed.

Drucker also noted that a private citizen who was extorted to pay a bribe to a criminal, say for "protection," would be considered a helpless victim of intimidation. Certainly extortion privately or corporately is never desirable. But this was clearly not an ethical issue on the part of the individual forced to pay. Drucker did not think that a corporation should be viewed differently, and he strongly objected to this "new business ethics", which asserted that acts that are not immoral or illegal if done by private citizens became immoral or illegal if done in the context of a business organization. They might be stupid, they might be illegal, and they might be the wrong things to do; however, they were not necessarily "business ethics".

Drucker's Analysis of Ethical Approaches

I said that Drucker took his examination of ethics seriously, and he did. He looked at the determination of right and wrong in questions of conduct and conscience by analysing cases that illustrated general ethical rules. This might be called cost-benefit ethics or ethics for the greater good. Essentially it means that those in power – CEOs, kings, presidents – have a higher duty if their behaviour can be argued to confer benefits on others. So it is wrong to lie, but in the interests of "the country" or "the company", or "the organization", it sometimes has to be done. This approach carries the name of "casuistry". Drucker called it "the ethics of social responsibility" and it had to do with his dislike of the term "business ethics".

Recently, the Hollywood movie *Bridge of Spies* starring Tom Hanks was released. The movie recounts the story of the negotiation for the release of captured American U-2 aircraft pilot Francis Gary Powers in exchange for Soviet spy Rudolph Abel, held in the US. Before it was known that Powers had survived and had been shot down over Russia and captured, President Eisenhower publicly lied about the fact that Powers was on a spy mission. I don't think that President Eisenhower's ethics were ever challenged on this issue. He had lied for the greater good, a higher responsibility.

In the same way, from a casuist's view, the bribe paid to the Japanese officials by Lockheed executives was a duty, a higher responsibility since Lockheed's leaders were trying to take care of Lockheed employees, not to benefit themselves. This sounds very high-minded, but Drucker maintained that it was too dangerous a concept to be considered in business ethics because it could easily become a tool for a business leader to justify what would clearly be unethical behaviour for anyone else.[6] Drucker continued his search.

The Ethics of Prudence

To be prudent means to be careful or cautious. It is a rather unusual philosophy for an ethical approach, but admittedly it has some benefits. When I first became an Air Force general, we were sent to complete a special course for new generals. During the course, we were given lectures and advice by senior military and civilian leaders. I do not recall if what was said on this subject was by the secretary of defense or by a senior general, but it struck us as pretty good advice. "Never do anything you wouldn't want seen on the front page of *The Air Force Times*," he said. That certainly was a strong motivation for ethical behaviour of his listeners.

Drucker gave a somewhat similar example. He said that Harry Truman, at the time a US senator, gave this advice to an army witness before his committee in the early years of World War II: "Generals should never do anything that needs to be explained to a Senate committee—there is nothing one can explain to a Senate committee."[7]

Now, this approach may be pretty good advice for staying out of trouble, but it is not much of a basis for ethical decision making. For one thing, it doesn't tell you anything about the right kind of behaviour. For another, there are decisions that a leader must take that are risky and may be difficult to explain, especially if things go wrong. No serving Air Force general would like to see a controversial action coupled with his or her name on the front page of *The Air Force Times*, much less be subject to adversarial questioning by a Senate committee. Nevertheless, these may be the correct decisions, which lead to these undesirable results.

The Ethics of Profit

Drucker also thought through what he called, "The Ethics of Profit". This is not what you might think. Drucker did not say anything about limiting profits. We'll talk about Drucker's views on maximizing profits later. Much to the contrary, Drucker wrote that it would be socially irresponsible and most certainly unethical if a business did not show a profit at least equal to the cost of capital, because failing to do so would waste society's resources.[8]

Drucker believed that the only logical rationale for the justification for "profit" was that it was a cost. He exhorted business leaders as follows: "Check to see if you are earning enough profit to cover the cost of capital and provide for innovation. If not, what are you going to do about it?"[9]

Drucker stated that profit as an ethical "metric" rested on very weak moral grounds as an incentive and could only be justified if it were a genuine cost and especially if it were the only way to maintain jobs and to grow new ones.[10]

I found it interesting that the rise in gas prices (prior to their dramatic fall) in 2008 prompted the following response by one refining company CEO when challenged by a Congressional investigating committee: "There is no 'profit'. Every dollar goes into exploration or research and development and is needed to run this business." If accurate, Drucker would have certainly agreed with the concept, although this would have probably been extremely difficult for someone not in the oil business to understand or accept (and clearly did not satisfy the committee, confirming Truman's advice to generals).

Confucian Ethics

Drucker called Confucian ethics "the most successful and most durable of them all." In Confucian ethics, the rules are the same for all, but there are different general rules that vary according to five basic relationships, all based on interdependence. These five are superior and subordinate, father and child, husband and wife, oldest brother and sibling, and friend and friend. The right behaviour in each case differs in order to optimize the benefits to both parties in each relationship. Confucian ethics demands equality of obligations, of parents to children and visa versa, and of bosses to subordinates and visa versa. All have mutual obligations. Drucker pointed out that this is not compatible with what is considered business ethics in many countries, including the US, where one side has obligations and the other side has rights or entitlements. Though he clearly admired Confucian ethics, which he called "The Ethics of Interdependence", they cannot be applied as business ethics, because this system deals with issues between individuals, not groups. According to Confucian ethics, only the law can handle the rights and disagreements of groups.[11]

Drucker's Conclusions

Drucker concluded that business ethics, as we know them today, are not that at all. If ever business ethics were to be codified, Drucker thought they ought to be based on Confucian ethics, focusing on the right behaviour rather than misbehaviour or wrongdoing. The bottom line is that Drucker believed that consultants should adopt the following into their personal philosophy of ethics:

1. The ethics of personal responsibility from the physician Hippocrates: "Primum Non Nocere," which means, "above all (or first) do no harm."[12, 13]
2. The mirror test: what kind of person do I want to see when I look into the mirror every morning?[14]

[1] Drucker, Peter F., *Management: Tasks, Responsibilities, Practices*, (New York: Harper & Row Publishers, 1973), p. 367.

[2] Cohen, William A., *A Class with Drucker*, (New York: AMACOM, 2008) p. 114.

[3] Adamopoulos, John and Walter J. Lonner, "Absolutism, Relativism, and Universalism in the Study of Human Behavior," citing a translation of Padcal by G. Hofstede in his book *Culture's Consequences: International Differences in Work Related Values*, accessed at http://eyewitness.utep.edu/3331/Lonner&Malpass1994%20Chap%2018.pdf, 25 May 2015.

[4] No author listed, "Lockheed Bribery Scandals," *Wikipedia Free Encyclopedia*, accessed at http://en.wikipedia.org/wiki/Lockheed_bribery_scandals, 25 May 2015

[5] Drucker, Peter F., *The Changing World of the Executive*, (New York: Truman Talley Books, 1982), pp. 242.

[6] Drucker, Peter F., *The Changing World of the Executive*, p.245.

[7] Ibid.

[8] Op. Cit. Drucker, Peter F. and Joseph A. Maciariello, *The Daily Drucker*, p.126.

[9] Ibid.

[10] Ibid. p.86.

[11] Ibid. pp. 248-254.

[12] Ibid. pp.366-375.

[13] Although Drucker, and others, declare to be part of the Primum Non Nocere part of the Hippocratic Oath, this is not true. See Wikipedia at http://en.wikipedia.org/wiki/Primum_non_nocere

[14] Drucker, Peter F., *Management Challenges for the 21st Century*, (New York: Harper Business, 1999), pp.175-176.

Chapter 7

Drucker's Consulting Model Was to Ask Questions

Since Drucker's model for his consulting engagements was to ask questions, consequently there was much that differentiated his consulting method from that of other consultants of all types. True, Drucker was an acknowledged genius. Most consultants are thought to be and frequently termed "very smart", a "good communicator", "charismatic", "an innovator", or perhaps "a born salesperson". But Drucker was a genius. Period. Probably this in itself caused differences in Drucker's approach to carrying out the function of consulting in a certain way, but there is more. Most very successful singleton consultants seem to partner, hire associates, and other employees. In short, they expand. It was a fact noticed by others looking at Drucker's consulting practice that he did not expand. Taking a look at the largest firms will help illustrate what I am talking about and what it means in reference to Drucker's consulting, and especially to his modus operandi.

The Big Three Consulting Firms and How They Got that Way

Many huge consulting firms are born of a single consultant. McKinsey & Company, the most prestigious and the largest with an annual revenue currently of $8.4 billion, is harvested by 20,000+ employees worldwide. Yet it all started with one man, James O. McKinsey, a University of Chicago accounting professor, who founded the company in 1926 with the idea of applying the principles of accounting to general management.[1] There are similar stories with other major firms. The Boston Consulting Group, or BCG, was founded by Bruce Henderson, a former Bible salesman, in 1963, the company's first month's billings were just $500.[2] In 2014, the company had revenues of $455 billion and 6,200 consultants included in a total staff of 9,700.[3] Bill Bain partnered with six others to form Bain & Company in 1973. He was a little different from the other two founders in that he had been a vice president of the Boston Consulting Group and resigned to establish Bain & Company.

Before that, he had been a director of development at Vanderbilt University. Today, the company has 51 offices in 33 countries,[4] and along with the other two consulting firms mentioned, claim status as one of the "Big Three" consulting firms.

Others noted that, even when alive, Drucker easily could have started Drucker and Associates or the Drucker Consulting Group, leveraged his abilities and his name, and multiplied his income a thousand times over. He died wealthy, but not the level of wealth of the three consultants mentioned. He never expanded past a single employee, and that one employee was Drucker himself. And while McKinsey quit teaching accounting in Chicago to devote himself full time to developing his consulting firm, Bruce Henderson had long since quit pushing Bibles, and Bill Bain surrendered his job at BCG to start his consulting giant, Drucker continued as a management professor almost until the end of his life. Yes, Drucker was a highly paid and much sought-after management consultant throughout his life. However, he defined himself as a scientist, specifically a social ecologist. Meanwhile, maintaining his practice as a "one-man band" may have led to the primary difference in his model of consulting, which even practitioners in "The Big Three" might apply beneficially today. A single independent consultant cannot possibly accomplish the output of the teams of consultants assigned to single-client projects of a large consulting firm. So Drucker may have been driven to a dramatically different approach by this single fact.

I have noticed that sometimes a more optimal model, whether physical or cerebral, is the accidental result of some constraint. When a senior cadet at West Point, I was in the audience when Walter Dornberger – former major general in Germany's World War II Luftwaffe, and then an employee of Bell Labs in the US, but once Werner von Braun's boss at Peenemunde, the secret German rocket centre during World War II, and the actual father of the V-2 Rocket – was questioned by a fellow cadet regarding the missile's dimensions. "We had no choice," Dornberger answered. "We spent an enormous effort on this because we knew the routes the missiles had to follow to be transported to the launch sites.

They had to travel through several medieval German towns to avoid allied air strikes and the narrow, curving roads dictated the missiles' dimensions. In the end, this turned out to be a significant advantage not only in transportation, but also in storage, propellant, and other factors. It was worth the effort for what we at first considered a really side issue."[5]

The Primary Difference in Drucker's Consulting Model

Most consultants seek to solve a client's problems by themselves, or at least with the client acting primarily as a catalyst. But Drucker went beyond simple communication and basic interaction with the client as the engagement progressed. Most seem to agree that this is what consultants get paid for. There are two old jokes about this. I'm certain if you've been around consultants, either as a practitioner or a client for any length of time, you've heard one and maybe both previously. But just in case you've escaped these trivialities, here they are. The first is a definition of a consultant. There are variations of this one. In one version, a consultant is defined as an individual who borrows your watch to tell you the time, and then charges you for the privilege.

In the other joke, the consultant strikes back and is the protagonist. A client has a problem within his organization, but doesn't know what or where it is. He hires a consultant and sends him to an empty desk, along with the company's organization charts. A few minutes later, the consultant rises from the desk. He shows the client one of the organization charts and with a black marker pen he draws an "X" prominently over one job position and gives the client instructions to eliminate that particular job. At the same time he presents his client with a written invoice for $1,000.

The client is shocked. "You spent less than five minutes looking at our organization charts, then you bring them to me and draw a single "X" on one of them and charge us $1,000. Give me a price breakdown," he demands.

The consultant scribbles a few lines on a piece of paper and hands it to the client. It reads:

Drawing an "X" on a specific job position on the company's organization chart	$1.00
Knowing where to draw that "X"	$999.00

Total	
$1,000.00	

The point with both of these little homilies is that they both assume the engagement model of consulting to be that the consultant and his expertise solve the issue and that the client is basically a bystander to this process. Neither situation described Drucker's model of the consulting engagement. The model they describe is that a client tells the consultant his problem either verbally or most likely in writing, and then gives the consultant a statement of the work to be accomplished. The consultant then independently solves the client's problem, be it by simply observing and reporting on the time shown on a client's watch, or inspection and analysis of something else.

The Client Is the Real Expert

I was once asked to sit in on a team of four consultants who were making a presentation on strategy for a major university that had hired them. They had used a variation of the GE/McKinsey nine-cell matrix to allocate resources over various departments and programmes. They were clearly experienced. They had collected data, analysed it, placed it into various cells in the matrix, and drew conclusions from an analysis they explained based on their interpretation of the data, including what resources were needed and how to allocate these resources.

Certainly a credible job, and I had no quarrel with the basic process that they used, although I did find fault with their interpretation of the data on which their analysis, conclusions, and recommendations were based. And this leads to one of the advantages of Drucker's model of the consulting process: it wasn't the consultant who provided the data or interpreted it. It was the client. It was the client who best knew and understood the situation, and after Drucker provided the guidance through questions, the client provided the correct data, as well. The client did this because Drucker asked questions that provoked the client's brain to start working. These questions acted as a catalyst, resulting in a much better analysis and solution from someone who better understood the facts and nuances of the situation than any one or more consultants could on their own as outsiders, no matter how brilliant or hardworking. It was simply a matter of asking the right questions of the brain. However, there is something else that made Drucker's questions even more powerful. We need first look at using our own brains to get answers.

Asking Your Own Brain Questions

Years ago I read an article in which the author recommended that talking to oneself was really quite useful in problem solving. The author maintained that if you talked to yourself and asked your brain questions as a separate entity, you would frequently be rewarded with effective answers. In fact, your brain would answer, or at least attempt to answer, any question you decided to ask.

I tried this technique and was surprised at just how easily it worked and how frequently it provided me with sometimes immediate and highly effective answers to a variety of questions with which all of us are faced on a daily basis.

Now you might think that you are doing this anyway as you worry about and obsess over some issue bothering you at a given time. But that's not what I'm recommending with this technique. What I'm suggesting is actually conversing with your brain to arrive at an answer. For example, instead of concentrating hard on whether you should adopt course of action A or course of action B, you merely say to yourself, "Hey, brain – what should I do, adopt course of action A or course of action B?"

Amazingly, you will frequently find that your brain will many times reply with a very workable answer that is usually the best course of action to adopt.

Why This Strange Technique Works

Psychologists tell us that one reason for this phenomenon is that the brain already has all the facts necessary for problem resolution stored away in memory. Some of these facts cannot be easily accessed directly. By eliminating the various psychological blocks when you struggle with finding a solution directly, questioning the brain as a separate entity eliminates much of the garbage that is preventing you from deciphering an answer.

However, sometimes the pressures and stresses we are under are too great. The problem is either too big or the situation is too demanding. Our brain cannot function consciously so easily and will not consciously come up with a workable solution, even if we question it separately. But the brain can work subconsciously, even while the conscious brain tends to blot out the useful information emanating from the sub-consciousness. The solution then, is how we can separate the two. Fortunately there are number of non-invasive techniques available without resorting to a surgeon's knife to separate the conscious mind from the unconscious mind, which wouldn't work anyway.

The answer is distraction. This may be done in a variety of ways. It is said that the inventor Thomas Edison used the simple technique of sitting in a darkened room. Others take a nap or simply go to sleep at night and find they awaken in the morning with the solution. I've had this happen to me without any effort, and maybe you have too.

The Power of Distraction in Problem Solving

Scientists at Carnegie Mellon, led by Dr John David Creswell, found that all these techniques simply distracted the conscious brain, frequently even for just a short period, while allowing the subconscious mind to do its job and continue to work.[6]

They investigated the brains of individuals attempting to solve problems that their conscious minds couldn't handle. Using the purchasing of an imaginary car, along with conflicting and multiple wants and needs, the subjects were divided into three groups. The first group was required to come to an immediate decision and consequently could do little about weighing the pros and cons in coming to an optimal decision. The second group was given time to try to consciously try to solve the problem to decide on the optimal car. The third group was given the same problem, but also a distracter task to perform. While it held their attention and distracted their conscious effort, their subconscious minds continued working on the car problem. The distracted group performed significantly better than the other groups at selecting the optimum car while considering other factors in the purchase situation. This group was distracted for only a few minutes, but clearly this method was more effective than even sleeping for many hours.

I have found similar results in playing games online. For example, Mahjong, is a game in which a variety of stacked tiles are displayed and the player is required to consecutively eliminate successive tiles that are similar while competing against time. Frequently stuck in attempting to identify similar tiles, by mere looking away and thinking of something else for a few seconds, I could look back and immediately identify duplicate tiles, which I had been struggling with and could not discover earlier. David Rock, analysing Creswell's research for *Psychology*, confirmed similar results in his own game-playing research.[7]

What can we learn from this about Drucker's consulting methodology? We know that asking questions, even asking questions of ourselves, can serve as a distraction to enable higher quality, and even more immediate answers to problems confronting us, consulting or otherwise. Now we can begin to see the value of Drucker's questions as a methodology for consulting engagements and that by simply asking questions, Drucker was frequently even more powerful than the largest consulting firms that supplied clients with solutions.

Drucker's Five Basic Questions

We've talked about the power of Drucker's questions and his questioning previously, beginning in chapter one. What better recommendation could Drucker's questions and his questioning have had than the recommendations of Jack Welch? Remember, we're talking about the most widely respected executive of our lifetimes, a man who caused the value of a major corporation to rise 4,000% during his tenure, and when he retired was given $417 million, the largest severance pay in history, and finally a man who credits Drucker and his consulting with a significant contribution to his accomplishments.[8] That's one heck of a recommendation.

Drucker's basic questions were even brought together in a single book,[9] edited by Frances Hesselbein, winner of the of the Presidential Medal of Freedom from President H. Bush, first occupant of West Point's Leadership Chair, once CEO of the Girl Scouts of the USA, and currently one of my presidential advisors at the California Institute of Advanced Management. Drucker said of Frances that she could serve successfully as CEO of any corporation in America.

These are the five vital questions of Drucker's, which Frances called "The Five Most Important Questions You Will Ever Ask about Your Organization":

1. What is our mission?
2. Who is our customer?
3. What does the customer value?
4. What are our results?
5. What is our plan?

As Drucker maintained, each of these is one of the five most important questions you will ever ask, and these are the most important questions you will ever ask of your clients, as well. So we had better understand exactly what Drucker was talking about.

What Is the Mission of Your Client?

Drucker advised his clients to decide what business they were in, which clearly involved knowing the organization's mission. Drucker's favourite mission statement was from a very old business. But this mission statement, though not recent and very short, almost a one-liner, was his favourite for a very important reason: it changed Sears Roebuck from a struggling mail-order house that continually flirted with bankruptcy into the world's leading retailer, all within 10 years. Simply stated, it was to be the informed and responsible buyer first for the American farmer, and later for the American family.[10] Like all missions, an organization's mission may change. Do I walk my talk? Does my own former organization, the California Institute of Advanced Management (CIAM), have an identified mission? You bet it does!

"The mission of CIAM is to provide a flexible, affordable, and high quality education based on the principles and values of Peter F. Drucker, the "Father of Modern Management," and to enable students to immediately apply their knowledge and ability with integrity and success."

Who Are Your Client's Customers?

As I noted in an earlier chapter, my friend, entrepreneur Joe Cossman, started selling garden sprinklers that consisted of a flexible plastic hose with holes in it. He sold mainly through supermarkets and similar outlets. One day he read that his hose was being used in the poultry business as an inexpensive way to cool poultry pens during the hot summer months. This caused him to redefine his business and opened an entirely new market for his product. Clients need to continually track sales to redefine customers.

Marlboro is the largest selling brand of cigarettes in the world. It gained millions with its image of the masculine man's cigarette, promoted by "The Marlboro Man" using manly representatives including weight lifters, sea captains, and cowboys. You probably would never have guessed it, but Marlboro was launched as a woman's cigarette with the slogan, "Mild as May" in 1924. It even had a red-tipped filter to hide lipstick stains. However, later the idea of a filter itself pointed to the possibility of a shift to a wider market of men – a market that was concerned about the risk of lung cancer, which the proper filter, not necessarily red, might reduce. Results were immediate once this market had been identified. It went from 1% to the number-four ranking brand.[11] Drucker clearly knew his stuff. Knowing your customers is clearly more than half the battle.

What Does Your Client's Customer Value?

What the customer values is frequently not what we think. Some years ago, Falstaff beer, once a major brewing corporation in St Louis and a popular beer in the US East Coast, attempted to expand into the lucrative California market. Early attempts failed, although blind taste tests confirmed that the brand was exactly what the Californians wanted. Some in the company wanted to change the product, which they said was clearly wrong for the California market. But shrewder marketers in the company determined that the error was not in the product, but in the perception of the product and Falstaff advertising, which did not properly promote the qualities of beer desired by the customer in the Californian market.

Of course, in the mid-1980s Coca-Cola made a similar and even bigger mistake on a national level when it attempted to introduce "New Coke" in response to "The Pepsi Challenge", which was slowly eroding Coke's market. Coke introduced "New Coke" as a revolutionary soft drink to considerable fanfare. You could almost hear Coke marketers shouting, "So you guys at Pepsi want a challenge do you? We'll give you a challenge!" Coca-Cola had carefully conducted blind taste tests and formulated a product that was consistently preferred over either its own original product or that of its rival, Pepsi Cola.

The problem was that taste was not the only reason customers bought Coke and not necessarily what Coke's customers valued.

Above all, they valued Coke's image. It represented America, as much an icon as mom, apple pie, and John Wayne. With this market, Coca-Cola's previous campaign of the "The Real Thing" resonated. However, America rebelled in mass against "New Coke", which appeared *not* to be "The Real Thing." After millions of dollars in development, testing, advertising, promotion, and taking on detractors nose-to-nose in the media, eventually Coke surrendered. At first, old Coke returned and was billed as "Classic Coke". Eventually "New Coke" was quietly withdrawn from the market.

The strange thing was that even blind taste tests proved that Americans really did like the taste of "New Coke", although most blind testers really can't tell the difference between specific brands. In one famous blind taste test conducted before several million viewers on television, one of the leaders of the rebellion and campaign against New Coke identified Pepsi Cola as his one and only "old Coke".

What Results Are Your Client Getting?

Drucker knew that, without measuring results, you were not going to make any progress. In fact, you couldn't tell if your client was succeeding or failing, and if progress was being made or not. So by results, Drucker wanted numbers: "Show me the money!" doesn't just mean cash. It means results. This was an important exception to his recommendation to place numbers behind a decision maker's gut instinct.

What Is Your Client's Plan?

You will probably be surprised how frequently your client will have no plan at all, or it will be woefully inadequate. Drucker was equally surprised. However, as with everything, Drucker had questions he felt important to ask before a client sat down to work out the plan. Drucker wrote that a leader must start with three questions to begin planning to create an organization's future.

The first was his familiar, "What business are you in?" You have that one pretty much covered if you used the mission question. But he had two more questions to be considered, especially if the plan was more strategic than tactical: "What will the business be in the future?" That is, will the business and the mission change? However, Drucker went further. He wanted to know, right then, if the client thought the business or mission should change. Drucker wanted to know, "What should it be for the future?"[12]

Although these questions need to be considered separately, they need to be integrated, too. This is because the present is connected with the future. We have short-range plans for projects, products, and initiatives. These have an impact on what our businesses will be in the short-term future, whether we like it or not. What should it be is a question of the more distant future. How far distant? That's up to you and your client. Ten years is not too far distant. I've seen organizations plan for the creation of a future 25 or even 50 years away. Regardless of the time horizon selected, the answers to the three questions must fit together. One doesn't suddenly jump from the business we are in today without intermediate steps into the future of what our business should be.

How to Develop Good Questions

Although it is Drucker's "The Five Most Important Questions You Will Ever Ask about Your Organization" that have received the most publicity, Drucker asked many questions of his clients, and they are scattered throughout his writings. Clearly this methodology was an important part of his consulting, and it can benefit the consulting that any individual or consulting organization does or any leader uses in looking to better his or her own organization, even if combined with more traditional methods. However, while Drucker's questions were always effective, they did not cover everything or anything in every possible consulting engagement. Drucker himself would have said, "I am not a guru, able to provide every possible question under the sun that might be useful or needed."

As a consultant, what questions do you think should be asked? Here are some guidelines for developing questions, which I think Drucker would have approved:

- Will the question act as a catalyst for further discussion with your client?
- Will the question arouse curiosity?
- Will the question promote an exploration of new ideas?
- Will the question challenge the client to a suggestion?
- Is the question open to a variety of different views and responses?
- Will the question require clients to answer how and why?
- Will the question help uncover controversies in the subject matter?
- Is the question directly connected with the client's operation?
- Will the question encourage clients to examine their own thinking?

When your list of questions is complete, go over them and ensure that they are asked in your client's language. You may need to have someone from that industry, or even that organization, review and recommend new wording, additional questions, or certain questions that should be eliminated. Sometimes your wording may offend clients in a particular organization, so this review and your own modification are well worthwhile. A review by someone in a client's organization once saved me from a tremendous political blunder due to a situation with a former CEO that I did not know about.

Drucker's engagement model, relying on questions, may be very different from the kind of consulting that you may wish to do. But his techniques were sound. They frequently yielded amazing results, and they are easily adapted and can be integrated into a variety of other consulting engagement models.

[1] No author listed, "McKinsey & Company," *Wikipedia*, accessed at https://en.wikipedia. org/wiki/McKinsey_%26_Company, 13 June 2015.

[2] No author listed. "BCG History," *Official BCG Website*, accessed at http://www.bcg. com/about_bcg/vision/our_heritage/history/default.aspx, 13 June 2015.

[3] No author listed, "Boston Consulting Group," *Wikipedia*, accessed at https:// en.wikipedia.org/wiki/Boston_Consulting_Group, 13 June 2015.

[4] No author listed, "Worldwide Offices," *Bain & Company Website*, accessed at http:// bain.com/about/worldwide-offices/index.aspx, 13 June 2015.

[5] I do not remember the date of this lecture, except that it was at West Point in fall 1958 or spring 1959. It was particularly memorable for General Dornberger's explanation of the dimensions of the V-2 rocket, but also for a question he answered as to which service should have responsibility for the new IRBMs (Intermediate Range Ballistic Missiles). The Army, Navy, and Air Force were all competing for this mission. Dornberger had been an army officer, in fact in the field artillery before being assigned duties in developing military rockets. West Point was an army academy, although it also supplied a number of Air Force officers, as did the Naval Academy, because the Air Force did not yet graduate its first class from its own academy. So it was no surprise when asked his opinion that Dornberger answered, "Well, it shouldn't be the Navy because there are no oceans in space." This evoked loud cheers from his audience. Then he continued, "But it should be the Army either, because there are no land masses either—this should clearly be an Air Force mission." Those of us who wanted to be commissioned in the Air Force were the only ones to cheer.

[6] John David Creswell, Bursley, James K., Satpute, Ajay B., "Neural Reactivation Links Unconscious Thought To Decision-Making Performance," Social Cognitive and Affective Neuroscience Advance Access, May 29, 2013, accessed at http://www.psy.cmu.edu/ people/Creswell,%20Bursley,%20&%20Satpute%20(2013),%20unconscious%20 neural%20reactivation%20in%20decision%20making,%20SCAN.pdf, 16 June 2015.

[7] David Rock, "Your Brain at Work," *Psychology*, September 18, 2012, accessed at https://www.psychologytoday.com/blog/your-brain-work/201209/stop-trying-solve-problems, 16 June 2015

[8] No author listed, "Jack Welch," *Wikipedia*, accessed at https://en.wikipedia.org/wiki/ Jack_Welch, 16 June 2015.

[9] Peter F. Drucker, edited by Frances Hesselbein, *The Five Most Important Questions You Will Ever Ask about Your Organization* (San Francisco: Jossey-Bass, 2008).

[10] Drucker, Peter F., *Managing the Non-profit Organization* (New York: HarperCollins, Publishers, 1990) p.4.

[11] No author listed. "Marlboro (cigarette)," *Wikipedia*, accessed at https://en.wikipedia. org/wiki/Marlboro_(cigarette), 17 June 2015.

[12] Drucker, Peter F., *Management: Tasks, Responsibilities, Practices* (New York: Harper & Row Publishers, 1973, 1974), p.122.

Chapter 8

Disregarding What Everyone "Knows" to Get to the Truth

Drucker said and wrote so much that was wise, profound, valuable, and witty – he may have more quotes attributed to him than any other management thinker of modern times. I am frequently asked if Drucker said this or that, which could not be located as an original source even after a thorough internet search. Sometimes it sounds like something Drucker might say, but I could not recall him actually having said it or remember reading it among his writings or speeches. There is, however, one particular remark that I clearly remember him making again and again, both in the classroom and in private conversations. Yet, only after I wrote and explained this in several of my books about Drucker did it appear anywhere in print, and I have never seen it among his published work. This is what he said … often: "What everyone knows is usually wrong." His continued use of this phrase clearly meant that he not only believed it strongly, but considered it important. I investigated its truth and discovered just how correct he was.

Drucker Was Right Again

Maybe through repetition I finally began to think more deeply about what his words really meant. This seemingly simple and self-contradicting statement is amazingly true and immensely valuable in every business and management decision and analysis. It is especially important in consulting because it opens a world of alternatives that we would normally disregard as unusable because "everyone knows something to be so", even though it may not be. What Drucker wanted to emphasize was that we must always question all assumptions, no matter from where they originate or how impossible they may first appear. This is especially true regarding anything that a majority of people "know" or assume without analysis or further questioning. This "knowledge" should always be suspect and needs to be examined much more closely, because in a surprisingly high percentage of cases, the information "known to be true" will turn out to be false, inaccurate, or true only under certain conditions. This can lead a consultant to overlook some uniquely valuable alternatives and to extremely poor or even flat-out wrong recommendations. I now consider this simple statement critically important regarding his work and especially in consulting engagements.

This was confirmed by my father, who, except for the war years of World War II, was a practising attorney and after the war switched from military intelligence to become a full-time military attorney. He said, "Don't believe everything you read in the newspapers. Believe only one-half of what you hear. And don't believe everything you see, either." Before the war he practised criminal law.

What Everyone Knows Is Usually Wrong

Of course there are many old "truisms" once thought by everyone to be true that we laugh at today. "The world is flat" or "the earth is the centre of the universe" are typical. Question some of these "certainties" in the past and you could be sent to prison or burned as a witch. The ancient Greeks knew that everything was made up of only four elements: earth, air, fire, and water. I don't think that you got imprisoned or killed for believing otherwise, but you were at the very least thought ignorant.

Of course, in modern times we learned that these views were mistaken. I often remind myself that when I took chemistry as a student in high school, I learned that a periodic table of elements had been formulated by the Russian chemist and inventor Mendeleev and that it established that there were exactly 93 elements, which were arranged by atomic mass, no more, no less. We got an "A" if we could name them all. Had we proposed that there could be more, I am certain that we would have been immediately corrected by our teachers. In the words of Richard Rodgers and Oscar Hammerstein in *Oklahoma*, things "had gone about as far as they could go", Today, there are 102 elements – or so "everybody knows". And what they forgot to tell us is that Mendeleev had only envisioned 63 elements... the other 30 hadn't been discovered yet in his time.

Many Things that Everyone "Knows" Today Are Also Wrong

Just about everyone, both Christian and non-Christian, knows that the Immaculate Conception refers to the birth of Jesus, right? Maybe so, but what everybody knows is wrong again. According to the *Catholic Encyclopedia*, the Immaculate Conception refers to the fact that "Mary was preserved, exempt from all stain of original sin at the first moment of her animation, and sanctifying grace was given to her before sin could have taken effect in her soul".[1]

Or I like this one. Consider the most famous sentence ever uttered by Sir Arthur Conan Doyle's famous detective, Sherlock Holmes. In fact, this may be the most famous sentence ever uttered by any fictional or even real detective. Everyone knows that this sentence consists of only the four words, "Elementary, my dear Watson." According to what everyone knows, the famous detective would say these words to his sidekick and recorder of his adventures, Dr Watson, who showed surprise at a particularly shrewd, but totally unexpected deduction made by the sleuth. Maybe everyone knows this, but they are wrong.

As pointed out by Paul F. Boller, Jr and John George in their book, *They Never Said It* (Oxford University Press, 1989), Holmes didn't utter the immortal words in a single instance in anything ever written by Doyle, not in any of Doyle's four published novels, nor in 56 short stories about the adventures of Sherlock Holmes and Dr John H. Watson. Wherever did people come up with such totally believed, but incorrect knowledge? If not Doyle's literary character, who did utter these immortal words? In reality, it was the English actor, Basil Rathbone, playing the part of Sherlock Holmes in Hollywood movies that responded with the famous sentence, not Doyle's character in anything he ever wrote. These words seemed to fit the character of Holmes perfectly in those days on the silver screen, and though not emanating from Doyle's creation, it became a known fact. However, I have noticed that more recent Sherlock Holmes movies on the silver screen and television no longer have Sherlock continuing the practice. That's a shame. They seem to be missing something for those who grew up in that era.

The Ancients Knew that 100% Agreement Is Suspect

Drucker's assertion rings true across the millennia. In Ancient Israel, the highest court in the land was called the Sanhedrin. It corresponded roughly to the highest court in the land, although it had a lot more power than the US Supreme Court does today.

The Sanhedrin judged the most important cases and had the power to exact capital punishment. However, in this high court, there were no prosecuting or defence attorneys. As far as we know, there were no appeals to the Sanhedrin's judgment, either. The Sanhedrin court consisted only of judges. The national Grand Sanhedrin had 71 judges, but each ancient Hebrew city had a little Sanhedrin, consisting of 23 judges. The actual number is unimportant to some factual points.

The judges could examine the defendant, the accusers, and any witnesses from either side brought before it. The Sanhedrin was the only court that had the power to try anyone, even the king. To exonerate a defendant required only a majority of one, while to find the defendant guilty required a majority of two.

But here's the most interesting rule of the Sanhedrin's judgment: more than 2,000 years ago, the ancient Hebrews made Drucker's most famous conclusion a rule of law. If all 71 judges found the accused guilty of a capital crime, he or she was allowed to go free! And these folks were supposed to be "wise". How did they ever come up with a rule like that?

Remember, there was no defence attorney to argue the defendant's case. But the ancient Hebrew judges knew that there is always a defence to be argued for every individual accused, regardless of the gravity of the crime or the persuasiveness of the evidence and witnesses. So if not a single judge considered that the defendant's case had merit, this was clear evidence to them that no matter how obvious the guilt, something was amiss in the situation and wrong in the court. Perhaps someone against the defendant was too charismatic or too persuasive. Maybe politics, corruption, "command influence" by the high priest or king, or something else was involved. In their opinion, this single fact meant that it was much more likely that the accused could actually be innocent and that this was so important that it outweighed everything else implying guilt. In other words, when every judge – men especially appointed due to respect for their experience and judgment – all knew something to be absolutely true, it probably wasn't true at all, and the defendant walked. That's pretty strong support for Drucker's assertion!

Today the impact of mass agreement on an issue has been addressed and confirmed in psychological research. In one experiment, subjects were asked to rate the attractiveness of individuals depicted in selections of photographs. However, there was only one real subject and the results were rigged. Unknown to the subjects, the other participants were part of the scientist's team of experimenters. These participants were to agree about the most attractive individual depicted in any particular set of photographs at random. It was found that the subject could usually be influenced to agree with any photograph that the group selected, regardless of merit, simply by the overwhelming support from the others. This experiment demonstrates the influence of social proof. At the same time it confirms Drucker's theory that when everyone is certain about a fact, the "fact" usually isn't a fact at all, or that something usually factual isn't factual in a specific instance.

Drucker's Wisdom Critical in Management and Therefore Consulting

I like this story, because it is illustrates not only that whatever everyone knows is wrong, but is also a great story of personal integrity by a CEO representing a major corporation. It happened more than 30 years ago. Yet I remember the whole situation as if it were yesterday. It began the morning of 29 September 1982. A young girl, 12-year-old Mary Kellerman, died after taking a capsule of Extra-Strength Tylenol (a paracetamol-based brand drug). Others died soon afterward, all from the Chicago area. It was soon discovered that someone had laced a number of the popular over-the-counter drug with cyanide. This led to a nationwide panic. One hospital received 700 queries from people suspecting they had been poisoned with the tainted product. People in cities across the US were admitted to hospitals on suspicion of cyanide poisoning. The Food and Drug Administration (FDA) investigated 270 incidents of suspected product tampering. While some of the product had been tampered with as some sort of a sick joke, in most cases this was pure hysteria with no basis at all in fact. This panic in itself demonstrates part of Peter's thesis, but there is more that is of some importance to both consultants and management decision makers.

At that time, the product was almost 30 years old. Over the years, Tylenol had built a well-deserved trust with consumers. This trust disappeared almost at once and sales of the product plummeted. Johnson & Johnson, the product's owner, launched a recall of $100 million in product and stopped all sales. The company advertised and advised everyone not to buy or use the product until further notice. Johnson & Johnson and its chairman, James Burke, received kudos for integrity and doing the right thing. However, when Burke announced that Johnson & Johnson succeeded in developing tamper-proof packaging and was going to reintroduce the product under its original name, virtually everyone predicted the demise of the product.

One well-known advertising guru was quoted in the *New York Times*: "I don't think they can ever sell another product under that name … There may be an advertising person who thinks he can solve this and if they find him, I want to hire him, because then I want him to turn our water cooler into a wine cooler."[2]

The product once dominated the market. "Everyone knew" that those days were gone for good. An article in the *Wall Street Journal* commented sadly that the product was dead and could not be resurrected; any other notion was an executive's pipedream. A survey of "the-man-in-the-street" found almost no one who would buy the product, regardless of what the company did to guarantee its safety or promote its sale. Virtually everyone predicted that this brand, which accounted for 17% of the company's net income in 1981, would never recover. Guess again. Only two months later, the product was back, this time in tamper-proof packaging and supported by an extensive media campaign. A year later, its share of the $1.2 billion analgesic market, which had plunged to

7% from a 37% high, was back to 30% of the market despite "what everyone knew".[3]

The product we're talking about, of course, is Tylenol, which eventually made a full recovery and more than 30 years later reached a high of 56% share of its market.[4]

Where would Johnson & Johnson have been had this established brand, built through 30 years of advertising, performance, and reliability, been allowed to disappear under its old name? "New Tylenol" probably would have gone the way "New Coke" did. How much would it have cost Johnson & Johnson to attempt to introduce and build an entirely new brand to replace Tylenol? Could this even have been accomplished? We'll never know. Nor do we know whether Peter Drucker was called in to consult with Johnson & Johnson. What we do know is that Johnson & Johnson did the right thing when this tragedy struck and then took the right actions to reintroduce the Tylenol product successfully. This was one of the first recalls of this type and it also introduced tamper-proof packaging for these types of products. Burke's actions are still studied in the business schools as an almost perfect example of a successful public relations strategy and execution. However, the basis of this was that Johnson & Johnson executives, knowingly or not, decided that "what everyone knows is not necessarily right", and as Drucker suggested, is usually wrong. Burke and his team went up against what all the experts and even consumers "knew" and went on to resurrect Tylenol to be even more successful than it was previously.

Drucker's Most Valuable Contribution?

Journalists interviewing me about previous books on Drucker frequently ask one question: "What was Drucker's most valuable contribution?" With so many insights, so many wonderful ideas, so much ethical and moral guidance that might have saved organizations or even countries from financial ruin, I found this a difficult question to answer. For several years my response was something along the lines of "It all depends." I pointed out that his "most valuable contribution" was situational, and depended primarily on what issue one was looking at. I avoided naming a single contribution that would cover all instances because I couldn't think of any.

However, after one interview, I rethought this issue and decided I could do a lot better with my response. I reviewed various Drucker prescriptions for a variety of problem areas. Was there a thread of commonality in his recommendations and solutions that might lead to a universal and most valuable contribution?

Why Krav Maga Training Has a Relatively Low Injury Rate

For combat, everyone knows you should train as hard as you fight, and the injury rate from combative sports is not insignificant. Krav Maga is a self-defence system developed by a Hungarian Jew, Imre Lichtenfeld or Imi Sde-Or, and brought to Israel when he escaped Europe during World War II. Krav Maga is Hebrew for "close combat". It is known to be brutal, and if practised in real life can cause permanent injury or death to an opponent.

In 1935, Lichtenfeld visited then-Palestine with other Jewish wrestlers to participate in the Maccabian Games, similar to the Olympics. However, Lichtenfeld could not participate because of a broken rib that resulted from his training practice on the way to the competition. This mishap led to his immediately abandoning what everyone knew about combat arts and the adoption of what is now the fundamental Krav Maga principle, which is not to get hurt while in training. Yet, the effectiveness of Krav Maga in actual combat is not to be denied, not only in Israel, but worldwide. Still, it is the prevailing wisdom in the athletic world that success comes from training as hard as you can so you're ready for the highest performance when it is for real.

Drucker on Customer Value

If it were a marketing challenge, Drucker would advise clients to think it through to determine what their customers considered value and to be extremely cautious that they didn't substitute their own definition of value for that of their customers or prospects.

This is a valuable insight and if you go down the list of failed products, you will find this at the core of many marketing problems.

A young Steven Jobs claimed that the Lisa computer would be successful because it was technologically superior to any of its competitors. The Lisa had an advanced system-protected memory, multitasking, a sophisticated operating system, a built-in screensaver, an advanced calculator, support for up to 2 megabytes (MB) of RAM, expansion slots, a numeric keypad, data corruption protection, a larger and higher resolution screen display, and more. It would be years before many of those features were implemented in any other computer. Still, Jobs was wrong. All these features resulted in Lisa's high price of about $22,000 in today's dollars, and buyers opted for what they considered important to them and of value – the far less expensive, although technologically inferior IBM, at less than a third of Lisa's cost.

How a 61-Year Old Won the World's Toughest Ultra Marathon

The Sydney-to-Melbourne Ultra Marathon in Australia was regarded as the toughest in the world. It was 544 miles long and took up to seven days to complete, with stops for rest permitted along the way. Most athletes ran all day and rested at night. In 1983, an unknown 61-year-old potato farmer by the name of Cliff Young entered the race. Many thought he would be lucky to finish. Young thought about it and realized that he could walk the distance if he chose since the rules allowed. The rules also did not require him to stop overnight to rest. So he didn't. Result: he won, shaving off almost a day from an athlete half his age who came in second place. Once again, what everyone knew was wrong.

Applying This Lesson as a Consultant

What was Drucker's most valuable contribution? He taught us not to listen to what "everybody knows," but to think it through and develop our own methods of success. There is no question that applying this lesson requires critical analysis, because while "what everyone knows is usually wrong" may be true, sometimes it may be the case that what everyone knows is actually true. So the problem is in how the consultant can know when common knowledge is true and when it is not. The first thing we need to understand is that what everyone knows, or "so-called" common knowledge, is simply an assumption. Now we have the problem nailed down. Our task is an analysis of an assumption believed by a majority. An assumption is any belief, idea, hunch, or thought that you, a group of people, or any experts, internal or external, have about any subject. These assumptions are crucial because we use our assumptions to guide our actions and decision making. This is sometimes complicated by the fact that frequently these assumptions are implicit and unstated. Psychologists tell us they are useful because if true, they provide a sort of short-hand way of thinking and decision making. However, decision making can be disastrous if we accept assumptions as fact without analysis.

In the Tylenol example, Tylenol would have been dropped as a product and Johnson & Johnson would have lost millions of dollars in revenue, as well as having to spend the money to develop and market a replacement product. On the other hand, maybe the Tylenol case is a unique example. Maybe in most situations, trying to reintroduce a product that had been withdrawn due to the deaths of consumers of the product, even if it was no fault of the manufacturer and it had behaved ethically in every way, would have resulted in zero sales and might have been an absolutely disastrous decision. So the consultant must always think and analyse.

Analysing an Assumption

The first step in analysing an assumption is to look at the source's source. From where did this assumption originate and is it still a valid and reliable source today?

Many years ago, I was involved in the selection of one of two designs from two different companies for a new aircraft for the Air Force. The companies were the Boeing Aircraft Company and McDonnell-Douglas Aircraft Company. Those who know this industry also know that the former company eventually acquired the latter, but this has nothing to do with my story. Both companies proposed modifying one of their standard airline designs that was already in production and in use.

Periodically we would meet with each aircraft company's design team individually to assess progress on each company's proposals, the acceptance of which would be worth hundreds of millions of dollars to the winning contractor.

On one occasion, we met to discuss ways in which we might lower the cost of each aircraft. It was the McDonnell-Douglas manager who stated, "You can save $10 million dollars for each aircraft produced if you will allow us to deviate on the size of the escape hatch by two inches. That would be the standard size of the hatch on our DC-9 airliners. They successfully passed all FAA tests with no problems." I promised to look into his request. It could save a lot of money.

Tracking Down the Origin

In this case, the initial source was the engineer who had put this requirement into the package listing design specifications that we had sent to the two aircraft manufacturers. However, frequently we need to conduct a process I call "peeling the onion" because the initial source may not be the actual originator. What we are looking for lies inside one or more layers of onion and we need to peel away the layers to get to the centre – the ultimate source.

As soon as I could, I contacted the engineer responsible for the aircraft specification that McDonnell-Douglas wanted waived. "We can't do it," he told me. "This requirement comes directly from our aircraft design handbook with specifications that we must use for all new transport-type aircraft."

This meant that the source was not the prime source. It had another source. This other source was the design handbook. Not only did it produce a predictable and repeatable result, but "everybody knew", because of its reliability, not only that these dimensions were the correct ones for the escape hatch, but that we were required to use them. It was as if Johnson & Johnson had investigated the sources for those who said that the demise of Tylenol was irreversible. These were the advertising and business experts who wrote for the business journals. These were good sources. They were frequently correct in their judgments regarding advertising and how "bad press", accurate or not, could ruin a product's reputation. They were reliable sources based on past history.

Is the Source Valid?

Both reliability and validity are concepts that come from testing. The validity of a test tells us how well the test measures what it is supposed to measure. It is a judgment based on evidence about the appropriateness of inferences drawn from test scores. But we're not looking at test scores here, we're looking at assumptions. So where did this particular specification in the aircraft design handbook come from? Knowing that source could help me decide whether this particular specification was valid for the aircraft we now wanted to build. In other words, we still hadn't located the original, prime source for this information.

So I peeled the onion again. I knew that every specification in the aircraft design handbook was referenced as to where it came from and what it was based on. Making this a requirement was good thinking. Usually they were based on the original tests performed. I asked the engineer to do the necessary research to find out what tests this particular design specification was based on and when they were accomplished.

Surprise, surprise – this specification was based on an aircraft test done with propeller-driven aircraft almost 30 years earlier. That aircraft travelled at about 120 miles per hour. The aircraft we were working on travelled at about 500 miles per hour. Obviously, in this instance, the design specification was not valid. We turned it over to one of our aeronautical designers. He advised us to forget what everyone knew (the design handbook) and the two inches at the air speeds we were anticipating for an emergency bailout would make no difference at all. We took his advice.

In the same way, the chairman of Johnson & Johnson and his advisers must have evaluated the sources cautioning them to abandon the original Tylenol product and introduce a new product. I can imagine them just considering changing the name as one option. They probably asked what the success rate was for a product that was reintroduced in this way and under similar circumstances. That would have been peeling the onion. They probably discovered that there wasn't much of a database to go on because no one had even attempted something like this. They had taken the high road all the way, and felt that despite "what everybody knew", it was worthwhile trying. This brings up another important aspect. Testing the assumption.

I can't tell you how many times, both as a consultant and as a decision maker in the Air Force, in industry, and as an academic administrator, I have seen that because everyone knows something to be true, others don't even want to test the assumption for truth and will want to dismiss it outright. The naysayers may proclaim knowingly, "that's the way it's always been done." Or "everybody does it that way." Or maybe simply, "We tried that long ago and it won't work." Long ago in direct-response advertising, I learned the value of testing a headline, artwork, the medium, the vehicle, or a concept and found that what everyone knew was simply wrong, or wrong in this particular instance. I've heard this reasoning, ultimately proved wrong, so many times that when I hear the argument, "no one else does that!" my instant retort is, "wonderful! Then we'll be the first."

All this reminds me of Roger Bannister's achievement. Bannister, an English medical doctor, broke a record in running once thought to be impossible. The experts knew that it could not be done. This was the famous "four-minute mile". No one had ever run a mile in four minutes previously. Today, the fastest-mile record is held by Moroccan Hicham El Guerrouj. He ran the mile in a time of 3 minutes 43.13 seconds in Rome, Italy, on July 7 1999.[5]

I've even heard that some high school runners break the four-minute mile. However, the fact is that when Bannister achieved this on 6 May 1954, many, if not most, knew that it was impossible and that's why it had never, and would never, be done. Bannister was knighted for his achievement. At 3 minutes 59.4 seconds, Bannister's time was less than a second faster than the fabled four-minute mile. Since this was deemed impossible previous to Bannister accomplishment, you might ask yourself why no one was knighted or received honours for running even faster since then.

I was in high school at the time and I remember a radio interview with a doctor of kinesiology shortly before Bannister broke the record. He stated emphatically that the human body just wasn't built to run that fast and it couldn't be done. He predicted that Bannister would never succeed. Bannister knew better. What everybody "knew" was wrong and Bannister understood this. Did Cliff Young, the 61-year-old Australian potato farmer who entered and won the ultra marathon in 1983, use this technique? I don't know. Maybe he tried it out before the race. However, it was certainly a case of what everyone knew being in error.

What everyone knows is usually wrong. It is wrong because people make one or more erroneous assumptions. To use Drucker's wisdom – maybe his greatest contribution – effectively, a consultant needs to look at the source of what everyone knows and determine its reliability and validity. Do your own thinking and critically analyse the assumptions made by others. Test the assumption with a small investment. Do this and you will surprise yourself at the number of times you will, like Drucker, prove that what everyone knows is wrong.

[1] New Advent, *Catholic Encyclopedia*, "Immaculate Conception," accessed at http://www.newadvent.org/cathen/07674d.htm, June 26 2015

[2] Jerry Knight "Tylenol's Maker Shows How to Respond to Crisis." *The Washington Post.*, p. WB1, 11 October 1982.

[3] Judith Rehak, "Tylenol Made a Hero of Johnson & Johnson : The Recall that Started Them All," *New York Times*, March 23 2002, accessed at http://www.nytimes.com/2002/03/23/your-money/23iht-mjj_ed3_.html, 22 June 2015.

[4] No author listed, "Hey, Where's my Tylenol? CVS Pulls Popular Pain-Reliever from Some Stores." *New York Daily News*, January 15 2013, accessed at http://www.nydailynews.com/life-style/health/cvs-won-stock-tylenol-stores-article-1.1240622, 22 June 2015

[5] No author listed, "Four-Minute Mile," *Wikipedia*, accessed at https://en.wikipedia.org/wiki/Four-minute_mile, 24 June 2015.

Chapter 9

How Drucker Used his Ignorance to Consult in Any Industry

A sked by a student about the secret of his success as a consultant in so many different industries, Drucker responded, "There is no secret. You just need to ask the right questions." We talked about this important aspect of Drucker's consulting in chapter seven. However, my fellow students immediately asked, "How do you know the right questions to ask? Aren't your questions based on your knowledge in the industries in which you consult? What about when first starting out with no experience – how did you have the knowledge and expertise to do this when you first started?"

It was then that Drucker responded with his amazing consulting secret. "I never ask these questions or approach these assignments based on my knowledge and experience in these industries," he answered. "It is exactly the opposite. I do not use my knowledge and experience at all. I bring my ignorance to the situation. Ignorance is the most important component for helping others to solve any problem in any industry, and ignorance is not such a bad thing if one knows how to use it. All managers must learn how to do this. You must frequently approach problems with your ignorance and not what you think you know from past experience, because not infrequently, what you think you know is wrong."

Ignorance Has Value

Drucker immediately launched into a story to prove this point. His stories covered the wide range of Drucker's reading and thinking – from the Catholic Church to Japanese culture, politics, history, Jewish mysticism, warfare, and of course business, and so did this one.

There was a tremendous fuel shortage in Japan immediately after World War II. Automobiles existed even right after the war, but they were immobilized by a shortage of gasoline. Soichiro Honda, a young manager, had significant experience in manufacturing machinery and even airplane propellers during World War II. He came up with the very creative idea of fitting a bicycle with a small engine as a substitute for automobile transportation, since this simpler, lighter vehicle would consume far less gasoline. He built a model as an experiment and it was successful. The problem was that due to the gasoline shortage there were also governmental restrictions in Japan on even manufacturing new engines that utilized gasoline. So it was a great idea, but it couldn't be immediately implemented.

Honda struggled with the idea. He knew something about manufacturing, but was totally ignorant about gasoline or fuel substitutes. Like Drucker, he brought only his ignorance to the problem. However, he didn't drop the project because of his ignorance. He wanted to introduce a product immediately, with tremendous marketing waiting, but it wasn't within his power to end the gasoline shortage or to lobby the government to at least allow him to manufacture the small gasoline engines for propelling the vehicle. After studying this, he came to the conclusion that the solution was in using another type of fuel. This helped him to focus on the problem. That was step one.

Because Honda was unfamiliar about potential fuels or fuel substitutes for gasoline, he began to do research. His complete ignorance led to knowledge and some level of expertise. He read an article somewhere that pine resin had been used, or at least tried, as a substitute for aviation fuel during the war. He reasoned that if pine resin could be considered by experts as a substitute for aviation fuel, why not as a substitute for ordinary automobile gasoline as well? Others thought it a worthless idea born of his ignorance. That Honda's idea was born of ignorance was undoubtedly true. Moreover, if this was such a good idea, why had more experienced manufacturers not already adopted it? Still, Honda reasoned that if pine resin, plentiful in Japan, worked with gasoline engines for aircraft, it should work with much smaller engines as well.

He experimented with pine resin as fuel for his engine himself, and much to his delight, he eventually got it to work reliably. So Honda developed a unique bicycle motor that ran efficiently on pine resin. Of course, there was a strong odour, and colleagues called his engine "the chimney." Through the successful commercialization and development of this innovation and eventually switching to gasoline when restrictions were lifted, he grew the company into the largest motorcycle company in the world. Honda also began to manufacture automobiles and today these, too, are sold worldwide, but these developments were actually unexpected benefits to solving his initial problem. None of this would likely have occurred had Honda not solved an "unsolvable problem" by approaching his challenge with his ignorance.

Analysing Drucker's Claim of Ignorance

Using my own ignorance, I began to investigate how to employ what Drucker had asserted regarding what managers should do in applying their ignorance to problem situations. I knew that Drucker didn't mean to exclude one's prior experience, knowledge, or expertise completely. If that were true, how would Drucker have known even where to begin? Moreover, his injunction to begin with ignorance had to be based on a model developed through knowledge, experience, and expertise. I suspected that it was his journalistic background that may have given him the inspiration to begin from ignorance, but then approach general problems in a logical fashion while gathering additional information so that he was no longer as ignorant as when he began.

In addition, I realized that as a manager or a consultant got involved in following Drucker's advice based on a question, whatever it was, without considerable knowledge he would be unable to accurately understand the issue. This meant that Drucker was not talking about tactical decisions that needed to be made immediately and on the spot. Such decisions had to be based on prior knowledge and experience. He was referring to decisions that one had the time to investigate thoroughly and reflect upon. Moreover, Peter had said on many occasions that managers needed to trust their gut feelings, but that this didn't mean ignoring intuition, either. Clearly the same was true in his consulting work.

I concluded that what Drucker meant was that a consultant or a manager should not jump in with an immediate solution. And while a manager's experience and intuition were not to be excluded, he or she had to approach these problems first with an open mind. Thus the manager needed to recognize and even emphasize his own ignorance in organizing resources to solve the problem. This point continues on from the previous chapter of this book, in which we discussed his oft-repeated phrase, "what everyone knows is usually wrong". To rely primarily on expertise or on what everyone knows is equally dangerous to the problem's optimal solution. That this was, in fact, what Drucker meant was confirmed some years later in a personal discussion over lunch.

The Beauty of Ignorance in Problem Solving

Starting with Drucker's concept, I began an investigation of problem-solving methodologies. I categorized two major approaches to managerial problem solving, both of which involved beginning from a point of "ignorance". Essentially these involved emphasizing the left-brain and right-brain methods; essentially logic and analysis versus reliance on creativity and emotion. Of course, both approaches can be combined. Most importantly, both are applicable by managers directly or by consultants assisting them. The important basic is to approach the problem with ignorance and you'll become knowledgeable as you proceed, since both methods involve amassing, organizing, and analysing additional information available.

Left-brain Problem Solving

A very long time ago, I was taught left-brain problem solving in the Air Force. It was and is used in staff studies. It is extremely effective, not only in defining complex problems, organizing and analysing data, and reaching logical solutions and recommendations, but in presenting this information to others to convince them of the validity of the problem solver's solution. This makes it absolutely critical for consultants.

I always understood that this was developed by the military in the 19th century. However, during my investigation, I discovered that this method was also used and taught at Harvard University. Later yet, I learned that other professionals, such as lawyers and psychologists, frequently use a very similar approach to analysing and reaching logical conclusions when confronted with difficult and complex problems.

Without a doubt, Drucker hit on a similar solution. And for years I overlooked the fact that he had hit upon it almost exactly, and published the information in his book, *The Practice of Management*, in 1954.[1]

The left-brain approach involves defining the problem, deciding on the relevant information bearing on the situation, developing potential alternative solutions to the problem, analysing these alternatives, developing solutions from this analysis, and finally making a concluding decision, even turning these conclusions into recommendations to consulting clients or even others higher up in an organization, such as boards of trustees and directors.

Building Ships at High Speed

Drucker was asking us to think on our own. He was not accepting "common knowledge" or the way things were done in the past as being necessarily correct. In fact, the phrase that I heard him use most in the classroom was, "what everybody knows is usually wrong". Drucker never claimed great knowledge about anything, especially in his legendary consulting. Instead he claimed great ignorance, which therefore required him to think. That's what an American industrialist did with amazing results during World War II, which is an outstanding example of this simple approach that Drucker recommended.

In response to high losses from German submarines, the British had developed a design for cheap cargo ships. These ships were so cheaply built and basic in design that they weren't even expected to remain in service for more than five years. Moreover, they only took about eight months to build, and this was important.

British shipbuilders were considered the best in the world, but it still took experts and skilled workers to build a ship, even a vastly simplified design like this one. Britain was fully engaged in all aspects of fighting the war. The manpower, shipyards, and production facilities to build the fleets needed simply didn't exist.

The US was not yet at war, so the manpower was available. However, the United States did not have a terrific record for merchant shipbuilding. In the previous decade, only two ocean-going cargo ships had been built in the United States. The hope was that with the British design, it might take about a year to build each ship, which could be built in England in eight months.

The US government looked around and Henry Kaiser got the job. Kaiser knew little about shipbuilding and was completely ignorant about cargo ships. However, he looked at the British design and proceeded not with his knowledge and experience, but with his own ignorance. But he did think about it. First Kaiser redesigned the assembly process using prefabricated parts so that no worker had to know more than a small part of the job and workers were much easier to train. The British knew that for close tolerances, heavy machinery was necessary to cut metal accurately. Kaiser didn't know this, and anyway he didn't have heavy machinery. In his ignorance he told workers to cut the medal using oxyacetylene torches. This turned out to be cheaper and faster than the traditional British methods. Kaiser thought about it and replaced riveting with welding. It was cheaper and faster.

He called his ships, "Liberty Ships". He started building them and it didn't take him a year for each ship. It didn't even take him eight months. He started building them from start to finish in about a month. Then they got production time down to a couple weeks and for publicity purposes, they constructed one Liberty Ship in just four-and-a-half days. He built almost 1,500 ships. Despite the fact that they were not built to last, a couple were still around and in use almost 50 years later.

Problem Definition

You can't get "there" until you know where "there" is was not one of Peter Drucker's assertions; it's one of mine. That's my way of emphasizing that in order to solve any problem, you've got to first understand exactly what the problem is. That's the "there" in a problem situation. The shipbuilding problem was not to be able to build the ships the British way, but to build merchant ships to get food and supplies to England despite the huge losses to intercepting German submarines. But it took some thinking to arrive at this definition.

Defining the central problem in a particular situation is the single most difficult, and most important task in most consulting issues. If you correctly identify the main problem in a situation, you can find many different approaches to solving it. But if the wrong problem is identified, even a brilliant solution will not correct the situation. You are well advised to take all the time necessary; be sure you are indeed looking at the central problem, for as Drucker wrote: "for there are few things as useless – if not dangerous – as the right answer to the wrong question."[2]

You can see why Drucker's instruction to begin with ignorance is so important. Previously with the shipbuilding problem, the problem had been defined incorrectly. It had been defined as, "how can the US build the ships the British way without the same human expertise, the experience of centuries, and physical facilities for building ships quickly enough to help England in its hour of need?" The fact was, that problem couldn't be solved. The British were the best. Build it their way and they would be the best, but it would take months. If Kaiser's ignorance hadn't been brought to the problem so that this problem statement was redefined, Kaiser and other potential American emergency shipbuilders might still be working on the problem or long since given up. Using the 1940's technology available at the time, and the state-of-the-art American shipbuilding of merchant ships, the problem just couldn't have been solved. Only ignorance could save the day! So the first step was redefining the problem.

One of the major errors made in defining the central problem is confusing the symptoms with the problem. For example, low profits are not a central problem, but a symptom of something else. Frequently a consulting engagement has more than one problem. The object then is to locate the *main* problem in the situation, the one that is more important than any other and is therefore "central." It may be causing many of the other problems. If you find more than one major problem in a particular situation, you should handle each one separately.

Once you have identified the central problem, write an initial draft explaining what the problem is. Try to keep this statement as simple as possible by making it as short as you can; a one-sentence central problem is usually best. Be aware, however, that even if you have spent some time in both identifying the problem and wording it as concisely as possible, in many cases you will have to go back and modify it as you proceed through the analysis.

Also be careful not to word the problem as if it were the solution by assuming one particular course of action is correct before you analyse it. Returning to Honda's problem, if he defined it as, "How to get the government to drop the restriction on building gasoline engines," he would have arrived at an entirely different course of action, which would have had nothing to do with pine resin. Remember, too, that your goal in using this methodology is to develop as many different courses of action as possible. Try not to word your statement so that only two alternatives are possible. For example, don't ask the question, "should a new product be introduced?" That allows for only two alternatives: yes or no. Occasionally there are some situations where only two alternatives need to be analysed. Usually, however, you can reword the problem statement in a way that opens it up to more than two courses of action.

In your statement, include important specifics about the problem. "What should be done about the possibility of introducing a new product?" is not the best problem statement. It allows for more than two alternatives, but it omits specifics about the problem that may be important to readers of your report who are not as familiar with the problem as you or your client.

Be careful about making your problem statement too long by incorporating various additional factors. Even if these factors are relevant, they will make the problem statement unwieldy, awkward, and difficult for any reader to understand.

With these cautionary notes in mind, begin formulating your problem statement. Phrase it as a question, beginning with *who*, *what*, *when*, *where*, *how*, or *why*. Or you may start with an infinitive, as in "To determine the best source for borrowing $xxx,xxx."

Drucker knew all of this and, after considerable experience, didn't even need to write it all out. Also, in many situations he simply asked the client a question or questions, and they were able to get to this important central issue at once. Drucker spent a lot of time describing what is needed to get to the right problem and so did I. He knew that working on the wrong problem was not only a waste of time, but also a waste of resources and money, and almost invariably resulted in the wrong solution.

Relevant Factors

Factors may be facts, estimates, speculations, assumptions, time and money limitations, and more. All must be documented, and many should be tested before they are even listed. Most importantly, the word relevant is critical because, even though there will be many different factors in any situation, you must determine and list only those that are relevant to the central problem you have decided upon. Kaiser's problems had a number of factors that were directly relevant to the problem situation. Therefore, additional data and information was needed. Kaiser knew what he didn't have. For example, he needed to know what resources he did have available. Kaiser looked into this, did his analysis, and eventually concluded that he could build these particular ships cheaper and faster. This was made easier because he discarded the unimportant and irrelevant and focused on what mattered in doing his analysis and seeking a solution.

Alternative Courses of Action

In this part of the left-brain decision-making process, Kaiser had to decide on alternatives to solve the problem. One option might have been to develop new tactics. Maybe he could have started a worldwide search for expert shipbuilders in neutral countries and offered them high wages. Maybe he could have designed new metal-cutting machinery and produced it quickly using his methods. It is possible he did consider these or other options.

Although theoretically it is possible to have an alternative with all advantages and no disadvantages, this is highly unlikely. If this were the case, the solution would be self-evident, and this problem-solving procedure would be superfluous.

All alternatives have both advantages and disadvantages. Jack Welch probably sold off some really valuable companies using his requirement of shedding any of his businesses that were either not being or capable of becoming number one or two in its industry. He knew that there would be mistakes in some instances. That was a disadvantage to this alternative. And there were enormous risks in this alternative. But there always are and Drucker cautioned clients how to deal with these risks, as I will explain in a later chapter.

Kaiser took an enormous risk with his solution. He had millions of dollars invested before he built his first ship. Many of the methods he used had never been employed previously and many were extremely innovative, to say the least. It was reported that because it took years and extensive training to enable novice fitters to tightrope across the high structures of the ship as it was completed, Kaiser also hired ballet dancers as fitters.[3] Yes, he really did. He thought that it would enable faster work in completing the ship's superstructure, and it worked.

The Analysis

During the analysis, the manager essentially compares the relative importance of each alternative's advantages and disadvantages. Some alternatives have few disadvantages, but no great advantage, either. In any case, the manager needs to think it through and document his thinking. That helps this left-brain method to be really effective in explaining the final conclusions and recommendations to others after a clear solution is developed.

In this case, the conclusions are from the analysis and the eventual decision should be obvious. I'm sure Henry Kaiser went through this process in detail in explaining what he wanted to do to managers, workers, and board of directors. He would have left nothing out, concluding that despite the risks, the best way to achieve the desired results was to implement the building of the British design in the way he outlined it.

Here is a good test of the clarity of your thinking so far: show the entire written document up to this point to someone who is not particularly familiar with the problem. Have this individual read your central problem, the relevant factors you have identified, the alternative courses of action with the advantages and disadvantages, and finally your discussion and analysis. Then ask what his or her conclusions are. If they are identical to yours, you have correctly worded your discussion and analysis. If the conclusions are different, you have made an error, either in the wording of the discussion and analysis or in the logic of your conclusions.

Conclusions and Recommendations

It is important to precisely list the conclusions arrived at as a result of your discussion and analysis. Do not add any explanations; they belong in the previous section. Also don't list conclusions based on information extraneous to your analysis; your conclusions are based solely on your discussion and analysis. Another common error here is to restate relevant factors as conclusions.

Finally, we get to recommendations to your client. You explicitly state the results of your analysis and your recommendations about what your client should do to solve the central problem you have identified and defined. As with your conclusions, do not include extraneous information or explanations; all such explanations go in the discussion and analysis section. If you are presenting this orally, your client can always ask additional questions; if this is a written report, your client can always contact you for additional information. However, if you have done the analysis correctly, there will be no need to explain your recommendations; your reasons will be obvious from your discussion and analysis.

Many consultants first learning this methodology ask about the difference between conclusions and recommendations. With a recommendation, you put your reputation on the line. You make it clear and unequivocal what you want your client to do. You are accepting full responsibility for the recommendations you make. A conclusion is written in the passive tense: "Marketing research should be done." Recommendations are written in the imperative: "Initiate marketing research." If a conclusion on your list reads, "A new accountant should be hired," the recommendation would be, "Hire a new accountant."

Did Drucker do all this in his head? I doubt it. There are limits even to genius. Knowing him, he did not allow for chance. Except for the rarest of general consulting issues, he would have had things well worked out, with notes ready and fully prepared with his questions, even if he didn't use fancy presentation slides.

The Right-brain Solution

The right-brain approach to problem solving still works by starting out with an assumption of ignorance. However, unlike the very structured procedure that is part of the left-brain approach, the right-brain method uses no fixed sequence of logical steps to arrive at a solution. It uses the subconscious mind, in which Drucker was a big believer and though not commonly known, used it frequently: "I first do my analysis homework and come to a conclusion. Then I put the answer aside and spend time with my feelings, intuition, pray about it, and leave it to my subconscious mind to come to a conclusion. If analysis and intuition both give the same answer, it is an easy decision. The problem is when one says yes and the other says no. Then courage comes into play."[4]

One of the best examples of the use of subconscious in American business was by the famous inventor, Thomas Edison. It is important to recall that while Edison had no formal education past high school, he was the inventor of numerous "high-tech" devices, from the light bulb to practical motion pictures. His right-brain approach, according to those who worked with him, was to go into a dark room and sit there – sometimes for hours – until a solution to the problem presented itself.

Donald Trump can be described variously as an American politician and current presidential candidate, business magnate, investor, television personality, and author. However, he makes no bones about the subconscious. In one instance, his subconscious mind worked on a problem even after his conscious mind had come to what proved to be the wrong decision. "The papers were being drawn up, and then one morning I woke up and it didn't feel right." Listening to the conclusions of his subconscious mind, Trump changed his mind. He didn't invest in a project that many experts, and his conscious mind, said was a sound investment. Several months later, the company about which Trump made his decision went bankrupt. The investors lost all their money.[5]

Another example of the use of this right-brain method was Einstein's description as to how he formulated the Theory of Relativity – and he didn't even need to go to sleep. He simply started daydreaming. One would think that anything as quantitatively complex or as mathematical as the development of this theory would require a good number of white-coated scientists working months at blackboards covered with hundreds of chalk-smeared formulas and equations, and advanced work in laboratories. Even if today's technologies were available to Einstein, these scientists would have used up an awful lot of computer time to conceptualize this theory. Yet Einstein stated that he thought the whole thing up by himself by simply closing his eyes and imagining himself riding on a beam of light and what would transpire as to time on Earth during his speed-of-light-trip. Daydreaming may not be as useless as you may have thought.

After your conscious mind has collected and analysed all the relevant factors in a situation, your subconscious mind sometimes comes to a better decision than your conscious mind. Why is this so?

1. *No pressure.* Your conscious mind may be under the pressures of time, a demanding client, or deadlines. Your subconscious mind doesn't recognize these pressures.
2. *Distractions.* Your conscious mind may be distracted by friends, family, business problems, noise, or even a lack of sleep – not so for the subconscious mind.
3. *Limited time.* Most consultants don't have the time to work on a single problem all day on a continual basis. But your subconscious mind has all night, and it will work effortlessly on a problem that needs solving.
4. *False knowledge.* For a variety of reasons, your conscious mind may be influenced by false assumptions or inaccurate facts. Your subconscious mind may know better.

Helping the Subconscious Solve Consulting Problems

If you want to use your subconscious mind to help you solve a problem, first learn all you can about the problem. As when you use the staff study method, that Drucker introduced in *The Effective Executive*, gather all the relevant factors and spend a great deal of time arriving at the central issue in the case. You can also mull over the alternatives, talk to other people and get their opinions, and do additional research. Do this until you feel slightly overloaded.

Before you go to sleep, set aside a half-hour to an hour to do nothing but think about the problem, analyse the data, and think about potential solutions.

Go to sleep in the normal way. Don't try to force a solution to your problem. Although the solution is usually ready for you sometime the next morning, it could come in the middle of the night.

If it does, be ready for it by having pencil and paper nearby, and quickly scribble down the solution and any other insights.

Sometimes answers come in indirect and strange ways. In 1846, when Elias Howe was struggling to invent the sewing machine, he was stumped. Howe had invented a machine that could push and extract a needle in and out of cloth. The problem was the thread. Since the thread went through an eye in the needle at the end opposite the point, the entire needle had to go through the material and back again in order to make a stitch. That was impossible. Howe was at an impasse. Then, for several nights in a row, Howe had identical dreams; Howe's subconscious mind was trying to tell him something. In the dreams, Howe found himself on a South Pacific island, where natives armed with spears danced around him. But the spears were very strange. Each spearhead had a conspicuous hole. Only after several days did Howe realize the solution to his problem: to construct sewing needles with eyes for the thread near the point rather than at the opposite end.

If you want outstanding solutions to your client's problems, use both sides of your brain and your conscious and subconscious minds, but first and foremost, according to Drucker, it's your ignorance with which you start that counts most.

[1] Drucker, Peter F., *The Effective Executive* (New York: Harper and Row Publishers, 1954), pp.422-436.

[2] Ibid., 421.

[3] John H. Lienhard, *Engines of Our Ingenuity*. "No. 1525: Liberty Ships," accessed at http://www.uh.edu/engines/epi1525.htm, 25 June 2015.

[4] No author listed, "What Would Drucker be Reading?" *Drucker Institute*, 12 November 2013, accessed at http://www.druckerinstitute.com/2013/11/what-peter-drucker-would-be-reading-79/, 25 June 2015.

[5] Donald J. Trump and Tony Schwartz, *The Art of the Deal* (New York: Warner Books, 1987), pp.27-28.

Chapter 10

Drucker Tells His Clients What to Do about Risk

Risk in management is unavoidable. Some of Drucker's clients did not acknowledge this. They thought that risk could be avoided and just wanted Drucker to tell them how. However, according to Drucker, risk could not be avoided, and it could be desirable. In fact, the assumption of risk was a basic function of any successful enterprise. Here's how Drucker reasoned. First, of necessity, in any organization economic activity consists of the commitment of present resources to an unknowable and uncertain future. Moreover, this is a commitment to expectations, assumptions, and predictions, almost everything, but not necessarily to facts. Yet future facts, while essential, cannot be known with certainty. That meant whatever decisions were made had risk 100 times out of 100.

If that were not bad enough, risks are not taken only by the one running everything at the top, but by everyone in the organization who contributes knowledge to the enterprise. That is, by every manager and every professional specialist at every level, as well as non-managers and non-specialists.

Even Attempting to Lower Risk Could Be the Wrong Move

Drucker saw that in attempting to decrease risk, managers and professionals of all types sometimes made assumptions that could lead to disaster. The most-used method of lowering risk is to assume either no change in the current situation or that the trend, whatever it is, will continue on into the future. The fallacy of either assumption can be seen almost every day, as many stock market investors make one of these two assumptions with eventually poor results. Drucker knew that change is inevitable and so advised his clients.

Years ago, I saw this in a weekly advertisement for an investment firm in the *Los Angeles Times*. Every Sunday they took out a full-page ad that showed for ten or more consecutive years they had provided investors a consistent return on investment. Then in bold, giant type, they wrote two words: "HO HUM!" The message being that theirs was a consistent, reasonably high return on their investors' money, which would go on forever with no risk whatsoever. Not quite. Obviously when the bottom fell out of the market, beginning with the "Great Recession", they no longer ran the ad.

One of Drucker's Few Errors Was of this Type

Drucker made one of these erroneous assumptions himself and learned the hard way how dangerous such an assumption can be. As a young journalist for the *Frankfurter General-Anzeiger* in 1929, Drucker predicted a rosy future and a bull market in his newspaper column. He had to eat crow a few weeks later with an article that he wrote, but that his editor entitled "Panic on the New York Stock Exchange". The panic he wrote about was the onset of the worldwide Great Depression, which lasted more than 10 years. Drucker at least admitted his error. That's a lot better than some of our journalists today who, in print or on television, attempt to put a positive spin to make it appear that what occurred was exactly what they had predicted and known all along, even though it was not.

Drucker never made the same mistake again. But he knew that risks in business and life could not be avoided. He concluded that, "While it is futile to try to eliminate risk, and questionable to try to minimize it, it is essential that the risks taken be the right risks."[1]

The Story of the Unlucky General
Who Took the Wrong Risk

Shortly after I was commissioned a lieutenant in the Air Force, I heard the story of the unlucky general. This was in peacetime, so he had no worries about an enemy. This general was given command of a large number of bomber aircraft billeted in "Tornado Alley", a part of the southwest United States. During tornado season, dangerous and destructive tornados build with sudden rapidity. The bomber aircraft were very large and most could not always be protected by hangars, sitting out during regular storms right on the runway, unprotected. Now that was good enough for rainstorms, thunderstorms, or even snowstorms.

However, tornados could destroy these multimillion-dollar air-craft with great ease. Today, they would have been valued at multibillion dollars each.

One day the conditions were right for tornados and a storm warning was issued. Being prudent, this general ordered his crews to man their aircraft and ordered all his aircraft to fly out of the tornado-threatened area to other airfields far enough to avoid the tornados. But after the airplanes landed at their emergency bases, the storms dissipated, and no tornados struck. The fuel and man-hours wasted amounted to tens of thousands of dollars. However, the general was not criticized for his actions in moving his aircraft. At least, not this time.

A few weeks later, the same thing happened. Again the storms dissipated after the general moved the aircraft, and no tornados struck. And again, the fuel and man-hours wasted amounted to tens of thousands of dollars. This time his commander suggested that the general look into the possibility of improving his ability to predict whether tornados were really going to strike or not. The general did, but the state of art at the time would allow him to do no better. No one could predict whether tornados would form and strike the base with any certainty.

And sure enough, a few weeks later the tornado warning came again. This time the general decided that enough was enough and he didn't move the aircraft. You guessed it. This time the tornados did form and several struck the base and destroyed or damaged several of these expensive aircraft. The general's boss immediately relieved him of his command. In plain language, he fired him. "But I didn't do anything wrong," the fired general complained. "I know," responded his boss, "but I don't like unlucky generals." In analysing the situation, this general had taken the wrong risks. Despite the expense of moving the aircraft, and his superior's mild criticism regarding the decision of getting them to safety, he should have paid the price and moved them anyway. The weather may have been unpredictable, but millions of dollars in aircraft still should not have been risked.

Picking the Right Risk Is Crucial

General Walter Short commanded the US Army in Hawaii, including the Air Force, which in those days was part of the army. The Navy Commander was Admiral Husband Kimmel. Both Admiral Kimmel and General Short thought that the danger of sabotage was greater than that of an air attack and that the Navy, responsible for air surveillance, could provide adequate warning of an air attack, roughly thought beyond the capability of Japanese forces, which were thousands of miles away. Short therefore parked his aircraft close together, almost wingtip to wingtip, where they could be easily and more efficiently guarded. He was lowering the risk of sabotage, but greatly raising the risk of destruction if there were an attack by air.

Consequently, when 353 Japanese airplanes launched from six aircraft carriers attacked at 7:48a.m. on Sunday morning, 7 December 1941, it was a complete surprise. Of the eight US battleships in port, all were damaged and four were sunk, as were many other smaller ships. No less than 188 aircraft were destroyed and another 159 from a total of 390 aircraft were damaged, almost all on the ground, The US suffered immensely, with almost 4,000 killed and wounded. Both US commanders were accused of dereliction of duty and relieved of command. They were forced to retire and played no further part in the war. In their defence, some commented on their previous efficiency or even on the efficiency of the wrong actions they took. But it was for naught. These leaders may have been very efficient in doing the wrong thing, but they were not effective in protecting their crews defending their charges, or saving the Hawaiian Islands when they came under attack.

Drucker learned to analyse the situation and to emphasize taking the right risks, because taking the wrong risk could be even more disastrous. Drucker's investigations led to the discovery of a critical factor in the process: while deciding on the right risk, one had to institute controls in the actions involved in taking the risk. Otherwise, even though it might well be the right risk to take, there might be other considerations and more important risks. Risks that, in the end, may result in mismanaged actions, intended objectives not reached, and failed results, even though taking a risk of some sort was fully understood and accepted. This is important for any client to understand. Moreover, it is useful in persuading clients to take this approach.

Risk Controls and their Characteristics

Drucker found that all controls invariably have three basic characteristics that make risks difficult to manage:

1. Risk controls won't be objective and they won't be neutral.
2. While they need to focus on the real results, the "real" results aren't always possible to control.
3. Risks are needed for both measurable and unmeasurable events, which cannot be measured or cannot be managed without difficulty.

The Near Impossibility of Objectivity and Neutrality When Dealing with Human Beings

This characteristic is a cautionary note. From 1924–1932, a study of lighting conditions was done at the Hawthorne Works, a Western Electric factory outside of Chicago. One experiment was to examine the effect of better lighting on productivity. It sounds simple enough. The control was based on increasing wattage of the light bulbs weekly and then noting the results in productivity. It was expected that productivity would increase as lighting got better every week, and sure enough, it did.

However, one week some joker decreased instead of increased the lighting intensity, removing all objectivity and neutrality. Guess what? Productivity improved anyway. It was hardly a miracle or an error in measurement. What had happened was that workers expected the lighting intensity to increase and this motivated them to work harder, more efficiently, and hence more productively. Today this is known today as the "Hawthorne Effect".[2] It demonstrates that the novelty alone of having research conducted, along with the increased attention to the measurement results, can cause at least a temporary increase in productivity. And it means that, as Drucker said, "Controls are not applied to a falling stone, but to a social situation with living, breathing human beings who can and will be influenced by the controls themselves."

Focusing on the Real Results

It is relatively easy to measure effort or efficiency, but much more difficult to measure real results with a control. Drucker explained that it was of no value to have the most efficient engineering department, for example, if the department was efficiently designing the wrong products. In somewhat the same fashion, Drucker differentiated leadership from management. Others have since similarly adopted his formula: that management was doing things right – read efficiently – while leadership was doing the right things, that is, the effective things to get the job done. So one could be very efficient as a manager, using whatever measurement you choose, and still not be a good leader.

Measuring efficiency is usually not so difficult. For example, one can measure the number of times a leader recognizes subordinates for accomplishing good work. That's considered a sign of good leadership. Think of the "One-Minute Manager", who was told to catch his people doing the right things more than catching them doing something wrong.[3] However, "good work" can be done on the wrong things, as well as the right things. Maybe salespeople are doing a marvellous job selling the wrong product. Is this "good work"? To complicate controls further, how do we know what are "the right things"? This is much harder to know when so many factors and multiple humans are involved. Since leadership is an art, in observation, its quality may most definitely be in the eyes of the beholder.

Focusing on the Right Results

Battle gives some real examples of what this means. Marine Corps Gregg "Pappy" Boyington was a World War II fighter pilot. He later wrote the book, *Bah, Bah, Black Sheep*. About 20 years ago they made a TV series about his experiences, under the same name. As a young pilot he had resigned his commission as a Marine Corps pilot and volunteered for General Chennault's "Flying Tigers" in China. He scored several victories as a fighter pilot. But his senior leadership thought that he drank too much, and he was so despised as a leader by his military superiors that when he left China to re-join the Marine Corps, he was not given a very good recommendation.

Although a superior pilot – and even when fighter pilots were badly needed during World War II – he was assigned a desk job with minimum responsibility in operations and no subordinates other than a secretary. It was only through luck that too many fighter aircraft were shipped to his location with no pilots to fly them in combat. He proposed to be given the job of squadron commander and that he would find and train his own pilots somehow. After all, the basic idea was to fight the enemy!

Boyington was given "temporary" command of a makeshift squadron and the authority to train a group of any pilots he could find and put them together in a squadron with a temporary unit designation under his leadership. Only in wartime could such a thing happen! He found pilots from wherever he could who were in non-flying jobs but were eager to volunteer for this "new squadron". He trained transport pilots to be fighter pilots, and pilots who were "grounded" for having done something wrong were allowed back in the cockpit on probation. He trained them hard, and when he felt that they were ready, he took the squadron operational and they began to fly combat missions.

They called themselves the "Black Sheep" Squadron. However, that Black Sheep Squadron shot down more enemy aircraft in a few weeks than most did in months. The responsible senior commander made the unit a permanent squadron and it became the highest-rated Marine Corps fighter squadron in the

Pacific theatre of operations. Boyington finished the war with a Congressional Medal of Honour, and a reputation as one of the finest fighter squadron commanders of any American service in the war. This once-despised leader who was barely trusted to command a secretary, retired from the Marine Corps with the senior rank of full colonel.

As in Boyington's case, the eyes of the beholder are not always very objective measurements. As Drucker said, you don't staff organizations because potential members don't have any weaknesses, but because they have the right strengths.

Moreover, Drucker would have said that the commander allowing Boyington to form this squadron of semi-misfits took the right risk. It could have failed, and planes and lives might have been lost. It was the correct risk and it paid off.

When Conditions Change, the Real Results May Change, Too

This chapter seems to have a lot of military examples, but here is another. When I was a cadet, I remember we studied the case history of an infantry officer who had been commissioned, barely got through commissioning training and, before his unit entered combat, his commander had already instituted paperwork to have him decommissioned and "busted" back to the rank of private.

This lieutenant was overweight and slovenly, his uniforms were rarely pressed, his shoes weren't shined, and he didn't shave properly. Then the entire division went into combat. This officer didn't change much, but he had a knack for leading under difficult circumstances and making the right decisions in combat. As the case description indicated, his men confidently followed in his "pudgy" footsteps. In combat, where it counted, he was a great success. Conditions had changed, and so did the real results upon which risks should be taken.

So one doesn't always measure leadership by appearances or even the lack of weaknesses, but by absolute results depending on the organization's mission. The failure or success of a leader is determined not so much by how hard a leader tries or how efficiently he or she works, but by the success or failure of the event or endeavour. This is a very crude measurement when we consider that so many factors are frequently not under the leader's control: resources available, quality of personnel, difficulty of the task, acts of nature, judgment, and a lot more. But that's all we have!

Non-measurable Events, Too

Controls are also difficult because some events in an organization, important to risk, simply aren't measurable. We already noted that you don't have true facts about the future. You don't know what may suddenly happen on the way to the future, either. The ubiquitous slide rule, once on the person of every engineer worthy of the name, disappeared almost overnight when the pocket electronic calculator hit the market in 1972.

The Seven Control Specifications

Drucker investigated further and determined that all controls must satisfy certain specific specifications, of which there were seven:

1. They had to be economical – the less effort required to gain control, the better.
2. They had to be meaningful – in other words, they had to be intrinsically significant or symptoms of significant developments.
3. They must be appropriate to the nature of what you are measuring – absenteeism of a yearly average of 10 days per employee sounds acceptable, but you could have only two employees and one was never absent while the other was absent frequently.
4. Measurements must be congruent to the phenomenon measured. As a writer, I'm always interested in book sales.

I once read a book by a famous entrepreneur who had written a best seller. He had bought a well-known company and promoted the company's product frequently on television, stating he liked the product so much, he had bought the company. His advertising promotions were great. However, when I read his book, I found it was at best fair. Yet it became a bestseller and sold two million copies, surpassing many better books on entrepreneurship in sales, including Drucker's Innovation and Entrepreneurship, which came out at about the same time. Not to mention several that I had written, the best of which had sold a little less than 100,000 copies.

One day it was revealed that the author had spent almost $2 million of his own money promoting the book. Now, book royalties are a lot less than you might think, frequently about 15% of the net amount received by the publisher. The net to the publisher may be only roughly 50% of the price of the book. Since this entrepreneur was not the publisher, I estimated that he had earned about $1 million in royalties for his total book sales. So he personally lost a million dollars selling his book. He may have been willing to pay a million dollars to have a two-million-copy bestseller just for bragging rights. But as a control measurement, book sales alone – the most frequent tool used to measure public demand for a particular book by readers – is probably a poor tool without other factors being noted and compared.

Control requirements 5, 6, and 7 are much easier and intuitive. They need to be timely. They are an expensive waste of time if the information received arrives too late to be of use. They need to be simple. As Drucker noted, complicated controls just don't work. They frequently cause confusion and lead to other errors. Finally, they need to be oriented toward action. Controls are not something instituted for academic interest. They are for implementing strategy once actions with the right risks are chosen.

The Final Limitation

The final limitation on controls is the organization itself. An organization operates with rules, policies, rewards, punishments, incentives, resources, and capital equipment. But its success comes from people and their daily, frequently unquantifiable, actions. The expressions of their actions, such as an increase in salary, may be quantifiable. However, their feelings, motivations, illnesses, drive, and ambitions are not. As an operational system, the organization cannot be accurately quantified.

What It All Means

Risk is essential and, as a consultant, this is what Drucker taught his clients. The key is to pick the right risks and then control those risks considering the many factors that make this control so difficult to comprehend and use. But knowledge is power, or at least stored power. Selecting the right risks and monitoring the seven important aspects of the risk controls identified by Drucker means effective risk management. One cannot do more, nor should the consultant consider doing less.

[1] Drucker, Peter F., *Management: Tasks, Responsibilities, Practices* (New York: Harper Business). p 512.

[2] No Author Listed, "The Hawthorne Effect" in *The Economist* (November 3 2008). This article is adapted from The Economist Guide to Management Ideas and Gurus, by Tim Hindle (New York: Bloomberg Press, 2008,) assessed at http://www.economist.com/node/12510632, 12 February 2015.

[3] Blanchard, Kenneth H. and Spencer Johnson, *The One-Minute Manager* (New York: William Morrow, 2003).

Chapter 11

How to
Think Like
Drucker,
Einstein, and
Sherlock
Holmes

I've written earlier that perhaps Drucker's greatest legacy was in teaching us to think. His valuable insights and theories, both published and in the classroom, did not come from scientific methods or mathematical calculations, but by the straightforward method of observation and using his brain and reasoning to logical conclusions. Like another genius of note, Albert Einstein, he did not arrive at his theories in a laboratory surrounded by microscopes, computers, and white-coated scientists, but in the laboratory of the mind. It is a fact that Einstein's most productive period was in 1905, during which he produced four ground-breaking theoretical papers, one of which eventually won him the Nobel Prize. None of the four were conceived and written in the sterile atmosphere of a laboratory, or even at a university, but while he was working at the Swiss Patent Office.[1]

The Development of the Theory of Relativity

Einstein himself described the first step in the development of one of his most famous theories, the Theory of Relativity, as conceived while he imagined himself traveling along the side of a beam of light. It is also distinctly possible that it was Einstein who provided Drucker with the example of developing his own methodology of reasoning and thinking, which in turn resulted in his many theories of management. Drucker observed companies in action. Collectively he described these companies as "his laboratory". He used his analysis and development of what he observed in this laboratory to develop his theories in his mind.

Einstein Revealed the Common Process

Although Drucker only gave us clues about the process, Einstein actually described it. In an article in the *London Times* written in 1919, Einstein wrote about what he called "Theories of Principle". He stated that these theories "…employed the analytical, not the synthetic method. Their starting point and foundation are not hypothetical components, but empirically observed general properties of phenomena, principles

186

from which mathematical formulae are deduced of such a kind that they apply to every case which presents itself".[2]

I do not know whether Drucker actually read Einstein's article. Drucker was only 10 years old at the time and did not speak English. However, Drucker did refer to Einstein, and it is possible that he read the article later. This article motivated me to better investigate the difference between synthetic and analytical research. To simplify some rather complex definitions, synthetic research starts with the known and proceeds to the unknown. Thus, one starts with a hypothesis or hypotheses and tests this hypothesis to prove or disprove it, usually by examination of a sufficient number of examples and testing mathematically for significant difference. Analytical research starts with the unknown and proceeds to the known. There is no hypothesis. One definition of analytical research is, "A specific type of research that involves critical-thinking skills and the evaluation of facts and information relative to the research being conducted."[3] The analytical process is how Einstein and Drucker arrived at their theories. This also extended to Drucker's consulting practice, both in his use of what he observed and his reasoning in considering a client's issues.

Enter the World's Greatest Fictional Detective

Sherlock Holmes, the great fictional detective of yet another genius, Sir Arthur Conan Doyle, also enters into this discussion of Drucker's thinking. I've already noted that Drucker likely used Doyle's definition of Holmes as a "consulting detective" to determine the definition of a management consultant. The dictionary and other sources were of little help in providing a definition at a time when neither Drucker nor his military supervisor understood the duties for which Drucker had been mobilized during World War II. It is likely that Drucker's insight as to this definition was helped by reading some of Sir Arthur's stories or novels after he fled Germany for England during the rise of Hitler in 1934.

While Sherlock Holmes had the amazing ability to deduce facts, his assistant, Dr John Watson, complained of his own inability to see all the facts that Sherlock seemed to see. To explain this,

Sherlock stated: "On the contrary, Watson, you can see everything. You fail, however, to reason from what you see. You are too timid in drawing your inferences." In other words, it was not only that one must observe, but one must analyse and draw conclusions from these observations.[4]

Academic Research is an Analytical Process, But...

Is academic research itself not an analytical process? It is. However, note that the theories developed by the three geniuses – Einstein, Sir Arthur Conan Doyle's famous detective (Sherlock Holmes), and Peter Drucker – did not start with hypotheses until after observation, and their resulting theories did not evolve from the scientific method as it is commonly understood, a process in which many subjects are surveyed and analysed through mathematical techniques and equations. Their analytical approach came from a simple model:

1. Observation, either real or, as in Einstein's case, imagined.
2. Analysis of what was observed.
3. Conclusions.
4. Construction of theory based on these conclusions.

Ed Cooke, a Grand Master of Memory, is a graduate of Oxford University in psychology, as well as the author of books on memory. He was the memory coach who convinced Joshua Foer that anyone could be trained to have a world-class memory in a year. Though Foer's tested memory was only average at the beginning, he was trained by Cooke to become the United States Memory Champion in about one year to prove Cooke's claim that he could train anyone in one year of concentrated study. In case you're wondering what concentrated study entailed, it took about one hour a day of training, and then several hours a day prior to the championship competition. (If you want to know more, I recommend *Moonwalking with Einstein* by Joshua Foer, Penguin Books, 2011).

Discussing what the mind was capable of, Cooke wrote that there were two ways of doing brain research: "The first is the way that empirical psychology does it, which is that you look from the outside and take a load of measurements from a lot of different people. The other way follows from the logic that a system's optimal performance can tell you something about its design."[5]

Cooke's description of the latter method matches how Einstein, Doyle, and Drucker all shortened the analytical method by focusing on the powers of ordinary observation and applying analytical reasoning in their methods of research, leading to practical results. It seems clear that all three followed this "other way".

Unexpected Insights at an Academic Conference

I found insights into the value of Drucker's methods about 15 years ago. I was invited to participate as a member of a special panel at an academic conference. The purpose of the panel was to discuss the influence of textbooks on management practice, or rather the lack thereof. During this discussion, and before an audience of marketing and management professors, one question was directed precisely at me. I was the only one of the five academic authors on the panel to have written both professional books for practising managers and textbooks for students. The question directed to me was why textbooks seemed many years behind the latest practices in management, while professional or "trade" books seemed to be frequently right on the cutting edge.

I pondered this question for several seconds and then responded: "The writers of textbooks must bring together research from many sources to confirm the main points or theories they discuss in their textbook. In some cases, there are also alternate theories to present regarding the various methods proposed for practice. Essentially, the time needed for the textbook writer to do the research must be added to the time it takes for the researcher to conduct the necessary experiments, to write about each in one or more articles, and to find a suitable academic journal for publication. For a top research journal, this in itself can take many months before such a paper is accepted. After a textbook has been published, it is used to instruct students in the classroom and rarely read by practitioners. It may take several years before these students are in supervisory positions and able to practise what is taught in the classroom. On the other hand, a professional book based on a theory resulting from personal observations is prepared using analytical research and can be applied much more quickly, as the professional book goes right into the hands of the practitioner, who can put it to immediate use."

More Insight from the Conference

What happened at this conference motivated me to do some research on my own. While preparing a lecture for doctoral students on the value of writing professional books for disseminating theory as Drucker did, rather than publishing in academic journals as is the method preferred by most scholars and academic institutions, I came across an unexpected fact. Many of the most widely publicized theories of management reached practitioners using Drucker's method of publishing a book and getting the information directly to the user. These include not only Drucker's Management by Objectives from *The Practice of Management* (Harper & Brothers, 1954) and other methods resulting from Drucker's own theories, but also Abraham Maslow's *Hierarchy of Needs* disseminated through his book, *Motivation and Personality* (Harper & Brothers, 1954) and Douglas McGregor's Theory X and Theory Y disseminated through his book, *The Human Side of Enterprise.* (McGraw-Hill, 1960). Sure, there were also a lot of articles published in research journals on all these topics, but this was only after the professional books had been published by the originators of these ideas and the theories had been put into practice and were well known and in common discussion by business professionals. The research was written to confirm or deny various aspects of the theories that the book authors proposed; or the authors themselves wrote these to help define their theories already published in books.

Drucker's Resulting Methodology and Thinking

Drucker empirically observed general properties of phenomena or through his questions and their answers, or had his clients report their observations. He did not start with synthetic mathematical formulae into which data was inserted to determine what was to be done, but used his powers of observation and reasoning in determining theory and then further testing this theory as he saw it applied.

This is perhaps why, although Drucker claimed that he always began with his ignorance about any problem, he insisted on measurements and numbers when seeking to measure performance and progress. But he eschewed quantitative methods for developing theory and its application to strategy. Less clear was what this process was, stating only when queried about his methods that he listened, and then added, that he listened "to himself". This comment was made in a humorous and not arrogant way. It is also probable that Drucker was speaking 100% accurately. He listened to his own logical reasoning in developing theory or in applying the resulting theory for action by his clients. That he followed an established process was clear, but unlike Einstein, he did not explicitly reveal it. It is highly likely that their methods were very similar, if not identical.

This important tool – Drucker's thinking processes – was part of Drucker's vast mental arsenal for his consulting and should not be overlooked. It is especially important since he did not use models of mathematical analysis to arrive at his conclusions and recommendations. I cannot state the mathematical equations, or his favourite methods of determining significant differences, because there were none. Still, if we can understand the processes of his thinking, we may do the same in our problem solving, decision making, and in assisting others through consultation.

The Missing Link in Drucker's Thinking in Developing Theory

So now we understand that the foundation of Drucker's thinking was analytical reasoning, but based on his own observations. While looking from the outside, he would draw on the logic of what a system's optimal or failed performance revealed, rather than "taking a load of measurements from a lot of different people". But Drucker used one final link that even Einstein may have overlooked, although Doyle, through the Holmes character, may have hit it. Drucker uncovered his theories by challenging "the known explanation" of what he saw. He actually challenged the assumed logic of the outcome of the events that he witnessed. Here are just a few clues about his challenging methodology that I have uncovered:

1. He examined ideas even if they appeared intuitively obvious.
2. He stood "facts" on their heads to see how they looked if basic ideas were reversed.
3. He was able to instantly discern certain things that others missed.
4. He adopted a Sherlock Holmes guideline that if all other conclusions had been examined and found to be lacking, then the one remaining must be the truth, no matter how unlikely or seemingly impossible. This latter "clue" to Drucker's methods merely confirmed the rationale for the first three. But let's us look at these first three clues to his thinking in more detail.

Examining that which Appears to Be Intuitively Obvious

Ask nine out of ten businesspeople the purpose of their business and they will look at you as if you were crazy. "Why, to make a profit, of course," or similar words would probably be the answer. Even a Drucker acolyte may simply repeat Drucker's quotation, "The purpose of a business is to create a customer," without understanding Drucker's reasoning or what Drucker really meant, but for certain the profit motive and profit maximization were both fair game for Drucker's genius. Let's examine his thinking in some detail.

The Profit Motive

The profit motive is a basic economic concept. On the face of it, there is little to question. A typical definition of the profit motive is:

"The intent to achieve monetary gain in a transaction or material endeavour. Profit motive can also be construed as the underlying reason why a taxpayer or company participates in business activities of any kind." Many economists also take the societal view that in order to maximize an economy's growth, one must also maximize profits. Drucker told us that profit is not the purpose of business and following that, he launched into an unheard-of concept: that profit maximization was not only meaningless, but could be dangerous.[6]

Drucker first called the profit motive itself into question. He claimed that there has never been any evidence for such a motive, and that the theory was invented by classical economists to explain a reality that their theory of economic equilibrium could not explain. For example, a good deal of volunteerism in which individuals, some quite highly paid in other roles, work long, hard, hours for the common good in a variety of organizations for little or no pay is unexplained by the profit motive.

The term "dollar-a-year men" first became popular during World War I. US law prohibited work without financial compensation, so many volunteers went on salary during times of war emergency for the princely sum of one dollar, frequently awarded with much ceremony. Even in those days, one dollar was not a lot of money, and for a year's work… well, the term attracted a lot of attention and publicity. Moreover, few can doubt that many talented individuals knowingly choose occupations that are less financially rewarding due to their personal interest or calling in more or less semi-permanent jobs, such as in the US Peace Corps, the Red Cross, or some cause that was important to them. Pat Tillman gave up a glamorous career as an NFL football star and a $3.6 million, three-year contract after the terrorist attack on 9/11 to become an army ranger. He served several tours of combat before he was accidentally killed by friendly fire during combat operations.[7, 8]

Drucker even challenged the notion that high corporate salaries were necessary to attract quality personnel "who would not work for less" due to the profit motive. Yet a variety of jobs attract high quality individuals with relatively low pay. Two examples are teaching and the military.

Drucker concluded that while profit can be motivating and a motivational factor, it need not be the primary motivator. And the notion of maximizing profit as the ultimate goal for a business, ignoring social issues or anything else is, according to Drucker, at best overstated.

Of course Drucker did not deny that profitability is neither a waste of time, immoral or both. This is not true and was not his point. He said that creating hostility to earning a profit was "the most dangerous disease of an industrial society", causing some of the worst mistakes of public policy and went along with the mistaken notion that there is an inherent contradiction between profit and an organization's ability to make a social contribution. Drucker pointed out that a business can only make a social contribution if it is profitable. It isn't a good thing for anyone if a company goes out of business. Yet, many forget that to continue into the future, a business must invest both in research and development and provide cash reserves for that future. Many times well-meaning observers make an erroneous calculation and conclude that a business is being "greedy", when it is doing exactly what it must do to continue to operate in the future. Drucker went on to prove that profitability – far from being a myth, immoral, or unneeded – is crucial for the success of both individual businesses and society. Moreover, he considered profit (as opposed to profit maximization) even more important for society than for an individual business. However, creating a profit is not the *purpose* of a business.

Is Profit Maximization a Dangerous Fallacy?

Now, if profit is necessary for sustainability, why isn't profit maximization a good thing? Many economists consider profit maximization a basic principle and important driver of capitalism. Drucker said that if you strip this principle down to its basic tenant, it is simply another way of stating that a business should buy low and sell at a higher price. That's pretty basic, right? However, Drucker noted that this simple description by itself doesn't begin to explain the success or failure of a business or its sustainability. A local retailer may have been buying low and selling high. If that's all that you know, you don't know enough to claim that the business is a success or a failure. Look around at businesses that fail. Weren't all of them buying low and selling high, or at least attempting to do so? If we look at the difficulties as many businesses struggle today, and the many failures that have already occurred, it is clear that buying low and selling high explains very little about why these businesses fail, just as buying low and selling high explains very little about those that are successful, or those that are accelerating their success despite the obstacles they face in any given environment or time period. There are many business successes, even in times of greatest economic challenge. For example, companies that attained great success in the Great Depression of 1929-1940 include Proctor and Gamble, Chevrolet, United Airlines, Hughes Aircraft, Camel Cigarettes, Kellogg Cereal, the Monopoly board game and hundreds more. Some say that more millionaires were created during the Great Depression than in any other period in US history. But look around and you'll see successes and failures on any street corner. Buying low and selling high explains very little.

Profit maximization seems to imply that you might prevent failure or increase the success of any business by simply raising prices and creating a greater differential between revenue and cost, that is, maintain (or increase) the profit margin. In point of fact, as business costs rise, be they gasoline, material, necessary services, taxes, or anything else, profit maximization is the immediate and simplistic response of many businesses. Yet these businesses still fail or succeed independent of the act of raising prices to maximize profit. Profit maximization by itself is just not the determining factor.

Not so long ago, I was told that a local restaurant had failed due to the rising cost of produce. Yet other restaurants in the same general area serving the same target market did not fail. Some were thriving and even increasing sales. Yet the cost of produce rose for all equally.[9] All this reminds me of a restaurant manager who once responded to an accusation of bad food and poor service with the response: "Bring me more customers and have them spend more money and I'll give you good food and better service." Well, I guess this is true as far as it goes.

The Purpose of a Business

After thinking about this, Drucker concluded that neither profits nor profit maximization are the purpose of a business, and that there is only one valid purpose for a business, and that is to create a customer. Drucker wrote, "The customer is the foundation of a business and keeps it in existence. He alone gives employment. To supply the wants and needs of a consumer, society entrusts wealth-producing resources to the business enterprise." In other words, society gives the business the means to gain employment for the business, by granting a customer in return for supplying the wants and needs of society's consumers. Yet profits and profit maximization as purposes still sound intuitively correct, even though they are clearly wrong for both the business and for society.

It was intuitively obvious that the purpose of a business was primarily profit. But Drucker analysed this intuitively obvious statement and came to an entirely different conclusion.

Standing "Facts" on their Heads

Drucker demonstrated again and again that almost any commonly "known" fact could be turned on its head and used to advantage in gaining an important insight. From this analysis came many of his comments that, as one experienced professor told me early in my academic career, made Drucker "eminently quotable".

I discussed "what everybody knows is usually wrong" thoroughly and validated its truth in many cases by example in chapter eight. But let's look at how Drucker arrived at this conclusion by turning the original upside down. The original belief is that knowledge known by everybody, or nearly everybody, is usually right. Actually Drucker was preceded in his warning to start questioning this notion by *argumentum ad populum*, which is Latin for "appeal to the people". In the argumentation theory, *argumentum ad populum* is considered fallacious based on the notion that "if many people believe it, it is so" as simply irrelevant as to its truth.[10]

But Drucker went a step further. He took the idea that if many people knew something to be true, this truth could be turned on its head.

He applied analytical reasoning and concluded that the exact opposite was true in so many cases and that he could make the statement
that what everybody knows is usually wrong. Of course Drucker
may have been exaggerating, and his statement may be equally fallacious because of this exaggeration. However, it is surprising just how
frequently Drucker's statement is correct if the assumption is that
because everyone or nearly everyone knows something is correct in
one situation, it is true in every situation. As I indicated earlier in the
book, even the US Supreme Court, the highest court in the land,
can be clearly in error according to our beliefs about many things,
including human rights; witness the Dred Scott decision defending
slavery. If that is so, we cannot even state that court decisions made
by a jury on a simple majority – even if unanimous – are always
correct. And as proven time after time, sometimes they are not.

Standing facts on their heads is relatively easy to do to come up
with some rather interesting truths. Here are two other well-known
Drucker quotes:

- "The most important thing in communication is hearing what
  isn't said"
- "The most serious mistakes are not made as a result of wrong
  answers. The truly dangerous thing is asking the wrong question"

As an exercise, you might consider examples of each and how
Drucker might have arrived at these conclusions by "standing a
known fact on its head".

Here's one that I thought of: "Success at sports comes from hard
work, not fun." Oh yeah? Why then do mountain climbers train, get
up early, freeze, sweat, and sometimes risk life and limb in practising
their sport? Obviously they must be experiencing some enjoyment
and fun despite the drawbacks and risks. In other words, they are
having fun. Is that really work then? I concluded that, "Success at
sports comes not from working hard, but from playing hard." After
thinking about it a little more, I concluded that this may be true for
just about everything, from babysitting to running a billion dollar
corporation. In any case, you get the general idea.

Instantly Discerning Certain Things that Others Missed

At one time it was believed that chess players must all have highly-gifted memories, since the champions see several moves ahead of their less-gifted opponents. But recent research proves this to be inaccurate, because that's not what champion chess players do at all. Nor are they more intelligent, necessarily, than you or me. What then is the big difference? The difference is that champion chess players can look at a given situation on a chessboard and instantly see possibilities, opportunities, threats, and what to do, while others cannot. This is because they can memorize entire chessboards with one quick look. Yet their memories of other things may be just as bad as everyone else's.[11] This ability is not something that they were born with, but rather a result of having experienced so much chess play that this incredible ability is automatic, and they need not even stop to think to be able to grasp a chess situation and apply this unique, but developed, talent.

Drucker could do the same. Given a management situation, he usually could instantly capture the important facts and immediately ascertain the important issues and what questions to ask and whom to ask. Now, you may think that this ability is unique to Drucker and can be duplicated by few if any others. And that would be true as far as it goes, but the same question holds. It is a case of repetition over about 10 years, the exact number is not clear, but years of experience nevertheless. Maxwell Gladwell noted this in is his book *Outliers*. Simply speaking, you may see celebrities or others who seem to come out of nowhere become instantly successful. A little investigation shows this to be untrue. In every case, the "instant success" has a long history of experience to get where they are.

Bobby Fischer, who some call the greatest chess grand master of all time, achieved this recognition at the ripe young age of 15. But most don't stop to consider that he had been playing intensely for nine years! According to Gladwell, 10 years, or about 10,000 hours, is the norm. He calls this the "10,000 Hours Rule" and points out numerous examples to back up his statement.[12] Does Drucker fit into this category? He started out as a journalist in about 1928. His first book, *The End of Economic Man*, was written about 10 years or 10,000 hours later.

Modelling Drucker's Thinking

Each of us is an individual, and so each of us approach consulting and thinking differently from everyone else. However, this doesn't mean that the basics can't be used by anyone to attain similar results. We can observe and use our own brains to do analytical research to evolve our own theories, which we can generalize for consulting or anything else. And while looking at what we observe, we can:

1. Examine ideas that appear intuitively obvious and find out whether they are true or not.

2. Stand facts on their heads to see how they look if basic ideas are reversed.

3. Keep at it with repetition for the 10,000 hours it takes until we too are able to instantly discern certain things that others miss in any situation in consulting, management, or the vocation of our desire. And maybe write like Drucker, too.

[1] No author listed, "Albert Einstein," *History*, accessed at http://www.history.com/topics/albert-einstein, 11 July 2015.

[2] Albert Einstein, "Time, Space, Gravitation," *London Times*, 28 November 1919 reprinted in Science, V. 2 ,2 January 1920, p.8, accessed at https://archive.org/details/science511920mich, 11 July 2015.

[3] No author listed, "What Is Analytical Research?" *Ask*, accessed at http://www.ask.com/business-finance/analytical-research-94534a536bf46028, 20 July 2015.

[4] Doyle, Arthur Conan, *The Adventures of Sherlock Holmes*, "The Blue Carbuncle" (Oak Park, IL: Top Five Books, iBooks, 2012), pps. 389-390.

[5] Ed Cooke, quoted in Foer, Joshua, *Moonwalking with Einstein*, (New York: Penguin Books, 2011). p.15.

[6] Drucker, Peter F., *Management: Tasks, Responsibilities, Practices* (New York: Harper & Row Publishers, 1973, 1974) p.60.

[7] No author listed, "Ex-NFL star Tillman Makes 'Ultimate Sacrifice'," *NBC.COM*, 26 April 2004, accessed at http://www.nbcnews.com/id/4815441/ns/world_news/t/ex-nfl-star-tillman-makes-ultimate-sacrifice/, 27 November 2015.

[8] No author listed, "Pat Tillman," *Wikipedia*, accessed at https://en.wikipedia.org/wiki/Pat_Tillman November 27 2015.

[9] Op cit Drucker, Peter F., *Management: Tasks, Responsibilities, Practises*.

[10] No author listed, "Argumentum Ad Populum," *The Free Dictionary* by Farlex, accessed at http://encyclopedia.thefreedictionary.com/Argumentum+ad+populum, 15 July 2015.

[11] Joshua Foer, *Moonwalking with Einstein* (New York: Penguin Books, 2011) p. 65.

[12] Malcolm Gladwell, Outliers (New York: Little Brown and Company, 2008) p. 41.

Chapter 12

Developing a Client's Self-confidence and Your Own, Too

Drucker wrote that no manager can operate effectively without taking risks. We've already discussed Drucker's advice on taking risks in chapter 10. However, until now we have ignored the fact that taking professional risks demands self-confidence. He also wrote that fear of job loss was inconsistent with a manager's ability to perform at a high level. The exact quote from one of his books is: "Living in fear of loss of job and income is incompatible with taking responsibility for job and work group, for output and performance."[1] But how can you not fear job loss, especially in times when loss of a job is a real possibility, regardless of tenure or prior highly successful performance? Maybe the whole company goes under. In that case, you are going to lose your job. Both of these issues and many others as well are solved by self-confidence.

The Answer Is Self-confidence

The answer to this and other questions is self-confidence. I've never seen a highly successful manager without a good deal of self-confidence, and I challenge you to find any "up and comer", "fast burner",—or whatever you want to call managers who seem to zoom right up the corporate ladder and past their contemporaries—who don't possess a healthy dose of self-confidence as well. Self-confidence is a necessity for significant success for us and for our clients. Unfortunately, the fact that it is a necessity doesn't in itself tell us how to acquire this important trait.

Sure, most who have already achieved great success usually have self-confidence. Unfortunately, those who are not in this category – and that's most of us as we progress in our careers – sometimes feel self-confident, but many times we do not. We are concerned with possibly losing our jobs in tough times, and we may sometimes choose the safest path when the way to enormous success involves more risk than we're willing to tolerate. We know what Drucker recommended to us, and we may agree with his recommendations. We know that if we were achieving the success of that small percentage of our colleagues that are shooting ahead at light speed, we would have the self-confidence that Drucker wrote about. However, to reach that kind of success, we first need to acquire self-confidence. We can't achieve great things without self-confidence, but we can't have the self-confidence without achieving them first. Or so it would seem.

Drucker's Secrets

You must acquire self-confidence yourself before you can instil it in others. Yet in my research into Drucker, I found there to be only three ways to gain self-confidence:

1. Being born with it.
2. Gain it slowly and laboriously over many years as you acquire experience, make mistakes, learn from them, and gain success.
3. Start building your self-confidence yourself, purposely, whenever you decide to.

Born with Self-confidence

Now there's a stunt if you could pull it off. However, unless you are into some kind of spiritual technology, that's just not possible. Or leaving room for the belief that nothing is impossible, it is not practical, and I don't think we can turn to Drucker for help if we want to do a rewind and begin our lives anew from the start. However, the truth is, no one is really born with self-confidence.

No one starts right out in life accomplishing what we think of as big things. We start as an infant and accomplish what we today think of as small things, like learning to walk and talk. But are these really small things? At the time you first learned to do any of these routine human accomplishments, if you had been able to think about it at all, you probably would not have thought that they were so small. The truth is, even with these "small things", we started out by doing still smaller things first and slowly increasing the difficulty of the subtasks until we could accomplish such a major task such as learning to walk for the first time.

Today, there is no longer any doubt that, unless you have a major injury, when you stand, put forth one leg and then another, you are going to move forward and walk. As you read these sentences, unless you are just learning the language, there is little doubt that you will understand what you have read. You automatically expect positive results.

With the more complex and challenging tasks and projects of adults and managers, you may fail to expect to succeed for only one of two reasons. Either you have been unsuccessful at similar tasks or projects in the past, or you have never tried to accomplish them in the first place. And by the way, people who believe that they would be unsuccessful at a particular task frequently never try it because of the belief that they would fail if they did.

You Learn to Crawl Before You Can Walk

How many infants have you heard of who simply took their bottles out of their mouths, placed them on a nearby table, hopped out of their cribs, and began to walk? I don't know about you, but I haven't heard of any. The correct sequence is that the baby learns to roll over, begins to crawl, gains self-confidence enough to stand up, gains a little more self-confidence, and takes a step. Usually the first step ends in a minor disaster and the infant falls. But the baby knows that at least a start has been made. Usually the parents are so elated by the attempt that they are full of praise and cheer enthusiastically, even though the baby may have not managed to take even a single step successfully. So the failed attempt is forgotten or is not thought about as a failure, but as a successful first attempt, and the child eagerly tries again not long afterward.

This illustrates an interesting fact about why people in general, and many consultants and executives, lack self-confidence later on in life. An infant learning a more mature task usually has someone cheering him on. But even if he didn't, who's to say that when he fell taking his first step, it was a terrible or a good attempt? The problem is that as we get older, there are others that observe us, either with or without malice. Moreover, many of these observers are judgemental and never fail to let us know when we do a poor job, less so when we do an acceptable one or even a pretty good one. So we get the idea that it is never a good attempt. In fact, an attempt is always a good attempt. It took my youngest son, now a successful management consultant, almost two years to learn to talk. I wasn't worried. It took Einstein almost four years!

A child wants to help wash the dishes and drops and breaks a plate in the process. Maybe the mother is nervous and irritable. So she yells at the child, who was eagerly and enthusiastically trying to help. Is the child as ready to rush forward to help with the dishes or other tasks in the future? Maybe, but not very likely. Worse, what if the mother is particularly upset because the plate was a prized possession? In addition to yelling, she tells the child that he or she is clumsy. If the mother continues to refer to the child as clumsy, eventually the child may even accept this statement as the truth. The growing child may internalize this "fact" and could have serious consequences later in having the self-confidence to accomplish other things. As the child gets older and leaves home, others may reinforce this erroneous belief. Children, in particular, are very critical of other children's failures. Some teachers can be even worse. Fortunately some don't listen.

Michael Jordan, who some call the greatest basketball player of all time, didn't make his high school basketball team and at five eleven was told he was too short to play varsity. He grew four inches one summer, but equally importantly, he trained vigorously, and by graduation he was selected for McDonald's All American Team and recruited by numerous colleges.[2]

A Closer Look at Those Who Were Born with Self-confidence

Individuals who are "born" with self-confidence usually developed it in their formative years and before they enter their professional lives. Mary Kay Ash, the woman who built a billion dollar corporation, Mary Kay Cosmetics, and gave away pink Cadillacs to her most successful saleswomen, didn't even go to college. Yet she had the self-confidence to begin her business with $5,000 only weeks after her planned support, her husband, died suddenly of a massive heart attack. Born with self-confidence? No, but as a little girl of seven she had more responsibility than many adults; she cared for her bedridden father daily so her mother could work. This included many ancillary chores and all the shopping for her family. Do you think that may have helped her in developing self-confidence as she grew older, before she even started her professional career?

Steven Spielberg is a fabulous moviemaker, director, producer, and screenwriter. He's worth over $3 billion. He was beaten up and received a bloody nose on two occasions by school bullies because he is Jewish. But Spielberg made his first film for a Boy Scout merit badge in photography at the age of 12. With the confidence gained from his first film, he went on and made a 40-minute war film and won first place in a film contest a year later. Then, three years later he wrote and directed a full-length science fiction film. It was shown at a local theatre and actually generated a profit ... of one dollar. He gained more confidence and made more films on his own, getting better and better. He applied to the famous School of Cinematic Arts at the University of Southern California, but they turned him down.

However, Spielberg had the self-confidence not to let that bother him. He attended California State University, Long Beach instead, and talked himself into a "part-time" job working seven days a week as an unpaid intern at Universal Studios. You know what he probably did next, and he did it. He made a short film on the Universal Studios' lot and had the self-confidence to get it to Sidney Sheinberg, then vice president of production for Universal's TV division, to view it. Sheinberg immediately signed Spielberg up as a TV director, although he was still not a college graduate and most TV directors had worked their way up after long years of experience, and possibly had also attended a famous school of cinematics. Spielberg was by then a very experienced and confident 23-year-old. He went on to become one of the top directors in Hollywood and made such films as *Jaws*, the *Indiana Jones* films, the *Jurassic Park* Films, *The Color Purple*, *Schindler's List*, *Saving Private Ryan*, *ET*, *Lincoln*, and many, many others.[3]

Okay, that's great. If you developed self-confidence before you began your work career, you have it already and others think you were born with it. What about the 99% of us that didn't do this?

Gain Self-confidence Slowly as You "Pay Your Dues"

Some of us eventually become successful this way and there is nothing wrong with doing this, except that it is usually a long and sometimes painful process. Basically, you enter work or a profession and do what everyone else is doing—work hard and do your best. Hopefully you stand out and your efforts are eventually noted and rewarded. If all goes well and as you progress upward, you gain more self-confidence at every stage. Of course there may be bumps along the way. Sometimes a promotion you think you earned goes to someone else. Through no fault of your own, you could suffer a layoff. Bad things seem to occur at inopportune times, such as soon after having purchased an expensive house, or if you are supporting a child in college, and if you are laid off it could be more difficult to find another job, particularly as you get older. However, if you persevere and are a little lucky, you will probably eventually reach your goals if they are not too high. However, the process is uncertain, takes time, and comes with no guarantees that you will get to where you want to go, even eventually.

Take Charge of Your Own Confidence-building

I like this method best. It is faster and has less risk than the previous method. Moreover, it gives you more control. The method of taking charge that I recommend is based on a simple principle. You can develop anything about yourself – physical, mental, or spiritual – by beginning with a small challenge and increasing it over time. In this way it is related to the slow, "pay your dues" method discussed previously, except that it is much faster, less risky, and guarantees results since you are not dependent on someone else, only yourself. Drucker noted that: "Every artist throughout history has practised kaizen, or organized, continuous self-improvement."[4]

And, "You will be a top producer if you put yourself where your strengths are and if you work on developing your strengths."[5] For example, exercise a muscle every day, and every day that muscle is going to grow bigger and stronger.

Arnold Schwarzenegger didn't start out with all the muscles that led him to win international bodybuilding championships before he became an actor or governor of California. However, by exercising with increasingly heavy weights every day, his muscles got bigger until after some years he was at world-championship level. This didn't start with Arnold. Milo, an ancient Greek athlete, trained by lifting a calf every day and carrying it a short distance. Four years later he was still lifting the calf, but he gained immortal fame throughout the ancient world because the "calf" was now a fully matured bull. I don't think anyone before or since has pulled off that stunt.

Now I'm not suggesting that you start lifting a calf every day to develop your self-confidence, although this would certainly do the job. But the principle for developing self-confidence works in a much simpler and easier way. All you need to do is to make the decision that you are going to take action to develop your self-confidence, and then do it. Select a relatively easy goal to accomplish and proceed until you reach it. Every time you complete a task or goal successfully, celebrate and congratulate yourself. Then set a higher goal or a more difficult task. It's just like training with weights. You build up the amount of weight slowly or run more swiftly as you develop your strength. Before long, you'll be doing things that you never thought you could. You will have acquired the self-confidence you need to expect positive results as a leader.

Move Out of Your Comfort Zone

Here's a great method. Every day select something different that is out of your "comfort zone". That is, something that you have never done previously and feel a little uncomfortable and uncertain about doing. This might be something physical like going dancing, ice-skating, or bowling. Or it could be about challenging a fear, going on a roller coaster or going bungee jumping or skydiving. The latter shouldn't be out of the question. After all, former President H.W. Bush skydives every year, and he's in his nineties as I write this! Even food can be used. If you have never before eaten sushi (raw fish), eating it for the first time is one way of getting out of your comfort zone. You can see that selecting a different thing every day can be fun. As time goes on, you can select more and more things to do that you find challenging. Of course, don't ignore challenges in your professional life either. Volunteer for tasks that are out of your comfort zone, from organizing a retirement party to company sports to making a speech. Don't select things that you have already done or are comfortable in doing. Challenge yourself! Do the uncomfortable.

Before long it will become more and more difficult to find things that you are unwilling to take on. At the same time, you will find that your new self-confidence has spilled over significantly into your professional life. You will find that others look to you because of your leadership and self-confidence, and that you are now considered one of the "up and comers" and "fast burners" and are slated for a promotion. Others will wonder how it happened that you suddenly caught fire. The truth is, you built your own self-confidence. You did it yourself. Drucker would nod approvingly.

Self-confidence Comes from Knowing that You Can Succeed

How is it possible that some leaders take charge and assume responsibilities for lives, jobs, and billion-dollar companies? How is it possible that leaders can take responsibility for the future of nations, if not mankind itself? How is it possible that leaders sometimes lead thousands or even millions of men and women in accomplishing something? Yet they may do all of these things seemingly without blinking an eye. Where do they get such tremendous self-confidence?

An old Air Force training manual on leadership says, "No man can have self-confidence if not convinced in his own mind that he is qualified to perform the job he is assigned."[6]

How the Military Builds Self-confidence

The military knows that if you build self-confidence in one area, it can carry over into others. So the military uses something called a "confidence course" to build self-confidence. It consists of man-made obstacles or events that each participant must traverse successfully. All are designed to be moderate to severe in difficulty, but doable if done right. One might be required to climb down a 100-foot rope suspended from a cliff. Another might force the participant to jump out to catch a swinging rope suspended over a pool of water. Do it right, and you catch the rope and safely reach the other side by dropping off before the rope starts swinging back. Do it incorrectly and you end up in the water. Another is called a "slide for life". It consists of a rope drawn across a lake from a 90-foot tower on one side of the lake, to the bank of the lake on the other. The participant jumps off the tower holding onto a pulley attached to the rope. As he slides across the lake to the other side, he keeps his eyes on a man signalling with a set of flags. On one signal, you raise your legs so that they are parallel with the water and you appear to be in a sitting position. At the next signal, you drop off about 20 feet above the water. Like a stone, you go skipping across the lake to the other side. If you don't let go and drop off the pulley, you land on the bank of the lake with some impact and can get injured.

While there is a real need for parachute training for some types of military duties, parachute training is frequently encouraged for all and given to almost anyone who applies for it for the same reason: confidence-building.

Anthony Robbins, the famed motivational speaker who has worked with groups and individuals around the world, started his career by learning that fire walks did the same thing. Yes, this is no misprint, I mean walking on a bed of white-hot coals for a distance of 12 feet or more. Robbins calls this seminar "Fear into Power" and makes it quite clear that he isn't teaching party tricks, but rather using the fire walk as a metaphor: "If you could do this which you think is impossible, what else can you do that you also think is impossible?" Before you put this down to pure quackery,

I should tell you that Robbins has been to Camp David in the past and helped the serving US president and other senior members of the government do a fire walk.

What I am saying here is that there are a variety of confidence-building means available, some commercially, and they all can work to raise your overall self-confidence. It's a fact. If you know that you can succeed at something, than you will have self-confidence that you can do it. The truth is, it is impossible not to. So the problem is how you can know you will succeed before you actually try something. The confidence course and the fire walks are only two ways of doing this. There are many others.

Little Things Mean a Lot

There is an old saying that nothing succeeds like success. This means that success breeds success, or that successful people tend to become more successful. In other words, if you have been successful in the past, you have a better chance of being successful in the future. But how can you become successful until you are successful? It's like the old question of the chicken and the egg. You can't have a chicken until you have an egg, but you can't have an egg until you have a chicken.

Fortunately, you can have a little success before a big success. And a little success counts just as much as a big success as far as our belief system goes. That means if you can win little victories in being successful at something, your psyche will believe that you can accomplish even greater things in the same area. Moreover, you will project this feeling outward and others will begin treating you differently.

Champion body builder, movie star, and former Governor of California, Arnold Schwarzenegger, described how his confidence began to develop while still in high school: "Before long, people began looking at me as a special person. Partly this was the result of my own changing attitude about myself. I was growing, getting bigger, gaining confidence. I was given consideration I had never received before..."[7]

Positive or Negative Mental Imagery Can Have Crucial Effects

Nik Wallenda is a seventh-generation descendant of a family of dare-devils going back to the Austrian-Hungarian Empire in 1780. On 4 June 2011 he completed a 135-foot long, high-wire crossing between to two towers of the 10-story Condado Plaza Hotel in Puerto Rico. This event was particularly significant because his grandfather, Karl Wallenda, known as the greatest tightrope walker who ever lived, had once attempted this "walk" and had fallen to his death. Karl Wallenda had walked across greater distances, and he did so without a net and continued with his breath-taking walks as he grew older. In his sixties he had completed a 1,200-foot walk with 30,000 people watching. He was age 65 at the time. He did the same fabulous stunts in his seventies that he did as a young man in his twenties.

Walenda's wife was interviewed on television regarding Wallenda's last walk. "It was very strange," she said. "For months prior to his performance, he thought about nothing else. But for the first time, he didn't see himself succeeding. He saw himself falling." Wallenda's wife went on to say that he even checked the installation and construction of the wire himself. "This," she said, "was something Karl had never done previously." There seems little doubt that Karl Wallenda's negative mental imagery and resulting lack of self-confidence for this particular walk contributed to his falling.

Nik Wallenda, who was the first to complete a tightrope walk across Niagara Falls and the first to walk across the Grand Canyon, as well as many other death-defying feats, said after the walk where his grandfather fell that this location had haunted him for years. However, "he was not scared at all."[8] Again, self-confidence.

Positive Images Can Significantly Improve Your Self-confidence

Just as negative images can hurt your self-confidence, positive images can help your self-confidence considerably.

One of the leading researchers in the area of imagery is Dr Charles Garfield. Dr Garfield is a unique individual. He has not one, but two doctorates: in mathematics and psychology. I first read of his work in the pages of the *Wall Street Journal* in 1981. The article spoke about Dr Garfield's research regarding what he called a kind of "mental rehearsal". Garfield found that more effective executives practised mental rehearsal frequently and less effective executives did not.

In his book, *Peak Performers*, Garfield describes how Soviet Bloc performance experts in Milan, Italy confirmed his theories. Garfield is an amateur weightlifter. However, he hadn't competed in several months. When he had, his best lift had been 280 pounds, although previously when he had worked out regularly, he had done more.

The Soviets asked him the absolute maximum he thought he could lift right at that moment. He responded that he might be able to make 300 pounds in an exercise known as the bench press. In this exercise, you are flat on your back, you take a barbell off two uprights and lower the weight to your chest. Then you return the weight to the starting position. With extreme effort, he just managed to lift that amount. As Garfield himself said, "It was difficult – so difficult that I doubt I could have done it without the mounting excitement in the room."

The Soviet performance experts next had Garfield lie back and relax. They put him through a series of mental relaxation exercises. Then they asked him to get up slowly and gently. When he did, he saw that they had added 65 pounds to the 300-pound weight. Under normal circumstances, it would have been impossible for him to lift this weight.

He began to have negative images. Before they established themselves in his mind, the Soviets began a new mental exercise.

"Firmly, thoroughly, they talked me through a series of mental preparations. In my mind's eye I saw myself approaching the bench. I visualized myself lying down. I visualized myself, with total confidence, lifting the 365 pounds."

Much to Garfield's surprise, he not only lifted the 365-pound weight. He was also astounded to discover it easier to lift than the lighter weight had been earlier.[9]

You Can Use Mental Rehearsal to Build Your Self-confidence

I have used mental rehearsal techniques for many years. I can guarantee that not only will you find them effective, but that they are easy and painless, with no after-effects.

The secret is to first relax as much as you can, then to imagine positive images. What I do is this: I lie back and get as relaxed as I can. Then I start with my toes and tell myself that my toes are becoming numb. I repeat this suggestion to myself several times.

From my toes, I go to my feet, legs, and torso. In every case I repeat the suggestion that the particular part of the body I am focusing on is becoming completely relaxed and numb. When I am totally relaxed, I go to work on my positive imagery. In my mind I will picture everything about the situation in detail. After I complete the rehearsal once, I repeat the entire rehearsal again. I do it several times at a sitting. If the situation is particularly important, I may repeat the entire mental imagery process a couple times a day for several days.

Does it work? Amazingly, I have rarely failed when I used this imagery technique. It is true that reality does not always follow my pre-planned script. Sometimes the changes are significant. However, the results gained by seeing a favourable outcome over and over again has a dramatic effect. I never lack self-confidence in any situation that I have mentally rehearsed.

With Self-confidence, Your Vision Has No Limits

George Washington is known as the "father of his country" because he had a big vision of that country's future. He conceived of an entirely new nation in his vision, with freedom and liberty. He held his vision through the most trying times that this nation ever faced. He was not only general-in-chief and our first president under our constitution, he was this country's number-one visionary. In fact, although the Continental Congress appointed him commander-in-chief in June 1775, he was commander of only one soldier… himself. There was no Continental Army. If Congress changed its mood and decided to accommodate George III, King of England, Washington would be left "holding the bag"... the most visible and conspicuous of traitors. But Washington's vision was so large that it carried him and his army through six years of war against the major power of the day to victory. Washington's vision was unsustainable except for one fact that stands out: his unshakable self-confidence that he would be successful, no matter what. You, too, can develop the self-confidence that Drucker suggested. Just take the first step.

[1] Drucker, Peter F., *Management: Tasks, Responsibilities, Practices* (New York: Harper & Row, 1974, 1974) p. 285.

[2] Lena Williams. "PLUS: BASKETBALL; A McDonald's Game For Girls, Too," *The New York Times* December 7 2001, accessed at http://www.nytimes.com/2001/12/07/sports/plus-basketball-a-mcdonald-s-game-for-girls-too.html, 26 July 2015.

[3] No author listed, "Steven Spielberg," *Wikipedia*, accessed at https://en.wikipedia.org/wiki/Steven_Spielberg, 26 July 2015

[4] Drucker, Peter F., *Managing in a Time of Great Change*, (New York: Truman Talley Books/Plume,1998) p. 79.

[5] Drucker, Peter F., Edited by Rick Wartzman, *The Drucker Lectures*, (New York: McGraw-Hill, 2010) p.174.

[6] *AFM 35-15 Air Force Leadership* (Department of the Air Force: Washington, D.C., 1948) p.30.

[7] Arnold Schwarzenegger with Douglas Kent Hall, *Arnold: The Education of a Bodybuilder* (New York: Fireside, 1997) p.24.

[8] Nik Walendra in No author listed: "Nik Wallenda: King of the High Wire," *Nik Wallendra Official Site* accessed at http://nikwallenda.com/index.php?option=com_content&view=article&id=11&Itemid=109 , 28 July 2015.

[9] Charles Garfield, *Peak Performers* (Avon Books: New York, 1986) pp.72-73.

Chapter 13

Innovation, Abandonment, and the Certainty of Eventual Failure without Change

There was one sure way Drucker knew that an organization or a company was going to fail, and even though absolutely counterintuitive, it is nevertheless absolutely certain and was an important element in his consulting practice. Simply put, if any organization continued to do what in the past had made it successful, it was certain that it would eventually go under. That sounds pretty strange, but if you think about it, it is not completely illogical and the "failures of success" are numerous throughout history.

Unlimited Examples of the Failures of Success

Examples of failures of success are so numerous that we needn't look far. Why can't a company or an organization continue to be successful indefinitely with what has made them successful in the past? As Drucker explained, usually the environment changes in some critical way and all the old rules are invalidated. Consider the following changes that are quite normal and happen all the time, but have the power to destroy any previous success, no matter its magnitude:

- Technology – something new, like the affordable automobile, comes along and downgrades the horse as the basic means of personal transportation. Everything connected with the horse declines or disappears as well. No more buggy whips, downtown stables and hitching posts, horse-drawn carriages, and the like. These and many other connected industries and products simply disappear... all failures.
- Economics – the economy falls into a depression or becomes significantly inflationary. The first condition might cause potential customers to hold on to their money to the greatest extent possible; the latter condition might cause them to not only spend more freely, but in a much shorter period of time. In some countries hit by massive and impossibly rising inflation, citizens have been reduced to hauling paper money around in a wheelbarrow rather than a wallet or purse (really!). Companies producing many types of previously successful

products and services fail during a recession or depression. Yet many other companies – from breakfast cereal and soap to movies – can flourish. Many argue that it was the Great Depression that created the market for the Monopoly game still popular worldwide today.

- Culture or social change – it became acceptable for females to wear a lot less at the beach in the middle of the last century. When the bikini was first developed in 1946, the developers had to hire an exotic dancer (some said a prostitute) to model it! She was the only one who would agree to appear nearly nude in public for photographs. Today, young women – and many older ones – don't give it a second thought.[1] Companies that determinedly continued to produce previous styles of women's bathing attire, which had been the basis of their success, went under.

- Politics, laws, and regulations – what was once legal becomes illegal and visa versa. The sale of alcoholic beverages became illegal in the US on 17 January 1920, and became legal again a little more than 13 years later.[2] The effects on business, management, crime, and a great deal more have been the subject of numerous Hollywood gangster movies since.

- Actions of competitors – if a competitor is successful in an action that you have not anticipated and allowed for, you can be in serious trouble. Apple opened the market for personal computers and dominated the market; IBM was very much a latecomer. In the personal computer market, it had been caught unaware. But once IBM finally decided to get into this market, it moved very quickly and with an excellent counter-strategy. Whereas Apple had not allowed anyone to create software for its operating system, IBM not only allowed this, but encouraged anyone and everyone to do so. As a result, the number of software programs, including games, business programs, and more available for IBM's operating system soon far exceeded Apple's. Through this strategy, computers based on IBM's operating system quickly moved into this market and dominated it even after a late start and entering with a product that was, for many years, technically inferior to Apple's system.

- Unexpected major events – the terrorist attacks on 9/11 led to reduced air travel and created demand for much greater security. The "Great Recession" caused major changes and failure for many businesses that were slow to adapt. Major outbreaks of disease in Africa, Asia, or the United States greatly affect formerly successful products or services. The rise of Japan, Korea, and China as major suppliers of cheap quality goods can immediately affect former successes in other countries. Swiss watches, once a universal name, would be replaced by upscale watches from Japanese manufacturers or unbelievably inexpensive watches from China. Most recently, the series of coordinated attacks in Paris by ISIS or ISIL on the evening of November 15 2015 created havoc and insecurity around the world, including in the US, which will cause the demise of formerly successful products or services, and not just in security.

The Bigger They Are, the Harder They Fall

In the mid-1980s, the entire billion-dollar vinyl record industry vanished almost overnight and vinyl record manufacturers lost millions when they failed to prepare for the growing threat from compact disc technology.

Slide rules, once a product that an engineer wouldn't have been seen without, went the way of the buffalo, gone except for very specialized roles and in museums. The handheld slide rules were manually manipulated, non-electronic, analogue computers. The basic models had two stationary rules, with a central sliding rule. A clear sliding piece with a crosshair, called a cursor, completed the basic model. With this device, engineers could accomplish a variety of complex mathematical and algebraic computations. Every single engineer in the world owned at least one. Major companies like Pickett and K + E dominated the industry. Yet, their markets disappeared within two years after the introduction of the handheld electronic calculator.

I could go on, but you get the general idea. The point is, like a light bulb that burns brightest just prior to complete failure, many of these companies and industries were at their best just a few years – or in some cases just a few months or days – prior to their demise. They optimized their success but it led eventually to failure, sometimes quicker than anyone could imagine, exactly as Drucker stated.

You might think that senior executives easily anticipate and readily prepare for change. This is rarely the case for several reasons. Most executives are where they are because they were promoted under the old paradigm of the organization's success. Their prior actions made them and their organizations even more successful. They are comfortable with the old way, not some new, usually unproven, idea. Even though they may not realize it, they are apprehensive about leaving what they know and are comfortable with. They invested heavily in the old modus operandi and tend to avoid anything that says that they must invest again and start over. It takes an exceptional individual to do this, or even to utter the words that imply that anything will change. However, the truth is that the new model may hardly be rocket science once accepting of the fact that there will be change, like it or not.

I have written about one of the most remarkable cases of an organizational leader who was able to recognize that future success based on great past success was not inevitable. He was not a business executive, but a military leader. His name was Henry H. "Hap" Arnold. He was the commander of the US Army Air Forces during World War II. To understand his vision, you need to know the whole story.

After the US Air Force was given the status of an independent military service after World War II, "Hap" Arnold became the first and only five-star general that the Air Force ever had. But getting there hadn't been easy. Arnold had fought his entire career for an Air Force independent of the US Army, with full career opportunities for the pilots who flew the airplanes central to any Air Force. Before independence, when the Air Force had been under the control of non-flying senior officers of the US Army, pilots were allowed to command only flying organizations. They were not permitted to head up non-flying divisions, corps, and others assignments. Without these assignments in their backgrounds, they could not reach the top posts in the US Army.

Soon after the United States Air Force was created, and despite a lifetime of fighting for this flying Air Force and equal career opportunities for pilots, Arnold wrote words then considered heresy by those who flew. General Arnold wrote that Air Force officers must be flexible and forward-looking in their vision of the future of this new military service. "We must think in terms of tomorrow. We must bear in mind that air power itself can become obsolete."[3] General Arnold said that at a time when airplanes were the essential vehicles in the Air Force's arsenal; space and other unmanned systems didn't exist except as experimental prototypes. Today, the need for pilots of unmanned flying drones is so great that it rivals not only the need for aircraft pilots, but for crews manning launch systems for intercontinental missiles and space systems. A situation General Arnold could never have predicted as he wrote these words.

Yet, almost every day one can read of a company failing due to not heeding Drucker's warning. Not long ago I read a headline in the *Wall Street Journal*: "Fat Lady Sings for Columbia House." The owner of Columbia House, Filmed Entertainment, Inc filed for chapter 11 bankruptcy. Columbia House was founded as a division of CBS Inc. Do you remember the direct-mail offers of the clubs records, then tapes, and finally DVDs – all by this famous mail order recording house? As an inducement to join the club, you could buy a tape or CD for as little as one cent. Their operations brought in as much as $1.4 billion a year. That's billion, with a B. It wasn't technology alone that did Columbia House in. It kept up with and improved its basic product. It was the way that consumers purchased and listened to music and other products that changed and led to its demise. On folding, the company still had 110,000 members, but it had years of declining revenue. The basic changes needed in marketing and distribution had never occurred.[4]

Stopping Success from Leading to Failure

- Understand that continuing what led to past success will invariably lead to eventual future failure due to one or more reasons, no matter what.
- Organizations must be willing to abandon what was formerly successful or even what may have once been its very essence.
- An organization must always be ready to take action to make even revolutionary changes.
- Plan your own "what-if" scenarios and how you would handle negative things before or as they begin to happen.
- Keep watch at every major happening, and ask what it will mean for your business and your products.
- Avoiding failure requires innovation, and innovation is one of two primary tasks of any business – the other is marketing.

Innovation Means Something Different

Drucker understood that as a consultant, innovation meant something different and maybe something completely new. But he also understood that resources in time, talent, capital, and facilities are needed every time an innovation is initiated and exploited. This led Drucker to a very important concept, which has come to be called abandonment.

The Revolutionary Posture: Abandonment of Profitable Products

Drucker's two questions to Jack Welch that contributed significantly to his phenomenal success as GE's head were: "If GE wasn't already in a particular business, would you enter it today?" and "If the answer is no, what are you going to do about it?" These questions led to the abandonment of successful businesses. According to Welch, Drucker's questions led him to shed profitable but underperforming businesses that had streamlined GE into its extraordinary success. Welch mandated that any GE business that was neither number one or two in its market would be sold or liquidated.[5, 6] These two examples of Drucker's theory of abandonment were discussed in his book *Managing by Results* in 1964, almost 20 years earlier. The questions are actually a powerful example of Welch's successful application of Drucker's theory.[7] These simple questions contributed greatly to Welch's accomplishments at GE and the universal success attributed to him as a leader and as a manager.

Should the Best-known Automobile Have Been Abandoned?

Henry Ford's Model T was named the world's most influential car of the 20th century. The actual title of the award was "The Car of the Century". No doubt the award was well deserved, as no less than 15 million Model Ts were built between 1908 and 1927. Although there were minor changes over this 19-year period, the Model T was primarily characterized by no change and maintenance of its initial design. This was exemplified by Ford's well-known declaration that Ford's customers could have any colour they wanted, so long as it was black. Ford's rival, General Motors, began to provide a variety of designs and options. Henry Ford responded with a one-liner: "The Model T design 'was already correct' and therefore would not be altered." The fact is that, at the end of its career, the Model T could no longer compete with more modern offerings. The design should have been abandoned years earlier, despite its having been the basis of Ford's success. Failure to do this cost Ford his company's leadership to General Motors for 40 years, which hardly offset the slim profits made at the end and Ford's brave declaration that it was "already correct".[8, 9]

Abandon with Finesse and Logic

Drucker saw that logically this meant that an organization must be prepared to abandon everything it does at the same time that it must be prepared to devote itself to creating the new. Abandonment must simultaneously be executed along with continuous improvement, exploitation of past successes, and innovation.[10] Drucker insisted that any proposal for a major new effort must always spell out what old effort must be abandoned.[11] I found this necessary early in my own career, as director of research and development, when my boss insisted on initiating products for development without simultaneously increasing my overall budget.

Drucker saw that all these processes must be systematic, and not done in a haphazard or ad hoc fashion. He thought that this process must start with clients rethinking what they were doing.

Rethinking Means an Examination of What the Organization Is Doing

Drucker thought seriously about what many clients and their consultants ignore: rethinking the environment and the actions of the organizations in it. Drucker considered rethinking as a preamble to abandonment. Drucker noted that rethinking should result in a long list of activities, programmes, or products that must be examined, analysed, and ranked by current and potential for further success. Once this is accomplished, those with the highest potential are given priority with the resources necessary to reach full potential. Those at the bottom (think "dogs" in the Boston Consulting Group's old four-cell matrix), should be liquidated and those in between should be given further thought and possibly refocused to be made more successful, but without a large increase in the limited resources expended. Drucker found that frequently the usual methods ranked programmes and activities according to what he called "good intentions". The Drucker difference was not to rank by good intentions, but rather according to actual, observed performance.[12]

Drucker warned clients to institutionalize the process, and he even recommended the period by which the process should be repeated: "Every three years, an organization should challenge every product, every service, every policy, every distribution channel with the question: if we were not in it already, would we be doing it now?"[13]

This last question assumes that conditions have changed and perhaps, even more importantly, that the organization has learned something new since the original action was initiated or in the interim. Drucker emphasized that if the answer to the above question was "no", the reaction must never be for additional study, but always, "What are we to do now?" Drucker was no fan of unnecessary study or research, but rather of action. With Drucker, the emphasis in his consulting was always on action.[14] He knew that only through action could failure be avoided and success be attained. Throughout he emphasized that abandonment was a necessity, but it was also an opportunity.[15]

When a product, business, or service is abandoned, it frees up resources: money, personnel, facilities, equipment, and time for new opportunities, or to take advantage of older ones that have a higher potential and have been ignored. These were "push priorities," which were easy to identify because the results of the push, if successful, produced their additional investments many times over.[16]

But there are other advantages to abandonment even if it is unknown where freed-up resources will be applied. Psychologically, it stimulates the search for a replacement to take the place of the old "something" that is no longer present. He also thought abandonment necessary to ignite a "ho-hum", existing business "to work *today* on the products, services, processes, and technologies that will make a difference tomorrow".[17] Finally, he told clients that abandonment even helps change management, since another of his beliefs was that the most effective way to manage change is to create it yourself, just as he recommended "predicting" the future by creating it yourself.[18]

Toward the end of his career, Drucker summarized a lifetime of observation of the abandonment concept by stating three cases where he could barely contain himself and boldly stated, "The right action is always outright abandonment."

1. If a product, service, or process was thought to "still have a few good years left."
2. If the only argument for keeping it is that it is "fully written off."

3. If a new product or service is being stunted or neglected because an old, perhaps declining, product is being maintained.

Drucker wrote that case number three was the most important reason for abandonment.[19] Even Steve Jobs had difficulty getting his people to quit emphasizing the once-potent Apple II, which had established the company and one could say the entire computer industry. I remember Jobs taking the reins in the development of the "Mac" and saying that those still enamoured with Apple II were working on "the boring project". At the time this was reported, I didn't understand why he had said this. Analysing Drucker's methods of consulting, I understood what Jobs was trying to do.

Discovering a Specific Criterion for Abandonment

Drucker simply did not provide specific criteria for abandonment. No four- or nine-celled matrix, no equations—nothing. Once again he recommended thinking. The potential products, processes, or businesses that might usefully be abandoned and the criteria for their selection are unlimited. However, he did provide a few guidelines. For example, in decision making he recommended looking at what he called "boundary conditions". These are specifications regarding intended objectives, minimal attainment goals, and other conditions that must be satisfied. He felt that clear thinking regarding the boundary conditions was needed to know when something must be abandoned, and by inference their understanding was also necessary for development of criterion for abandonment.[20]

Though he cautioned clients and those who helped them to beware of "the tyranny of numbers",[21] he also commented that budgeting – the most widely-used management tool – did provide a forum for evaluating and analysing the existing situation, along with other measurement and controls as well as organized information needed to be reviewed as candidates for abandonment were sought.[22] It follows that quantitative criteria for deciding what should be eliminated and what should remain could be determined, but again, beware "the tyranny of numbers".

You've Got to Have a Plan...
But then, the Plan Must Be Implemented

Once a candidate for abandonment has been identified and criteria for specific abandonment established, organize everything with a plan. This should include specific objectives, the number of people of various capabilities needed, the tools, money, information, and other resources necessary for completion of the abandonment, and unambiguous deadlines.[23] It's very much the same way as planning for new product development. Drucker noted that the "how" of abandonment was of no less importance than the "what". If this detail is ignored, the whole abandonment will be postponed in the hope that the abandonment will be abandoned. The reason is simple: abandonment policies are never popular and will be actively opposed by many, as Jack Welch discovered.[24] The abandonment at GE, which led to GE and Welch's incredible success, involved the displacement of more than 100,000 employees during the first years of his tenure as he discarded underperforming businesses and acquired new ones. It was also the source of the disparaging nickname given to him of "Neutron Jack". However, supporters argue that not only did this boost GE to the heights it ascended, but ultimately benefited employees, as well as stockholders. Without these final systematic steps of planning and execution, all this is just good intentions that, Drucker added, should rarely include the adjective "good".

To Dream or Not to Dream, That is the Question

It would be foolish – even dangerous – to abandon successful products, organizations, strategies, or businesses while they are still very profitable and have significant potential. When will new ideas for the future arrest the inevitability of failure without change about forward thinking, and when are they a costly waste of time and "not sticking to one's knitting"? Drucker agreed that tactical improvement of success works to the point that change is so needed that not changing will make failure immediately inevitable. How, then, can we recognize the possible onset of environmental conditions with significant magnitude that we must prepare for revolutionary change? Sorry – that's where the judgment of the manager comes in.

What to Recommend to Clients

- Make an effort to know what's going on, not only in a single industry, but in the world. Familiarize yourself not only with new products, but with trends in the environment that even remotely could affect operations in future years. This means a regimen of continual reading of trade journals, newspapers, the internet and other relevant media, and thinking about what this means or will mean in the future. This process should never cease
- Ask yourself not what will happen, but what could happen based on current and anticipated developments
- Play a "what-if" game about your current business. What would you do if …
- Watch developments closely. If sales drop over several quarters, find out why. Do the same if sales expectantly increase. Do not automatically assume that everything will "return to normal". There is no normal. If sales increase or decrease in certain areas, find out why. Recognize that nothing lasts forever, prepare yourself mentally for change, and take immediate action when necessary, regardless of your previous investment of time, money, or resources. Never forget the accountants' credo that sunk costs are sunk costs and that nothing lasts forever
- While you should not change just for the sake of change, establish a programme of continual review of every product, strategy, tactic, and policy. Aggressively seek opportunities to change and use change not only to stay ahead of the competition but to make sure what you are currently doing is not obsolete
- Adopt new ideas and change from previously successful methods to ones that are even more successful for the future. In this way, you'll not only succeed, you'll succeed in a big way

Much of Drucker's reputation came from doing what didn't come naturally to managers or most clients. All consultants seeking to follow in Drucker's path need to recognize this. It is truly difficult to recognize that in just about any business failure exists and the seeds of success lie dormant – and the same is true in reverse. The seeds of future failure also lie dormant in any success. The consultant, any consultant, must recognize this and be prepared to lead a client to the next success by abandoning what once was a "darling" of the company and its executives.

[1] No author listed, "1946 The Bikini Is Introduced," *History*, accessed at http://www.history.com/this-day-in-history/bikini-introduced, 8 August 2015.

[2] No author listed, "Prohibition in the United States," *Wikipedia*, accessed at https://en.wikipedia.org/wiki/Prohibition_in_the_United_States, 8 August 2015.

[3] Arnold, H.H. *Global Mission*, (New York: Harper & Row Publishers, Inc., 1949) p. 615.

[4] Corrigan, Tom, "Fat Lady Sings for Columbia House," in *Wall Street Journal*, 11 August 2015, pg. B1.

[5] Mulligan, Thomas F. and James Flanigan, "Prolific Father of Modern Management," *Los Angeles Times, Business Section*, November 12 2005, p. A-1, accessed at http://articles.latimes.com/2005/nov/12/business/fi-drucker12, 12 August 2015.

[6] Heller, Robert, "The Drucker Legacy," *Thinking Managers*, accessed at http://www.thinkingmanagers.com/management/drucker 12 August 2015.

[7] Drucker, Peter F., *Managing for Results*, (New York: Harper & Row Publishers, 1964) pp. 143-146.

[8] No author listed, "The Model-T Ford," *Frontenac Motor Company*, accessed at http://www.modelt.ca/background.html, 12 August 2015.

[9] No author listed, "Ford Model T," *Wikipedia*, accessed at http://en.wikipedia.org/wiki/Ford_Model_T, 12 August 2015.

[10] Drucker, Peter F., *On the Profession of Management* (Boston: Harvard Business Review Book, 1963, 1964, 1966, 1985, 1987, 1989, 1991, 1992, 1993, 1994, 1998), pp. 116-117.

[11] Drucker, Peter F. *Managing for Results*, p. 221.

[12] Drucker, Peter F. with Joseph Maciariello, *Management* (New York: HarperCollins, 1973, 1974, 2008) pp. 163-166.

[13] Drucker, Peter F. *Classic Drucker* (Boston: Harvard Business School Publishing, 2006, 2008) p. 29.

[14] Drucker, Peter F., *Management Challenges for the 21st Century* (New York: Harper Business, 1999) p. 74.

[15] Op. Cit. Drucker, Peter F., *Managing for Results*, p.143.

[16] Ibid. p. 144.

[17] Drucker, Peter F. *Innovation and Entrepreneurship*, (New York: Harper & Row Publishers, 1985) p. 155.

[18] Op. Cit. Drucker, Peter F. with Joseph Maciariello, *Management*, p.61

[19] Op Cit. Drucker, Peter F., *Management Challenges for the 21ˢᵗ Century*, pp. 74-76.

[20] Drucker, Peter F., *On the Profession of Management*, pp. 25-26.

[21] Drucker's feeling echoed those of David Boyle, author of *The Tyranny of Numbers: Why Counting Can't Make Us Happy* (Flamingo, 2001).
I confess, I have not yet read the book. However, the description provided at amazon.com very well represents Drucker's feelings as I knew them:
"Never before have we attempted to measure as much as we do today. Why are we so obsessed with numbers? What can they really tell us? Too often we try to quantify what can't actually be measured. We count people, but not individuals. We count exam results rather than intelligence, benefit claimants instead of poverty. The government has set itself 10,000 new targets. Politicians pack their speeches with skewed statistics: crime rates are either rising or falling depending on who is doing the counting. We are in a world in which everything is designed only to be measured. If it can't be measured, it can be ignored. But the big problem is what numbers don't tell you. They won't interpret. They won't inspire, and they won't tell you precisely what causes what. In this passionately argued and thought-provoking book, David Boyle examines our obsession with numbers. He reminds us of the danger of taking numbers so seriously at the expense of what is non-measurable, non-calculable: intuition, creativity, imagination, happiness ... counting is a vital human skill. Yardsticks are a vital tool. As long as we remember how limiting they are if we cling to them too closely." Accessed at http://www.amazon.com/Tyranny-Numbers-Counting-Cant-Happy/dp/0006531997/ref=sr_1_1?ie=UTF8&qid=1439394 476&sr=8-1&keywords=The+Tyranny+of+Numbers+Boyle, August 12 2015.

[22] Op. Cit. Drucker, Peter F. with Joseph Maciariello, *Management*, pp. xxvi-xxvii.

[23] Op Cit. Drucker, Peter F., *Innovation and Entrepreneurship*, pp.154-155.

[24] No author listed, "Jack Welch," *Wikipedia*, accessed at https://en.wikipedia.org/wiki/Jack_Welch, August 12 2005

Chapter 14

How
Drucker
Helped
His Clients
Innovate

L et's be honest. Many of our innovations come from flashes of sudden inspiration. I seem to get an enormous number of such flashes when waking in the morning, which tells me that my mind has been hard at work while I slept. Joe Cossman was an unbelievably productive innovator who thought of so many new product innovations that it was a miracle he found the time and resources to pursue even a small percentage of them. But somehow he exploited enough to become extremely wealthy, mainly like Drucker as a "one-man band". Most worked out and probably made him a million dollars or more every time one was introduced. A few failed, but there was no question that his batting average, as well as his productivity, were excellent. The Cossman Ant Farm was one of his most successful efforts.

Cossman's Ant Farm – the Most Successful Toy Innovation of the 20th Century

Cossman's famous "ant farm" was one huge success. The idea of constructing an educational toy by assembling an ant colony, with the correct kind of dirt, using a wooden framework of about 12 x 12 inches, surrounded by clear panes of glass so that the "farmer" could peer in and watch the goings-on, was not new. It had probably been around for 80 years or more when Cossman introduced his version. However, that's where his innovation started. The older version never attempted a mass market for children; the clear panes of glass were hazardous because they could easily break and would be dangerous. The original ant colony concept worked when used under the supervision of a teacher in the classroom, but it could not be promoted as an individual child's toy, and not only because of the danger of the breaking glass. The glass-wood interface was not perfect, and the ants frequently escaped, much to the dismay of both teachers and students. Parents would have been even less amused to have ants running around the house.

Joe's version of the "ant farm" was intended for use as a "learning toy" for individual children at home. Thus, it was designed for personal ownership and not as a class project. Moreover, it was a toy *system*. He replaced the wooden frame and glass with clear plastic. This made it lighter and unbreakable under normal use, and this design was therefore safer for children, more secure regarding the ants' ability to escape, and much less expensive to manufacture. But Joe didn't stop there. Even the name chosen, "ant *farm*," was an innovation.

But how could he distribute the farm with the ants to retail stores around the country? Simple: another innovation. A farm had livestock, and each ant farm that he sold had a "stock certificate" accompanying it, which could be mailed in to receive guaranteed delivery of the "livestock" necessary to populate the farm.

Cossman had great success with this product due to his successful innovations, and the product is still selling today, years after he is no longer with us. Joe Cossman said that once you focused on a certain product, service, industry, or business, flashes of inspiration flow at a rapid pace.

Flashes of Innovation

Drucker thought that flashes of inspiration were an excellent innovation tactic. However, he told me that there would always be more good ideas than time, money, and the personnel available to develop them. He accepted that the "bright idea" – a vague and illusive innovation rushed into development without much real analysis – could be successful. He did not disagree that one could even hit a "home run" with a single bright idea such as this. And he was happy to give me other examples of single bright ideas that had made millions for their originators – including the zipper, or to call it by its original name, the "slide fastener," the ballpoint pen, the aerosol spray can, and more. But he said these were not the norm and should be ignored as a model of how innovation should be approached and managed as a purposeful business activity. He said there was significant danger to the project if purposeful analysis was not a part of the process.

Joe Cossman and Peter Drucker were both my friends. In some ways, they had a lot in common. After another of Joe's innovative products, called "My Son, The Musician," which was based on a flash of genius, Joe would have heartily agreed with Peter's approaches to innovation. And since Joe, too, devoted time to consulting and advising others how to innovate, he would have suggested many of Drucker's recommendations to his own clients. Joe's product, "My Son, the Musician" taught Joe an important lesson.

"My Son, the Musician" Has High Sales But Is Pulled Off the Market

Joe Cossman had such high sales with "My Son, the Musician" that it almost put him out of business. The inventor of "My Son, the Musician," which was the clever name Cossman thought up, was guaranteed to end parental problems with potty training of growing infants through technology and a clever innovation. The technology part was a device consisting of a bowl containing a liquid-sensing device connected to a music box. When the bowl sensed a liquid, such as urine, it would immediately begin to play a selected nursery tune. So the child really was making his or her own music. Cossman tested the product with his own son, who was about the right age at the time. It worked perfectly every time.

Without the type of purposeful analysis that Drucker recommended, Cossman wrote advertising copy, rushed the item into production, engaged salespeople, and began to promote the product. There was tremendous interest and demand even prior to the product's introduction, perhaps one of the largest in the history of any of his toy products. Cossman thought that sales of "My Son, the Musician" might rival that of his top products from the past, including the ant farm.

His enthusiasm disappeared when a child psychologist, who had seen a unit in a local store, called to tell him the bad news. "My Son, the Musician" would absolutely encourage the child to go to the toilet when he understood that music could be created by using the toilet bowl properly. Moreover, this would be reinforced every time the child "played a tune" and the act of urinating would become associated with music.

Such associations are extremely powerful. You've probably heard of the Russian scientist Dr Ivan Pavlov's experiments with dogs. Every time he fed the dog, Pavlov would ring a bell. The dog would salivate when he saw the food. Before long, the dog would salivate when he heard the bell, whether Pavlov fed him or not. A strong association was created between the sound of the bell and the involuntary physiological act of salivation. Cossman connected the dots and knew that his product, though it worked perfectly, was in trouble.

"Bright Ideas" with Incomplete or Poor Analysis Lose Money

It doesn't take much imagination to understand the consequences of the music being played long after the child had stopped using "My Son, the Musician" as a learning device and unfortunately, even after the child had grown to adulthood. Cossman confirmed this potential problem with other psychologists. The initial sales of "My Son, the Musician" may have been very encouraging, but if continued, lawsuits from parents and former users of "My Son, the Musician" would have inevitably resulted and put him out of business. The innovation "My Son, the Musician" was a very bright idea. "The problem," Drucker maintained, "is that bright ideas are the riskiest and least-successful source of innovative opportunities." He estimated that probably only one in 500 made any money above investment costs and suggested that relying on the bright idea for innovation was akin to gambling at Las Vegas and almost certain to lead to similar results in the end.

The solution, he maintained, was analysis of innovative ideas through a systematic process. This, he declared, was purposeful innovation, the kind that all in business must pursue regardless of specialty, discipline, or functional area. He strongly recommended the abandonment of "the bright idea" as a standard operating procedure. Instead, Drucker recommended another approach.[1]

The Unexpected, but Still Analysed

Drucker wrote that the unexpected was the richest source of opportunity for successful innovation, much better than the "bright idea". But it was one that was not only neglected, but frequently and actively rejected by managers of all disciplines, before they were so focused on what was expected.

For example, during World War II, rubber was in especially high demand for all military vehicles. The Japanese controlled the primary sources of rubber, but we were at war with Japan, and the US was getting more and more desperate. Synthetic rubber existed, but was expensive. So General Electric launched a programme to develop cheaper synthetic rubber. In 1943, a GE engineer combined boric acid and silicone oil in this attempt. Unfortunately, the strange material that resulted from this combination couldn't be hardened. Thus it failed at what was expected: a synthetic rubber substitute.

However, the engineer noted that it had strange and unexpected properties. It would bounce when dropped, could stretch to a much larger size without tearing, and when pressed against printed images such as a newspaper, it would transfer the image from the newspaper. The amazed engineer showed his managers. Still focused on what was expected, nothing resulted because, though surprised, they saw no benefit from the product as a substitute for rubber. Some effort was expended, but no real analysis was performed on this material, which ventured far from its original purpose, so the product was abandoned. Several years went by and the war ended.

One day an advertising consultant by the name of Peter Hodgson, who was looking for unusual products, came upon this unique and unexpected result to solve the original rubber problem with a substitute. Someone said once that if you are a hammer, everything looks like a nail. Hodgson was a hammer. He looked on it as an unexpected but innovative gift, and took it to a party to demonstrate its uniqueness. Since other advertising people were probably in attendance, he would find out what they thought about it. It was the hit of the party.

Hodgson purposefully analysed the product further as a possible party favour and invested $147 in it. The results of this investigation and his meagre investment soon caused him to shift his target market to focus on children. He packaged the "liquid solid" into one-ounce plastic containers in the shape of a ball. He gave the product a new name. "Failed Synthetic Rubber" obviously wasn't it. It wouldn't have worked; neither was a name like "Raw Goo" likely not to be something for which parents were likely to shell out hard cash to have around the house. He came up with the name "Silly Putty". Under this name, it became one of the most successful toys in history, surpassing Cossman's ant farm, and achieved worldwide fame. It made millions and millions of dollars for Hodgson and his backers, but not a cent for GE or its original inventor. It was an unexpected bright idea, but the GE engineer who invented it failed to see it as Hodgson did. It was unexpected, but GE did not have a toy division or anyone who might have seen the possibilities in this direction. Hodgson had a broader background to see other possibilities and he followed Drucker's advice about the unexpected, and conducted an analysis before rushing forward.

Some Successful Innovations Are Spelled "In-con-gru-i-ties"

Incongruities are unexpected, too, but in a different way. One expects a certain result, but instead the exact opposite occurs. Frequently this has to do with economic results. In the 1950s, someone found that companies that dominated markets were more profitable. This led to portfolio management and the well-known BCG matrix, in which relative high market share was considered desirable and became either a "cash cow" or a "shooting star". If you could acquire a large share of "the market", success and high profits were yours. Many companies jumped on the bandwagon and, by simply expanding the definition of the market, dominated it with high sales. Some, however, got into industries about which they knew little or nothing, and as a result they had little to contribute in product or service. Yet small companies specializing in areas in which they could excel made money and high profits even if they sometimes actually reduced – rather than expanded – a market by focusing on where they could best serve a customer at whatever was the right price and thus be more profitable. That's unexpected. In this way and through such an incongruity, small organizations can defeat larger and more powerful competitors for specific market segments.

Famed coffeemaker Starbucks was a little company that became big by spotting incongruities in the marketplace where it could satisfy customers better than larger competitors. However, one time, as a giant company, it too fell into the trap of focusing on expansion instead of customers. In an interview with news reporter Katie Couric, CEO Howard Schultz explained, "We made expansion a strategy instead of an outcome of service."[2]

The expansion didn't lead to great profits, but great losses. Fortunately for Schultz, he spotted the incongruity of what he was doing and turned things around before disaster struck.

"Process Need" Innovation

"Process need" has to do with the old proverb that "necessity is the mother of invention". Someone needs something done and simply works on this something until he figures out how to do it. I have heard the same story of Thomas Edison uncovering the right light bulb filament to enable a successful light bulb many times. The problem was that the filament kept burning up. So he kept trying different filaments until he discovered one that worked without burning up. The first time I heard the story, it was 999 attempts before he discovered the right filament. Then I heard that it was 1,000. Then 2,000. Several weeks ago I heard the story and the number stated was now 10,000. I decided to investigate the story myself. Here's what I found out.

For one thing, Edison was hardly the first inventor to work on the problem and light was actually produced by electricity in 1802 by Humphrey Davy. But the light it produced lasted only a few seconds and was too bright for any practical use. Then in 1840, a British inventor by the name of Warren de la Rue got a bulb to work acceptably, but the filament was platinum and far too expensive for any commercial use. Another advance was made by an English physicist, John Wilson Swan, using carbonized paper filaments. He worked on this for almost 30 years, beginning in 1850, and he developed something that worked but was not commercialized. Finally, two Canadians, Henry Woodward and Mathew Evans, developed used carbon rods. They worked. However, their attempt to commercialize failed and they sold out to Edison, who eagerly grasped the baton from the two inventors and charged on.[3]

Edison got into the act in the late 1870s. By January 1879, he and his associates had tested about 3,000 filaments, but still the filaments only lasted a few hours. Finally, by the end of 1880, he managed a 16-watt bulb that lasted 1,500 hours using a carbonized cotton thread. Edison himself said, "I tested no fewer than 6,000 vegetable growths, and ransacked the world for the most suitable filament material." So it's likely that the latest figure that I heard, 10,000, is not far from the truth.[4] Whether 999 or 10,000 attempts, process need innovation works because the innovator simply works at something that is needed until he succeeds.

Industry and Market-structure Innovation

People tend to keep doing things the same way ... forever, and this carries through to industries, markets, and frankly, everything. As a manager, consultant, professor, and military man, I can't tell you the number of times I've been told by well meaning – and some not-so-well-meaning people – that "you can't do it that way – it's not the way it's done". I loved to hear those words as long as what was proposed was not unethical, immoral, or illegal. I discovered that many times folks were doing things the same way for years, even though the reasons they had started in this direction had long disappeared.

This is precisely why Drucker maintained that most innovations came from "cross-fertilization", where an individual from an entirely different industry or specialty moved out of his or her old environment and was given responsibilities in an entirely different environment. It is true that sometimes not having a certain product, industry, or market experience is a detriment and causes the executive to make errors due to this lack. But I have found that such errors are caused more by a lack of judgment than experience. The truth is many highly placed executives create major innovations because they don't know that it can't be done that way.

As a pre-med student in the early 1980s, Michael Dell discovered that he could get a vendor's licence to bid on contracts selling computer upgrade kits all over Texas straight out of his room in a residential building. With very low overhead, his prices were low and he won contract after contract. This led him to challenge the conventional method of selling computers through retail stores and go directly to the customer. This innovation revolutionized computer sales and allowed customers to essentially design their own computers at a competitive price. His net worth at the end of 2014 was $22.4 billion.[5]

Billionaire Bill Bartmann was once listed by *Forbes* magazine as the 25th wealthiest man in the US, right ahead of Ross Perot. Bill was on my board of advisors at the California Institute of Advanced Management, until he unfortunately died due to an unexpected allergy during surgery. He was one amazing individual, having accomplished so many phenomenal things that it would fill a book, and in fact it has. I highly recommend his book, *Bouncing Back* (Brown Group Publishing Group, 2013).

Bill made his biggest fortune in a highly innovative fashion by completely turning an industry on its head. This was in the money-collection industry, where the standard operating procedure was to threaten, hound, and otherwise coerce those owing money to pay up or else. In the immortal words of the *Godfather* "to make an offer which you can't refuse". Bill Bartmann bought these credit notes for 10 cents on the dollar. However, instead of hiring guys to threaten loss of reputation, home, or damage to bodily parts, Bartmann hired an assortment of head-hunters, personal coaches, and placement experts to assist those owing money in job finding, rebuilding careers, and restructuring loans so that most, while maintaining their self-respect, were able to pay off every penny. Now that's innovation and market structure innovation! And of course, Bill made a fortune in the process while helping others. He will be sorely missed at CIAM, by employees of his own company and by the many that he helped.

Demographic Change and the Potential for Innovation

Demographics describe the characteristics of any given human population. These characteristics may pertain to education, religion, ethnic group, culture, income, number of children, and just about any other factor that can be measured. It is important to understand that these characteristics are not static; they change over time. People live longer and tend to be in better health at older ages than in generations past. They say that today's age demographic of the '80s were previously the '60s of times past. Can you see sources for innovation in this? These changes have caused an explosion in the interest in and maintenance of health, which has led to health maintenance organizations, health newsletters, vitamins, spas for seniors, and more. I saw an article in the newspaper this morning reporting on how new technologies allow those in retirement to live better, live healthier, live even longer, and enjoy themselves in the process.

Sometimes demographics may change at warp speed. For example, the US population has doubled since 1950. Moreover, the composition of the US population is dramatically changing. According to an article in the *New York Daily News*: "The latest census data and polling from the Associated Press highlight the historic change in a nation in which non-Hispanic whites will lose their majority in the next generation, somewhere around the year 2043."[6] But at even greater velocity of change has been the rising costs of education. My younger son paid his own way through graduate school for an MBA. It cost him $40,000. Ten years later, the same school charged $120,000.

Drucker and His Education Solution and Predictions

About 20 years ago, Drucker predicted that the future of executive education was online. His prediction was based partially on technology and convenience, but also on the fact that computer literacy and computer ownership was growing even faster than the demand for executive education and that education could be provided at a much lower cost.

Many traditional educators disparaged the idea of "distance learning." They said it had to be done in the classroom face-to-face by lecture, just as it had been done in ancient Greece 2,000 years ago. They said that discussions had to take place and questions asked and answered in a classroom environment, or it just wasn't effective. Students might be exposed to information and ideas online, but they just wouldn't and couldn't learn in this way.

Well, Drucker was right again. Research found that learning online was even faster and more effective than classroom learning in many instances. Back in 2011, current Republican presidential candidate and former Florida Governor Jeb Bush, and James Baxter Hunt, Jr, twice the governor and the longest-serving governor of North Carolina, who happens to be a Democrat gave a joint speech on containing the rising costs of education, which was published afterward in *Inside Higher Ed*. They noted:

"The 2010 US Department of Education's 'Review of Online Learning Studies' found that students who took all or part of a course online perform better, on average, than those taking the same course through traditional face-to-face instruction. Similarly, a study conducted in the same year by the internationally known scholars Mickey Shachar and Yoram Neumann, which analysed 20 years of research on the topic, showed that in 70% of the cases, students who took distance-learning courses outperformed their counterparts who took courses in a traditional environment."[7]

Today, many old traditional universities such as Harvard, Stanford, and the University of Southern California all have online programmes. Others, such as Boston University, even offer doctorate degrees entirely online. The California Institute of Advanced Management started with a so-called "blended" or "hybrid" MBA programme with six lessons of every course face-to-face in the classroom and five online. After three years' experience, we started an alternative 100% online programme with all the features of our blended programme. Using these and other Drucker-recommended concepts, we were able to offer much more to our students, including completion in 11 months and practical consulting experience in every course, either online or in the classroom. Moreover, we were able to do all this at a much lower price than most graduate schools.

Innovation Opportunities Due to Changes in Perception

How we look at things is critical. There is a very old example from psychology, which is still used in many textbooks. When I first encountered it, I was amazed. It was an ambiguous picture of either a young, attractive woman, or an older, ugly one – all in the same picture. It just depended on how you looked at the illustration. You could see either, depending on your perception at that moment and which you perceived first, the young girl or the old woman. Once you saw one, it was very difficult to see the other. In my own experience I had to look away, or close my eyes to see the different image, and at first I had some difficulty in perceiving both. Of course after repetition I could move back and forth in my perceptions. I thought of how I might better demonstrate this in the classroom.

After some experiments, I found that I could control what picture viewers would see by simply showing them a few images in which a few lines were drawn first. In this first instance, the viewers would only see the young woman or the old one, but could not see both in the same drawing.

I would alter each picture. In my doctored versions, in one picture viewers could only see the young, attractive woman. I put that in one set of envelopes, and the doctored picture in which viewers could see only the older, ugly woman in another set. In my class, with a devilish gleam in my eyes, I handed out envelopes with the young woman's picture to half of my class on the left side of the room, and the envelopes with the older woman's picture to the remaining half on the right side of the room. I then instructed everyone to open the envelope and look at the picture for 10 seconds and return the pictures to the envelopes. Finally, in the last step I project the ambiguous picture on a screen in which both images existed and either could be perceived.

I then asked innocently: "How many see a picture of a young, attractive woman?" The hands on the left side of the room would go up. Students on the right side of the room would look puzzled, and I would appear puzzled, too. "How many see an older, unattractive woman?" I would ask. The hands on the right side of the room would be raised, and now those seated on the left side of the room would look puzzled. What fun!

Perception is always relative and depends on how you look at things. Although many perceptions depend solely on optical illusions, others may depend on your mood, values, beliefs, or what you see or "know" from previous experience, as in my experiment in the classroom. Others are illustrated by the old Indian fable about blind men feeling different body parts of an elephant – feet, trunk, tail, ears, tusks – and the different perceptions of the animal each individual imagined based on extrapolating the single part each had felt.

All this is confirmed by police line-ups. You've seen them on television and in the movies: the police put the arrested individual in a line with other people facing an eyewitness. The other people in the line are innocent of any wrongdoing. The eyewitness is asked to pick the one guilty individual from the line-up. Does this sound fool proof? Since DNA testing, a lot of folks judged guilty due to police line-ups have turned out to be innocent. As reported in *Time*: "According to the Innocence Project, eyewitness misidentification has been a factor in 72% of convictions that have been overturned by DNA testing. The National Registry of Exonerations, which works in conjunction with the University of Michigan, traces 507 of the 1,434 exonerations back to mistaken witness identification."[8]

How can we take advantage of perception as a source of innovation? Once a rip in clothing was cause for the quality inspector to reject the product and it was destroyed, or if the tear was minor, it might be sold at a significant discount. However the 1960s began the onset of the Hippie Generation. It became popular to wear torn or faded clothing. Almost overnight, stressed, faded, frayed, and yes, even ripped, jeans became status symbols that were desired by many young, prospective buyers. In response to this new perception of what was considered desirable, jeans manufacturers began to manufacture clothing intentionally produced to resemble clothing that was once considered damaged. However, it could be said that clothing that even the Salvation Army would no longer accept became articles of pride. Perception is everything, and innovations can take advantage of perceptions as they change.

Perception is Everything

A few years ago, a woman in Spain by the name of Susana Seuma lost the use of a leg in an automobile accident and it cost her career, which required two good legs. When a tragedy likes this strikes, there are many solutions that appear to limit or destroy a former career for the future. Ms Seuma's solution was not only highly innovative, but unique. It was based on her secret desire to be a mermaid and her perception that relying on this means of locomotion – at least in the water – was the solution to her career challenge. She had always wanted to be a mermaid—you know, a female creature with a tail like a fish but with the upper body of a woman. So Ms Seuma strapped on a fan-shaped monofin and donned glimmering spandex over her body. After mastering the art of swimming with this adornment, she founded the Sirenas Mediterranean Academy in 2013 and to date has taught the art of being a mermaid, or at least swimming like one, to 500 attendees at her school.[9]

If Knowledge Is Power, then New Knowledge Is New Power

You might assume that new knowledge would immediately become the source of innovation and competitive advantage, which would help spirit companies to advanced positions in their industries and at the same time satisfy needs and wants, some of which were not even recognized until the innovations were introduced. Sad to say, this simply is not true. It frequently takes years – sometimes decades or longer – before new knowledge is applied in worthwhile innovations.

Alexander Fleming is generally credited with the discovery of penicillin in 1928. But the first documented cure didn't occur until 1942, 14 years later. However, the first published paper on the use of fungi as a cure goes back to the 1870s, which would mean the time between knowledge and innovation was considerably longer. However, hold on. The blue mould of this antibiotic on bread was observed to help speed the cure of wounds of battle in the Middle Ages. So the time between knowledge and innovation would more accurately be described as several hundred years.

The knowledge needed to develop the internet became available in the early 1960s. The knowledge for the internet's close relation, the personal computer, has been around since 1962. Even ideas not requiring high technology take an amazing amount of time. Consider the marketing plan. Search for examples prior to World War II, and you will come up empty. Postwar articles in the *Journal of Marketing* began to tout the idea of a marketing plan similar to plans of strategy, which became more familiar during the war. But it took more than 20 years before most organizations began to innovate and adopt the process and produce the marketing plans resulting from it.

What this says is that there is "gold in them thar hills". That is, there is knowledge uncovered and available today that is the source of innovations, yet unexploited for the future.

Drucker told us that we must innovate. However, he did not leave it at that. He told us what we should avoid and how we should approach innovation to build and maintain the success of our organizations with the best sources of new ideas. Drucker found specific ways to approach innovation, and one commonly held method to absolutely avoid in helping his clients to innovate effectively and successfully. As a consultant, you can help your clients the same way.

[1] Drucker, Peter F., *Innovation and Entrepreneurship*, (New York: Harper & Row Publishers, 1985) pp. 130-132.

[2] Schultz, Harold with Katie Couric, *CBS Sunday Morning*, 27 March 2011.

[3] No author listed, "History of the Light Bulb," *Bulb.com*, accessed at http://www.bulbs.com/learning/history.aspx, 18 August 2015.

[4] No author listed, "Light Bulb," *Idea Finder*, accessed at http://www.ideafinder.com/history/inventions/lightbulb.htm, 18 August 2015.

[5] No author listed, "Michael Dell," *Wikipedia*, accessed at https://en.wikipedia.org/wiki/Michael_Dell, 19 August 2015.

[6] No author listed, "Fast Growth of Latino Population Blurs Traditional US Racial Lines," March 17 2013, accessed at http://www.nydailynews.com/news/national/fast-growth-latino-population-blurs-traditional-u-s-racial-lines-article-1.1291138, 21 August 2015

[7] Bush, Jeb and Jim Hunt, "New Higher Education Model," *Inside Higher Ed*, October 6 2011, accessed at https://www.insidehighered.com/views/2011/10/06/bush_hunt_essay_on_why_public_universities_need_to_embrace_online_education, 21 August 2015

[8] Sanborn, Josh, "Behind the Messy Science of Police Lineups," *Time*, October 3 2014, accessed at http://time.com/3461043/police-lineups-eyewitness-science/, 21 August 2015

[9] Moffett, Matt, "Where Can You Find Mermaids? In a School, of Course," *The Wall Street Journal*, front page, A8, 28 August 2015.

Chapter 15

Drucker's Group Consulting and IATEP™

If you work with two or more clients simultaneously, you are engaged in group consulting. Accordingly, workshops, seminars, training, and even plain, good old-fashion classroom teaching are all forms of "group consulting." A review of Drucker's career demonstrates that he did an enormous amount of group consulting in his seminars, workshops, classroom teaching, and "A Day with Drucker", an annual event sponsored by a major Los Angeles graduate school.

Drucker's Group Consulting

I recall Drucker's seminars in the Los Angeles area well from when I was his student in the classroom. He was always involved in presentations for various organizations. One of the two largest universities in the Los Angeles area, the University of California Los Angeles (UCLA), sponsored an annual event called "A Day with Drucker" for which he was always in demand and immensely popular. He did the same for private organizations and corporations.

Although he invariably stressed application, Drucker was trained in the European method, which relied heavily on the formal lecture. Because of this, it was sometimes more difficult for him to integrate class participation. This was evident even in questions and answers. To his students, it sometimes appeared that it was better not to even volunteer and raise one's hand to answer a Drucker-posed question until four or five previous volunteers had done so first and their responses rejected as something short of full acceptance. Only then could one venture an answer that might be judged adequate. However, when he didn't use questions to elicit a "school solution" response, but rather as a stimulus to thinking, he was extremely effective. And as noted in an earlier chapter, his clients were sometimes unfamiliar with being asked these types of questions instead of being given precise instructions as what to do, like they were by other consultants. His procedure also supported his concepts of self-teaching.

If you ventured a theory in your response that was not backed up by observed and quotable facts, you were sure to be challenged. And if you quoted his written work, you'd better be absolutely certain that your quote was accurate. Even then, "quoting Drucker to Drucker" was rarely a good idea.

He sometimes distributed and used case studies in the classroom. These were not quite the case study methodology for which the Harvard Business School is famous, but the basic ideas were definitely similar. Harvard's claim at the time was that detailed analysis in investigating and finding solutions for multiple cases best prepared graduates for immediately assuming general management responsibilities on graduation. Drucker recognized that application was essential for understanding and constantly reminded us that what we learned was useless unless the knowledge was applied. In this, he was preceded by the ancient Chinese sage, Confucius, who proclaimed: "I hear, I forget; I see, I remember; I do, I understand." Drucker emphasized the doing and understanding. In his seminars, Drucker usually concluded with a final instruction: "Don't tell me that you enjoyed my presentation; tell me what you are going to do differently Monday morning."

Again, regardless of his lectures, or any discomfort with his class discussions on a particular day, he stressed application and action. The doing led to the understanding that he knew was necessary for mastery of what he taught as well as helping the client, or client-student, toward the client's own frequently highly effective solutions to problems or strategies.

Several years ago, when I was named president of a brand new graduate school, I wanted to implement the best, fastest method that I could for executive students that had little time, but badly needed the information in an advanced degree, and they needed it as quickly as possible. Combining very powerful methods that I had been taught during my military career beginning at West Point, Drucker's concepts, and other pedagogies developed in some of our research schools, my colleagues and I at the CIAM came up with the method that we called IATEP™.

Immediate Application of Theory for Enhanced Performance (IATEP™)

IATEP™ stands for Immediate Application of Theory for Enhanced Performance. It combines several of Drucker's most important concepts in a teaching and learning environment:

- The advantages of teaching for self-mastery of a subject
- The unusual value of self-instruction in learning
- Immediate application for a complete understanding

While Drucker had a predecessor in Confucius for the necessity of doing or applying for real understanding, he actually had forerunners in these ideas for all three of these concepts. Nor was Confucius the only example of intellectual thought from ancient times, which predated Drucker's position on learning.

The Roman Touch

The Roman philosopher, Seneca, was important in laying the groundwork for Drucker's advice that teaching a subject provided a significant advantage in learning about that subject. Seneca had written millennia earlier precisely that the best way to learn something was to teach it. Drucker repeated that assertion: "No one learns as much about a subject as one who is forced to teach it." The advantages of teaching for learning became apparent to him as he began to consult and to conduct group consulting.

The final element in Drucker's model is the example of his own self-education. Recall from chapter two that Drucker did not formerly attend a university and study management, and he most definitely did not study social ecology, the practice that he particularly claimed in later years, in a classroom. He formally studied law at the University of Hamburg and obtained his doctorate in international law at the University of Frankfurt. He never formally studied management. So how did he get to be the "father of modern management"? In three words: "He taught himself." That's the third Drucker concept in this important model.

This third concept is critical, because teaching oneself is an amazingly effective method with great potential that has not been as much used as it should be in either consulting or learning. Drucker used it when he asked clients questions—recall his famous two questions of Jack Welch when Welch became head of GE: "What businesses would you get rid of if you could and which would you keep? And since you can, what are you going to do about it?"

What is IATEP™?

IATEP™ is a system that I developed for use at the CIAM shortly after I cofounded the school in 2010. In appeared that teaching in a group setting bore a close to group consulting. IATEP™ was developed to optimize Drucker's three concepts for group consulting in a classroom setting. We were going to demand a lot in our MBA; we – and our students – needed all the help that could be supplied. My "official" definition is "an advanced learning and teaching model whereby performance is permanently enhanced through self-instruction, understanding, and immediate application of theory to action."

Today, a "flipped classroom" is considered a revolutionary concept in teaching and learning. Yet it merely combines blended online work with a basic method that was first proposed and adopted in an academic setting more than 100 years ago. More about that shortly. Through this 19th century development, I learned some important things that I have integrated and combined with Drucker's original ideas.

The method used in almost all models of teaching since the Middle Ages requires a teacher lecturing to an awed group of students to impart knowledge. In the "flipped classroom", this basic element is flipped. The students, after having taught themselves a subject away from the classroom, demonstrate their knowledge to the professor or the leader of the group consulting and others present by recitation and demonstration. The "flipped classroom" has received a lot of publicity recently, but it is far from new.

IATEP™ incorporates one final element that improves on Drucker's basic concepts, but is nevertheless a crucial component and completes the process started by the other elements of self-teaching, learning, and demonstration in the classroom and the real world. This final element is most important for absolute mastery. Drucker used his own examples as case studies for class discussion. He did this as effectively as anyone could. Yet the case study methods, as discussion or not, is a simulated method. So it has one weakness, which is nevertheless significant. It is bloodless. Student don't encounter realistic problems in any situation, such as difficult clients and teammates, misunderstandings, misinformation, technology that doesn't work as advertised, the weather, even erroneous solutions introduced by persuasive classmates, and countless other elements in the environment that may prevent the execution of an otherwise best solution and strategy in any given situation. However, through incorporating the practice of actual consulting for real organizations into learning, the real challenge of theory implementation becomes clear. This real-world application of Drucker's principles and theories adds a dimension useful in training or educational group consulting.

The "Flipped Classroom" and the Implications of the Basic Model

One can look at Drucker as a "finished" genius whose work cannot be improved on. My view is that we stand on the shoulders of a genius like Drucker. So I'd like to spend a few minutes looking at the concept of the "flipped classroom" and show how it ties in with Drucker's concept of learning best by teaching, which itself came from ancient predecessors and how we can build on Drucker's consulting ideas.

A few months ago, our new librarian received an e-mail promoting a "revolutionary" system of academic instruction for graduate business programmes known as a "flipped classroom". Much to my surprise, I found that the whole concept incorporated many of the ideas that are a part of IATEP™. Naturally I Googled the term "flipped classroom". I discovered that in 2008, two high school chemistry teachers in Colorado, Jonathan Bergmann and Aaron Sams, sought to find the time to reteach lessons for absent students. They hit on lectures posted online. This proved not only successful for review, but for absent students as well. The basic idea was to stand the usual instructional approach on its head, for students not to have to depend on in-class lectures or the instructor's teaching, so that they could teach themselves ahead of time outside of the classroom. In class they demonstrate their knowledge through examination or engage in exercises or collaborative learning. One main point is that the scarce resource of time is maximized, and the basic concept really has little to do with today's technology, although it is certainly helped by it.[1]

More reading on my part uncovered the fact that the "flipped classroom" had to do with the "Thayer Method". This got my immediate attention. I am a West Pointer. Colonel Sylvanus Thayer is called the "father of the military academy", the United States Military Academy being the official name by which West Point, my alma mater, is known. West Point is the original source on which IATEP™ is partially based. Colonel Thayer (technically he could be referred to as Brigadier General Thayer since he was promoted to that rank as a special honour a day before his retirement) was one of the early graduates from West Point, having graduated in the seventh class in 1808. He is still the longest-serving Superintendent of West Point, having served from 1817 to 1833. In those 17 years, he completely remade the institution. The importance of Thayer's tenure and the instruction methods he developed are confirmed by the fact that they are still utilized at West Point today.

Until Thayer, the academy was subjected to the influence of politics and mismanagement, which involved everything from who was accepted, who graduated, and even how long a term one was required to remain a cadet until graduating.

The age of cadets varied between 10 and 37, as there was no specific age for admission, or even educational level. I recall hearing that even a candidate who couldn't operate a firearm because of physical handicap (he only had one arm) was admitted as a cadet in those early days. Thayer got everything into order. Cadets took a prescribed course of instruction and graduated only after successfully completing the required courses over a certain period of time. There were required physical and mental standards for admission. The US was young and engineers were needed, so Thayer established West Point as the first engineering school in the country, and like it or not, every cadet studied engineering. Graduates built railway lines, bridges, harbours, roads, the Panama Canal, the Pentagon, and supervised the development of the atomic bomb. But maybe Thayer did something else. Could this be the same Thayer referred to in "The Thayer Method?" I Googled further and discovered that this was exactly the same Thayer who was also the "father of the military academy".

The Thayer Method

As I said earlier, being a West Point graduate, I knew exactly what the Thayer Method had to refer to. Let me give you a sampling. My first semester as a cadet and the first day in mathematics class, the professor showed us six hardbound textbooks. He held up each book in turn, announcing as he did each title: "*College Algebra, Plane Trigonometry, Spherical Trigonometry, Plane Geometry, Solid Geometry, Calculus.*" Of the last, he said, "We'll only get through the first few chapters in *Calculus*. But by Christmas break you'll have completed every page and worked every problem of the other five books." We thought he was joking. He was not.

We had already received a schedule before our first class and, as he had stated, we now saw that every chapter of every book was covered and that a number of sample problems were suggested for us to ensure that we had mastered an understanding of the material.

He then asked, "Any questions regarding the first lesson?" I don't think there were any because we all assumed that the professor would teach us what we needed to know. We were all wrong. Did I say earlier that those two high school innovators copying Thayer's methods found out how to overcome the scarcity of time? I guess that they did.

Let me now jump ahead to a description written by a doctoral student about his professor who had taught at West Point as a visiting professor:

"In describing his experience teaching at West Point, Dr Stapell started by describing the first rule that West Point teachers are given – you're not allowed to lecture – at all! What? Isn't that what college teaching is? And wouldn't you expect a place with such a military history and an authoritarian approach to underscore this traditional teaching method – of having one expert individual lecture and provide information to a bunch of young, dutiful students? They don't lecture at West Point? At all? … according to Dr Stapell, this educational method is 100% activity-based."[2]

Returning to 1955 and my own mathematics professor's introduction, he then told us, "You will teach yourself the material required for every lesson in every class." When you come to class I will ask if there are any questions about the material. If there are, I will answer them and provide the answers to your questions. When all questions are answered, you will each be assigned problems to work in class based on the lesson. They will not be the same as those recommended that you solve. All cadets will be given a limited amount of time to develop solutions to these problems, which you will all develop simultaneously on the blackboards. There are 15 of you and there are exactly 15 boards. When I give the command, cease work, you will stop all writing. I will then call on different cadets to explain the solutions to me and the class. I will grade all solutions every day after your class is dismissed, so you will both recite and be graded every day. I strongly advise you to work every problem and make certain that you understand the solution. You are responsible for teaching yourself and you will be graded every day."

This was my introduction to the Thayer Method, a variation of which was used every day, in every class, for the next four years. Periodically tests were given to review major subject areas.

The basic element in the Thayer Method was that the professor does not lecture; he facilitates learning. The students teach themselves in every subject. Returning to Drucker's comment: "No one learns as much about a subject as one who is forced to teach it." Thayer's method was used in every course, and it was tough, but amazingly effective.

After my graduation, I was commissioned in the Air Force, and my first assignment was as a navigator-bombardier in the B-52 nuclear bomber. During the Cold War we spent much time on ground alert, ready in case the Soviet Union launched a surprise attack against the United States as the Japanese had done at Pearl Harbor 20 years earlier. We were encouraged to take graduate courses when off duty. I signed up for courses at Oklahoma State University (OSU), which translated my transcripts from West Point into semester hours. At a time when OSU required 130 semester hours to obtain one of its own undergraduate degrees, I was given credit for an astounding 244.4 semester hours earned from my four years at West Point. No wonder a top-tier school like the University of Chicago admitted me as a full-time student some time later, despite my less-than-outstanding grade point average as a cadet! If completing almost twice the normal load of semester hours over a standard four years of college doesn't get your attention, I don't know what will.

I do not know how Thayer developed his method. What we do know is that he had graduated as valedictorian from Dartmouth College before attending West Point. After his West Point graduation, he fought in the War of 1812 and directed the construction fortifications at Norfolk, Virginia. After the war, he spent several years on special assignment in Europe traveling and studying at École Polytechnique in France. Clearly he was highly regarded, both technically and for his ability to innovate, when he was selected and assigned to become superintendent and reform West Point by President Monroe in 1818. After his retirement from the army, he returned to Dartmouth and is honoured at that university as well for having founded their School of Engineering, much as he had instituted engineering at West Point.

More than Maximizing Time

If we just looked at the time saved by the Thayer Method, that would be pretty good, but there's more. West Point is basically a school for leaders, right? So a lot is crammed into four years, plus academics, but it is what you learn that is important. Well, the *Princeton Review* must have thought that much was learned. West Point is always ranked highly by the *Princeton Review*, but a few years ago, the *Princeton Review* named West Point the number-one public liberal arts college in America. At about the same time, *Forbes* ranked West Point number one nationally among the best US colleges[3] and *US News and World Report* ranked West Pont as the number three engineering school in the country.[4] Come on boys, which is it best in – arts or sciences?

Why Makes the Thayer Method Work?

Because of the "flipped classroom" publicity, a lot of this is being researched today. Here are some thoughts from one practitioner of the flipped classroom: "If some students don't understand what is presented in a real-time classroom lecture, it's too bad for them. The teacher must barrel on to pace the lesson for the class as a whole, which often means going too slow for some and too fast for others.

Moving the delivery of basic content instruction online gives students the opportunity to hit rewind and view again a section they don't understand or fast-forward through material they have already mastered. Students decide what to watch and when, which, theoretically at least, gives them greater owner-ship over their learning.

Classroom time is no longer spent taking in raw content, a largely passive process. Instead, while at school students do practice problems, discuss issues, or work on specific pro-jects. The classroom becomes an interactive environment that engages students more directly in their education.

In the flipped classroom, the teacher is available to guide students as they apply what they have learned online."[5]

Drucker attempted to get his students as well as his consulting clients to do their own thinking in applying his principles to their issues to solve problems, make decisions, and to build their businesses successfully. IATEP™ is a method of teaching, learning, and guiding clients and students alike in doing this. With a little thought, any of Drucker's ideas can be adapted to your group consulting, too.

[1] Tucker, Bill, "The Flipped Classroom," *Education Next*, Winter 2012 / Vol. 12, No. 1, accessed at http://educationnext.org/the-flipped-classroom/, 31 March 2015.

[2] Geher, Glenn, "Great Leaders are Made," *Psychology Today*, April 3 2014, accessed at https://www.psychologytoday.com/blog/darwins-subterranean-world/201404/great-leaders-are-made March 25, 2015.

[3] Alberts, Hana R., "America's Best College," *Forbes* August 6 2009, Accessed at http://www.forbes.com/forbes/2009/0824/colleges-09-education-west-point-america-best-college.html, 31 March 2015.

[4] No author listed, "Best Undergraduate Engineering Programs Rankings," *US News and World Report*, 2015, accessed at http://colleges.usnews.rankingsandreviews.com/best-colleges/rankings/engineering-no-doctorate, 31 March 2015.

[5] Horn, Michael B., "The Transformational Potential of Flipped Classrooms," *Educational Next*, SUMMER 2013 / VOL. 13, NO. 3, accessed at http://educationnext.org/the-transformational-potential-of-flipped-classrooms/, 31 March 2015.

Chapter 16

People Have No Limits! A Critical Concept for Every Consultant's Mastery

I f you consult on staffing or human resources issues, you need to know this, lest you fall into *the* trap that one professor fell into. There was a very popular set of books some years ago written by a man by the name of Laurence J. Peter. Peter was an associate professor of education at the University of Southern California (USC). In 1968, he published what he called the Peter Principle. Some say this was the most famous academic principle to come out of USC. It probably was the one that gained the greatest attention. But please remember that Laurence J. Peter was *not* Peter Drucker.

In a nutshell, the Peter Principle proclaimed: "In a hierarchy, every employee tends to rise to his level of incompetence." At which point he or she was able to rise no further. Since this principle made no exclusions, it follows that in accordance with the Peter Principle, eventually every position in an organization tends to be occupied by an employee who is incompetent to carry out his duties. Moreover, until that time, such work that is accomplished must be accomplished by those employees who have not yet reached their incompetence levels.[1] So without outside intervention, in time the organization would be filled by incompetent people, even though they may have demonstrated high competency and done remarkable things in their previous assignments. One solution was that we smile and benignly tolerate incompetence so long as we had someone available to do the real work of the organization, since the incompetents might do minimum damage and even create barely meaningful jobs.[2] However, many assume that Professor Peter (again, not Drucker) was speaking tongue in cheek with this recommendation.

While the Peter Principle cautioned that an employee promoted to a new job should be qualified for it, the main point was that since these risings were inevitable and the organization could not demote these incompetents who had arrived at their final and incompetent level, it had to eventually get them out of the way where they could do no harm, perhaps making room for new incompetents.

Drucker eschewed this concept totally, and it is critical for the consultant to recognize that Drucker believed that people have no limits. Past failure does not mean future failure, though a consultant may find individuals who are misassigned and not performing optionally, this does not mean that they have reached any limit of competency in their careers. Therefore, in reviewing the issues in any organization, the consultant must understand that people have no limits. This was Drucker's argument against this once-popular preposition.

Peter (Drucker, that is) said, "No!"

Most supporters of the Peter Principle did not see themselves as having arrived that their level of incompetency. This did not affect their view of the book because they might claim that while they still had a way to go, others – especially superiors or competitors in the hierarchy – had already attained this ultimate yet negative level and might be viewed in this category. Since the majority felt themselves not yet incompetent, the book probably gave a feeling of comfort for those still striving against competitors viewed as untalented, but perhaps lucky or with connections. The book rose in popularity and became a national best seller. Drucker said that it was all nonsense, and he hated it when asked if he was the author of the Peter Principle, with the title referring to his first name.

Other than Drucker's strong feeling of the power and importance of people in an organization, he objected to the Peter Principle on several other grounds. He believed that the whole idea was overly simplistic. He didn't contest the fact that many failed as they moved into successively higher levels of an organization. He thought that this was a tremendous waste, much of which could be avoided by the individual himself through proper training on his own or with the help of the organization. He agreed with Laurence J. Peter that more thoughtful placement and promotion could reduce this unwelcome phenomenon. However, he also felt that as those who worked more with their minds, what Drucker called "knowledge workers", became more important in the workforce, increasing numbers of managers were likely to be placed into positions in which they failed to perform adequately in specific situations due to developing technology. In other words, so long as the work was purely physical, it was fairly easy to measure performance, and physical skills were easier to move to other jobs demanding primarily physical inputs.

To put it crudely, a ditch digger dug ditches and could do so adequately in a variety of situations. But the transfer of knowledge-working skills to new assignments was at times much more challenging.

Drucker maintained that, "We have no right to ask people to take on jobs that will defeat them, no right to break good people. We don't have enough good young people to practise human sacrifice." However, this was not a case of an individual rising to a level where he could no longer perform competently. After all, the selection of the right person for the right job was the manager's responsibility. Perhaps even more importantly, the very notion that people rise to their levels of incompetence was dangerous to the whole organization.

The Dangers of the Peter Principle to the Organization

The Peter Principle was dangerous to the organization because of what appeared to be the obvious solution: get rid of the incompetents before the entire organization becomes overloaded with incompetents who make more and more incompetent decisions. Dismissal clearly has a negative impact on the individual. But Drucker saw that dismissal could affect the organization:

- Unless the acts of incompetence are well known, understood, and agreed to by others in the organization, dismissal or reassignment to a less-important post could affect organizational morale and its view of management fairness
- Presumably the so-called "incompetent" had a history, perhaps a long one, of previously successful performance. So dismissal or reassignment would cause loss to the organization of demonstrated ability and experience

The Man Who Lost $1,000,000 as Soon as He Got Promoted at IBM

There is a story that Thomas Watson, the founder of IBM, once asked to see a newly promoted vice president who not only failed on his first assignment, but his failure cost the company a million dollars, which probably was more like 10 or 20 million in today's dollars. The young man reported to the IBM chief ready for the worst. "I guess you called me in to fire me," he said on entering Watson's office. "Fire you!" exclaimed Watson, "We just invested $1,000,000 as part of your education." Drucker would have applauded.

The Hidden Pressure from the Peter Principle

If accepted as fact, the Peter Principle also puts a hidden and significant additional pressure on its employees not to make a mistake lest they be seen as incompetent. However, mistakes are an inevitable part of action and are always possible and must be weighed considering a reasonable balance with risk. Trying to avoid all mistakes is hardly conducive to willingness to take risks or even assumption of full responsibility, both of which are essential for success. Demanding "zero mistakes" is attainable, and in certain very precise cases must be sought and achieved. For example, around a nuclear facility you absolutely must insist on zero tolerance for potential errors affecting the lethal properties of the product that you are dealing with.

However, mistake avoidance for all situations is not a worthy goal. Accomplishment and progress, for example, are the goals a manager or a consultant should be seeking. A focus on avoiding mistakes as a primary goal will lead to an emphasis on risk avoidance and little progress. An organization in which members are trying to make as few mistakes as possible in order to avoid the appearance of incompetency will achieve little in innovation, one of the two prime qualities that Drucker found essential to any organization's success. Without it, an organization will eventually be overwhelmed by its competitors. Rather than mistake avoidance, employees should be encouraged to dare the impossible. This is the only way that they and the organization can achieve the extraordinary, and this is the true route to success.[3]

One More Nail in the Coffin

Implicit in the Peter Principle is the assumption that if a manager is incompetent for one particular job, he or she cannot succeed in any job at the same, or higher, level. It assumes that if a manager demonstrates incompetence and fails in one job, he or she cannot rebound to become a success in another. Both assumptions are in error and therefore not only unfair, but incredibly wasteful in human potential, for history is rife with "incompetents" who later proved to be great successes at different or even higher levels of responsibility in the same or similar organizations.

Disproving the Peter Principle

Now it's true that Professor Peter was talking about hierarchical organizations. My first three examples aren't quite in that category, but they are still worth considering for openers. Rowland Hussey Macy studied business, graduated, and then opened a retail store. It failed. He started another. It failed too. This happened four times, and he failed at each attempt. True, Macy was an entrepreneur and not a member of a hierarchical organization as specified by Laurence J. Peter. However, were his stores divisions of a Fortune 500 company accepting the Peter Principle, Macy would have been discharged after his first attempt, as he would have clearly demonstrated his incompetence at retailing, business, and entrepreneurship. He never would have had the chance to succeed and we may not even have known about him. However, Macy's fifth attempt did succeed, and even though on the first day it brought in only $11.08 in sales, Macy died a very wealthy man. More than 150 years later, Macy's still exists and although suffering like other retailers during the recession, it still has almost 800 stores and recently announced it was going to hire 85,000 seasonal workers for the coming holidays. Not a bad legacy for someone who had clearly risen to his level of incompetence four times before his overwhelming success.

Winston Churchill is certainly an interesting case. Some still argue the point, and Churchill himself maintained that his failure would have been worth the cost in resources and human flesh if the allies had maintained the fight just a little bit longer. He wrote that final success would have shortened the war and saved a million casualties. He was speaking about World War I and referring specifically to a fight he was responsible for initiating and maintaining, the battle called "Gallipoli" on the Turkish front. However, even if Churchill's calculations were correct, politically he should have known that the whole campaign simply wasn't sustainable. So one could say that his disaster would have been called proof of Peter's theory had he not been so successful later. And after all, politics was supposed to be Churchill's forte. Nevertheless, Churchill "reached his level of incompetence" as defined by Laurence J. Peter as first lord of the admiralty during World War I.

Here's what happened. As first lord, Churchill succeeded in convincing the British war cabinet to undertake the biggest allied disaster of the war, the Dardanelles Campaign, including an allied landing at Gallipoli. This resulted in the worst allied defeat of the entire conflict, with over 200,000 casualties. Churchill was forced to resign as First Lord of the Admiralty and forced into a much lower position in the army. As a graduate of Sandhurst, the British "West Point" with previous military experience, he volunteered and joined the British Army. Once having commanded admirals, general, and field marshals, he served on the front lines in France as a lieutenant colonel. He shared all dangers. His hut mate in the trenches was blown apart during an artillery barrage. Churchill himself survived the war and became a successful combat officer. But he failed miserably in his top job as Sea Lord.

Yet the same man, with much higher responsibilities, first as first sea lord, then as prime minister during World War II, saved England and possibly the world during the year that the British stood alone against Hitler and his minions. Moreover, this one-time incompetent is now considered the greatest British political figure of the 20th century, and maybe of all time.

Politicians are obvious examples at disproving the Peter Principle. Ronald Reagan was defeated twice as a Republican nominee, finally succeeding in becoming nominee and president of the

United States as well on his third attempt. Abraham Lincoln failed at just about everything. He failed in business, ran for the Illinois State Legislature and was defeated, went into business again and went bankrupt, ran for speaker and was defeated, was defeated in a nomination to Congress, was rejected for an appointment for the US Land Office, was defeated in a US Senate race, and two years later defeated again in a nomination for vice president. Then in 1860 he became our 16th president and saved the Union. To the best of my knowledge, not even his detractors, and certainly not historians, call him incompetent.

Certainly one of the most hierarchical of organizations is the military. But did you know that none other than General Colin Powell would have easily been classified as having risen to his level of incompetency? In further disproving the Peter Principle, he did not. As a "one-star", brigadier general, he had displeased his boss at a critical time and made two serious mistakes. As a result, his two-star boss gave him a mediocre effectiveness report. Since only 50% of brigadier generals went on to promotion to two-stars (major general), Powell was certain that he knew which 50% he would be in. His career would have been at an end. Then, if that weren't enough, it was felt that he may have mishandled a case of sexual harassment. In his own words, he questioned himself: "Was this 'strike three' (as in three strikes and you're out)?"[4] Boy, was he showing up as an incompetent!

Despite this, Powell's 30-year previous record of outstanding performance and accomplishments earned him his second star. And of course, later he was promoted to three- and then four-star positions and eventually he became Chairman of the Joint Chiefs of Staff, the US military's highest-ranking officer.

What Exactly Does Drucker's Denunciation of the Peter Principle Mean for Consultants?

Drucker was probably the first to put people on the positive side of the account ledger. People are not an expense, they are an asset, and every consultant looking in on an organization from the outside must recognize this. Drucker's consulting took this approach, and so should yours if you intend to follow his principles. So it's not that people have risen to levels of incompetency. Given that they have had success, maybe considerable success in past assignments, something else may be wrong. Consider the following before recommending or taking any other action:

- Was this the right person to put in this job?
- Rome wasn't built in a day – is more time needed?
- Are the resources needed available?
- Can you help?

As a consultant, there may not be much you can do about finding the right candidate, i.e., the right person for the right job. This may have happened before your involvement. However, the last three on Drucker's list all involve care, feeding, and development. You can clearly impact all three, and if early, help get the right person in the job as well.

The Right Person for the Right Job

I've devoted a good deal to this because it is the most important, and yet the most often neglected by managers and consultants. This process may have started and been completed long before the consultant came on the scene. However, even if it is too late to do anything about finding the best person for the job, you may get in early enough to help, or even be responsible for the entire process. Drucker said that you need to staff to strengthen an organization, so let's start there.

Drucker recommended three prime rules to staff for strength:

1. Think through the requirements of the job.
2. Choose three or four candidates for the job rather than deciding immediately on one candidate.
3. Don't make the final selection without discussing the choice with knowledgeable colleagues.

The Requirements of the Job

A poorly designed job, one in which the requirements have not been thought through, may be an impossible job that no one can do. An impossible job means that work intended to be accomplished can only be accomplished poorly or maybe cannot be done at all. Being impossible or nearly so risks the destruction, or at best, the misallocation of scarce and valuable human resources. To design a job properly, the objectives and requirements of the job must be analysed to decide on those few requirements that are truly crucial to the job's performance. That way the executive seeking to fill the position can avoid filling it with a candidate who minimally meets all requirements, rather than staffing for strength for the few critical areas of the job that are essential.

Developing the Essential Job Requirements

Thinking through the requirements of the job means developing those basic requirements that an executive must have to accomplish the job successfully. If this is done, it will minimize the chance that a selection is made on less relevant factors. Let's start with the factor of likeability. It is true that good professionals can work together without liking one another. Likeability does not guarantee success. We have all seen examples of very likeable individuals who fail miserably in jobs at all levels of an organization. However, the chances of success are greater when there is at least no animosity between boss and subordinate at the start.

Years ago, when I spent some time as an executive recruiter, I learned that the modus operandi for a recruiter was to submit three to five candidates to the hiring executive for any position. All of these candidates met the basic requirements, which the head-hunter had helped the hiring executive develop in a "job order, including job specifications". However, these individuals were of differing personalities, backgrounds, and physical appearance. As explained to me by a more experienced executive recruiter, this was to ensure that "the chemistry was right". "Sometimes a candidate won't personally like his potential boss," I was told. "Sometimes, a potential boss won't like the candidate. And there are times when neither one will like each other.

However, with three to five candidates, chances are that in at least one case the candidate will like the potential boss, and visa versa. But in all cases, the candidate must meet all the main requirements for the job."

This sort of occurrence is far from uncommon. In the executive recruiting business, there is a saying: "Once a candidate meets face-to-face with a client, all bets are off." What this means is that personality and "chemistry" prevail in most cases over experience and accomplishments documented in resumes. There is nothing particularly wrong with these aspects of a candidate being considered. Personality and the ability to fit into different organizations are extremely important. Meeting basic, well thought through job requirements, including "chemistry", cannot be ignored. We need to think through the requirements of a job and staff for the strengths that are needed. If a candidate doesn't meet an essential requirement, don't promote or hire him or her for the job.

Choose Multiple Candidates for a Job before Selection

The fact is that many promotions or hiring selections are made with only one or two candidates being considered. Managers get in a hurry or they are overly impressed with a single candidate for a position. At the very least, think through and come up with back-up candidates. However, the correct way, according to Drucker, was to consider three or four candidates, all of whom met the minimum qualifications of staffing for strength and to do this right from the start.

Sometimes the reason that this wisdom is ignored is that the hiring executive makes assumptions about a candidate's suitability before considering all candidates' qualifications against the prime job requirements. So just getting the requirements nailed down will be immensely helpful.

In one organization, the staffing executive, who had been with the company a year, wanted to appoint a particular manager from within the company to a senior position. He sent the recommendation, which had to be approved by his boss, forward. His boss asked to see the résumés of at least two additional internal candidates for the job. His boss was also curious about a particular aspect of the staffing executive's choice for this promotion.

The staffing executive used the old ploy of straw candidates. He picked three, rather than two, additional candidates for the position. He thought this would give the impression that he had considered many subordinates for the promotion and would show how superior the candidate really was. He did not think the three additional candidates were anything special. In fact, he selected them for that reason. He sent all four résumés to his boss. In addition to demonstrating questionable integrity in his ploy, he made two major errors. First, he did not think through all the job requirements. His boss had. In addition, he relied on his personal knowledge and opinion of the candidates without investigating other aspects of their work at the company. That would have been bad enough. However, he even failed to read the résumés he sent forward. He merely attached a strong letter of recommendation for the candidate that he wanted to get the position.

What the staffing executive did not know is that one of the three additional candidates had been with the organization for many years and had a strong reputation and a long list of accomplishments. However, for the past year he had been on special assignment away from corporate headquarters, so the staffing executive did not know him. As it happened, his background and proven experience were particularly suited to the obvious requirements of the position to be filled. He was so well suited, that he should have been the prime candidate recommended.

This was one reason that the staffing executive's boss had asked to see the résumés of additional candidates. If this manager was not even included in consideration, he wanted to find out why. If he was included, but not the candidate selected, he wanted to see if he was missing some important information before he approved the promotion. The staffing executive was fortunate enough not to overlook forwarding his résumé. Then he probably would really have been in trouble. However, had he looked closely at the résumés, he would have immediately grasped the fact that he was not recommending the best candidate for the position. Of course, he may have known something about this candidate not known to others, but in this case, he did not.

What his boss saw was that the executive was clearly not recommending the best candidate for the job. In a face-to-face interview with the staffing executive, he soon determined that he did not know who should have been the obvious candidate or this candidate's background as well as he should have. He could perhaps be forgiven, since this manager had been absent during most of the staffing executive's time with the organization, but it still did not reflect well on his ability as a high-level manager. Had he promoted the wrong manager, it might have caused a number of problems in the organization, not to mention not having the manager most suitable for the job. After a discussion of the requirements and the qualifications of the candidates, both he and the staffing executive agreed that this ignored candidate – and not the candidate who the staffing executive had earlier recommended – should be promoted to the job.

Discuss Your Choice with Colleagues

Had the executive I mentioned discussed the appointment with his staff or colleagues, he wouldn't have embarrassed himself in front of his boss. I want to state emphatically that Drucker was not saying that any staffing is a group decision. It is not, and you must take responsibility for the outcome regardless if those you consult give you erroneous information or possibly pass on a poor recommendation. You are still responsible. However, it makes sense to share your plans and get others' opinions and ideas whenever it is possible to do so. Even if you decide to promote someone who others don't recommend, at least you'll know the pitfalls of your appointment and learn more about what others think and know regarding the various candidates you are considering.

After the Assignment Is Made

Once you have made the assignment, or as a consultant you have assisted with it, your work is not done. You are responsible for what happens next, and there is always "care and feeding" that is involved. New appointments do not automatically hit the ground running. It would be well to prepare the way as much as possible, including with training. Sure, you can leave it to the new promotee to work it out. If it's the right selection, the individual may know himself in what areas of the new position he needs help or additional training. But why wait? There is much that you know already that the new appointee probably does not. Unless letting the individual struggle is part of his or her development, why do it? You want your new promotee to be successful and make you look good don't you?

Without doing the promotee's job, you want to do everything possible to ensure his or her success at that job. As a retired CEO once told a group of recently promoted vice presidents about leading their subordinates: "Don't you let them fail!"

Is This a Work in Progress?

It would be nice if every manager could hit the ground running in every new job. However, this isn't always possible, especially in a new job that is new not only to the placed executive, but also to the organization. Whether new or old, it may present a challenge for a new occupant. A manager can ease the way by clearly laying out requirements, meeting frequently during the early weeks with the individual in a new position, helping or assisting without doing the new appointee's job for him, but above all, not letting him fail. So don't be too hasty in immediately replacing a new assignee. Some need time to develop, and sometimes the assignment itself may have been made with insufficient thought on whether adequate resources such as money, personnel, equipment, or facilities have been allocated. Moreover, this can change given the way the new assignee operates or plans to operate. You may never be able to anticipate this precisely because there are many different ways of approaching any task, and this depends on the capabilities and thinking of the one now has the position.

Remember that as the boss, or the consultant, you are there to help and never forget the injunction: "Don't you let him fail".

Drucker's People Approach

The idea that managers rise to their level of incompetence is a dangerous myth. If a manager isn't performing, of course he needs to be relieved of his duties. But to automatically fire a manager due to failure with no further thought is, as Drucker maintained, a human sacrifice, pure and simple. There may be an equally challenging job available at which he will be successful. Find something or put him in a holding position until you do. Don't waste individuals who have previously done well over long periods of time due to one job failure. In any case, you can minimize these problems by performing due diligence in the ways recommended:

- Think though the requirements of the position and staff for strength
- Have multiple qualified candidates before settling on one
- Share your intentions with colleagues before promoting
- It's not over just because the assignment has been filled
- Much falls under care and feeding

Do this and you will have an excellent "batting average" of promoting the right person to the right job. Once in the job, it is still your responsibility to get the person off to the right start. Your success average needs to be equally high in this area.

Take these actions and your organization is on the way to being top heavy with the best and most qualified managers. If it's your organization, these are your responsibilities. If you are advising and recommending in these matters as a consultant, you too, have major responsibilities for success, all of which have to do with the importance of people, and the Peter Drucker Principle that people have no limits.

[1] Peter, Laurence J.; Hull, Raymond, *The Peter Principle: Why Things Always Go Wrong.* (New York: William Morrow and Company, 1969), p. 8.

[2] Asghar, Rob, "Incompetence Rains, Er, Reigns: What the Peter Principle Means Today," *Forbes*, 13 August 2014, accessed at http://www.forbes.com/sites/robasghar/2014/08/14/incompetence-rains-er-reigns-what-the-peter-principle-means-today/, 27 October 2015.

[3] No author listed, "Macy's," *Wikipedia*, accessed at https://en.wikipedia.org/wiki/Macy%27s, 27 October 2015.

[4] Powell, Colin, *My American Journey*, (New York: Random House, 1995) p. 269.

Chapter 17

10 Things Considered

I don't believe one can consider Drucker's unique steps toward becoming and then performing as a management consultant without learning a great deal that anyone can use in building their own successful consulting career. Here's what I've gleaned from his example in this area.

1. None of our upbringings or the opportunities from it are necessarily bad or necessarily good. They just happened, that's all. Caesar Millan didn't have any of Drucker's stuff, and he even entered the US from Mexico illegally. He didn't attend college, but he learned enough about dogs to become the "dog whisperer" to the extent that he has had his own successful television show for years, and undoubtedly commands consulting and speaking fees for his consulting about our pets, which may not be all that dissimilar from what Drucker's were once. We all have resources for becoming good, maybe even great consultants, which we can analyse and document. We just need to realize what resources we have, think, and then put them to use.

2. You don't need to build a giant consulting organization to do a lot of good, gain a lot of fame, and make a lot of money as an independent consultant. Drucker answered his own phone, even at the height of his fame. There is no reason why we can't do the same or similar things "they" tell us not to do.

3. Honesty is not just the best policy, it is the only policy if you want long-term success, and that's something you can't let slip. How often do we see really big names in every field who let their integrity slip and that's the end? So even though it may be a disadvantage in the short run, you must maintain your integrity at all costs.

4. Obstacles will always appear. The first thing that happened to an acquaintance of mine when he started his own consulting practice was that he got sued. It took him three years to win the case. Consider how you would best deal with such problems while struggling to get clients? Drucker had to shelve his goal of becoming a professor teaching graduate courses at a major university for about 15 years because of "a little thing"

like Hitler coming to power in Germany. So he did what he needed to do and eventually he not only reached his initial goal, but accomplished a lot more.

5. Don't depend on others for education in your profession or as a consultant. Some corporate managers maintain that their companies will pay for advanced education, or send them to the right courses or seminars if they really need them. Don't bet on it. Drucker didn't even depend on his parents, who wanted him to go to college. He took an apprenticeship and spent lots of time reading and educating himself, even while he struggled balancing law school and working full time. Drucker was not superhuman. He just calculated what he was going to have to do under the circumstances of pre-war Germany and Austria, and later post-war US and did it. He didn't wait for either parental help or a corporate or government hand-out.

6. Writing a bestselling book doesn't guarantee your success. But it sure can't hurt, and if your timing is correct or lucky, it can take you right to the top. Moreover, just about anyone can write, or can learn to do so if they are willing to make the effort. Drucker didn't even know English perfectly when he started.

7. Sure, serendipity helps, but consider serendipity as a process. Do enough things (maybe even read enough books like Walpole or Drucker) and positive serendipitous happenings are sure to come your way.

8. Drucker's mentor, Marvin Bower, cautioned not to discuss your client's work. Drucker may have stumbled on this one. As a result, he lost the good will of a major corporate icon, Alfred P. Sloan. Of course, Drucker didn't know that he had written anything to offend, but this is not the issue. It is in the eyes of the offended that counts. Drucker should have been more careful. He might have even received Sloan's blessing had he approached him, and he apparently had access. However, Drucker learned his lesson and you would be hard-pressed to find a client's business publicized in the manner of GM by Drucker from that time on.

9. The client is the real expert. An argument can be made that Drucker didn't tell clients what to do so much as guide them to tell themselves. Perhaps he took away a little of the glamour with asking more questions than providing answers and PowerPoint presentations. Drucker's model of the management consultant wasn't the image of the man on the white horse riding up, telling people what to do, making things right, and riding off as someone asked, "who was that masked man?" as rapid hoof beats sounded in the background with the words: "Hi ho, Silver."

10. Although Drucker gave us much through his values, principles, and genius, I believe that Drucker's most valuable contribution was that he taught us how to think. Then he expected us to do it followed by action.

I can only end this book the way Drucker would have ended it: don't tell me how much you enjoyed my words – tell me what you are going to do differently on Monday morning.

Bill Cohen
Pasadena, California
February 2016

Appendix

Essays on Drucker's Consulting by Clients and Experts

How Peter Drucker's Consulting and Philosophy Worked for Me

By Frances Hesselbein

Long ago, in 1976, I came to New York from the mountains of Johnstown in western Pennsylvania, a big-steel, big-coal, big-hearts community, to be the new CEO of the Girl Scouts of the USA, the largest organization for girls and women in the world.

I carried with me every Peter F. Drucker book and film I owned – and I owned them all. In my two previous CEO positions, our leadership and management decisions were pure Peter. We found the Drucker philosophy and resources exactly right for us.

We had thrown out the old hierarchy – the up-down, top-bottom, superior-subordinate language – and had launched our own Girl Scout management system, where we moved our people across the organization. We called it circular management.

It worked, and became the exciting structure for over three million girls and women. Our belief: "Only the best is good enough for those who serve girls."

In 1990, after 13 incredible years as CEO of the Girl Scouts of the USA, following an exuberant final year I left the best people and the best organization in the world. I was ready to write a book and not travel so much, but six weeks after I left, I found myself the president and CEO of the Peter F. Drucker Foundation for Non-profit Management.

I thought I was to be the chairman, but Peter said firmly, "You will be the president and CEO or it won't work."

So six weeks after leading the largest organization for girls and women in the world, I found myself the president and CEO of the smallest foundation, with no money, no staff, just a small board sharing a love for Peter Drucker and a commitment to keep Peter and his philosophy moving across the country and around the world.

For the first several years, Peter travelled from Claremont to New York for our board meetings. He spoke at every conference. When the time came for us to travel to California, it was joyous to be with Peter.

While Peter left us in 2005 and we now have a new name, The Frances Hesselbein Leadership Institute, we are still the Peter F. Drucker Foundation for Non-profit Management. We carry in our hearts and minds Peter's popular phrases: "Think first, speak last" and "Ask, don't tell." We quote Peter everywhere it is appropriate. He still inspires us to this day and always will.

About Frances Hesselbein

Frances Hesselbein is President and CEO of the Frances Hesselbein Leadership Institute, founded as the Peter F. Drucker Foundation for Non-profit Management and is its founding president. Prior to this, Hesselbein served as the CEO for the Girl Scouts of the USA. Hesselbein was the first CEO to rise from being an unpaid troop leader to the top job in 67 years. She led a turnaround, increasing minority membership and attaining a membership of 2.25 million girls with a workforce of 780,000, mainly volunteers. Peter Drucker wrote that Hesselbein could be the successful CEO of any US corporation. She held the first chair of leadership at West Point and received the Presidential Medal of Freedom from President Bush in 1998. Hesselbein is a trustee of the California Institute of Advanced Management.

Becoming a "Master Questioner" Like Drucker

By Penny (Ping) Li

In 2013, I was one of the first MBA graduates from the California Institute of Advanced Management (CIAM), and I also became one of its first directors. In learning to consult using Drucker's methods, I completed 11 consulting engagements. What I learned and applied most was that Drucker became such a successful consultant by the very simple secret of asking the right questions.

When I first heard about Drucker's methodology of questioning, I didn't think that I had much to learn. I was a TV journalist in China for eight years. My daily work was all about asking questions. In my job I interviewed people every day with the goal of giving my television audience a better understanding of what people were doing in our city. These were what you call "human interest" pieces in the US.

One day I met Rui Wang, a little six-year old Chinese boy with cerebral palsy. I had never interviewed anyone that young. He watched his twin brother leave home for school every morning, but Rui had to stay at home, as the cerebral palsy made him immobile. Rui exercised very hard every day under his grandpa's guidance. Rui's grandfather was raising him, as both of Rui's parents deserted him after being told that he would never recover from his disease.

Rui was covered with sweat from his exertions in trying to walk. I asked him my first question right away: "Rui, you must be tired from practising walking every day, right?"

"No," he answered bravely, "I'm not tired at all."

But I could see that this little boy was totally exhausted. I persisted: "Rui, you are very brave, but I don't believe you. I can see with my own eyes that you are sweating. Are you telling me the whole truth?"

"Yes, Um … no … sort of. I hurt a little."

"Why don't you stop for a few moments and rest?"

"Because if I don't work hard, I'll not recover, then I'll be a burden to my grandpa, my brother, and to the country!"

I knew what to do and kept "digging" deeper. I also thought that while we were talking, Rui was resting, even if he did not realize it. So I expanded my interview as long as I could. Finally, I could not stretch the interview longer. My last question was, "Rui, do you have a dream?"

I could see he was excited when he answered me. "Yes, I do have a dream! I have a dream that one day I will go to school with my brother and sit next to him and learn in a real classroom." I swallowed with difficulty and bid Rui goodbye.

In my documentary I showed my audience a brave little boy who was not only very intelligent, but very thoughtful. His pure and innocent heart was full of hope while his mind constantly focused on his dream. My documentary was so well received that many donors called our hotline in tears to make a donation for Rui. They wanted badly to help him achieve his dream. As a result, Rui received so many contributions that he was able to begin medical treatment and therapy. I was privileged to one day see him accepted as a student by a school and attend classes with his brother.

So when I met with my very first consulting client in the MBA programme at CIAM, I thought that I already had a special ability of asking questions, maybe even better than Drucker! All I needed to do was to ask his famous five questions and that was it!

The client was an owner of a bus charter company in Los Angeles and wanted to expand his business into a full-fledged tourism company. He thought that since he already had the buses, he just needed to bring in tourists worldwide. I remembered that we had learned the five famous questions that Drucker asked clients, including asking about the mission, customers, and plan. I began asking my questions one by one. Below are the answers he gave me:

Q: What is your mission?
A: To be more profitable
Q: Who is your customer?
A: Everyone!
Q: What does your customer value?
A: Oh, we have the lowest price
Q: What results do you seek?
A: Tell me how I can attract customers worldwide, especially from China and India, as both countries are my targets now (this answer makes more sense compared with other four answers)
Q: What is your plan?
A: My plan? I need you to provide me with a business plan and tell me what exactly I should do! I'll follow your recommendations!

Obviously, the first meeting with my client was quite short, and I felt anxious afterward as I realized that thinking I was a master consultant-questioner like Drucker was just plain wrong. I had no idea how to get the client to reveal the information that I needed in order to help him! I realized that asking questions of my interviewees for TV stories and asking questions of my consulting clients regarding their businesses were entirely different.

Peter Drucker once said that the consultant is not able to understand a business as well as the client does. The consultant will not be the one who provides answers to the client's issues or problems; instead, the correct consulting process is based on asking the right questions to make the client think about the problems from different angles and be able to figure out what to do on his or her own.

I got a copy of a consulting report that Drucker had done for Coca-Cola in the 1990s. It is called, "Challenges Facing the Coca-Cola Company in the Nineteen-Nineties". Drucker made it clear in its introduction that, "This report raises questions.

It does not attempt to give answers." Instead of telling the client what was wrong or what they should do, Drucker asked many questions in the report, a lot more than his famous five. However, I observed that the questions he asked the client were actually leading questions, such as: "What is it that should be promoted?" "What alternatives are there?" and many more.

Since Drucker said that clients knew their organizations much better than the consultants, the clients may have been thinking about what actions might be wrong, and what actions would probably be right to correct the problems. But the consultant wasn't the one with the real knowledge – the client was. Therefore, the consultant's job was to help the client eliminate wrong ideas or actions, and get him to become aware of the right actions to take.

With Drucker's principles and methodology in mind, we were able to ask better questions based on our marketing research. For example, when we asked the first question, "who is your customer?" we came up with more questions regarding the analysis of demographics (age, education, ethnicity, occupation) and lifestyle (income, housing ownership, consumer behaviour). We guided the client to think with us about who should not be his customer or what group of people he would not be able to consider as a target market. Within seven weeks, we provided our client with an in-depth consulting report on how to attract Asian tourists and received very positive feedback from him. He told us that he was much clearer about the mission and in this instance why he should concentrate on providing high quality service instead of continuing to lower the prices, which was the way he had looked at his problems earlier. As Drucker said, it was not the right answers that we needed to focus on, but the right questions.

After the completion of 11 consulting projects with my classmates at CIAM for various companies, I learned that we, the consultants, are not the ones to provide answers. Our function is to ask the right questions, wisely, learning about the organization with the clients, in order to help them challenge some assumptions and reframe the original issues and problems. By being asked the right questions, the clients were not only be able to figure out a better solution on their own, but also learn how to see the same problems from multiple angles to arrive at optimal solutions.

I think now that while my questioning of Rui performed a real service to be proud of, the techniques I used were wrong for eliciting the right questions for my consulting. They worked for Rui because he had already learned the correct questions and answered them. All I had done was to show an audience what he had done. And in a sense, I have repeated that in this essay. All I have done is to show you Drucker's questions and his answers and helped show you what he has done.

About Penny (Ping) Li

Penny Li is Director of Admissions at the California Institute of Advanced Management. She was one of CIAM's first MBA graduates and completed 11 consulting engagements as a student using Drucker's methods, receiving written and video testimonials from several consulting clients. She developed a major project for a United Nations' competition that recommended applications of Drucker's consulting procedures. During the production of a televised charity event, she organized a media aid project fundraiser that raised $150,000 for 6,000 children with cerebral palsy. A video that she directed on student consulting, based on Drucker's consulting principles, was selected as a finalist in the sixth annual Drucker Forum held in Vienna, Austria.

The Drucker Consulting Experience

By Eric McLaughlin

I was one of those fortunate individuals to have the privilege of attending Claremont Graduate University with multiple classes from Peter Drucker, qualifying exams for my doctorate, and a letter of recommendation for my first teaching position. My consulting company focuses on the health care industry and my experience with other consultants has jaded my perceptions considerably. The scene I have witnessed numerous times is a salesperson making a pitch to management with the emphasis on how the "product" can achieve remarkable results. The consulting report produced invariably consists of a canned format with the client's name and logo prominently displayed on numerous pages and the report contains an abundance of tables, graphs, charts, and recommendations that would apply to any organization, as the data is completely generic. Thousands (and sometimes hundreds of thousands) of dollars would be charged for this "customized" product.

Peter Drucker's approach to consulting was diametrically opposite to that of the pre-packaged, written recommendations of the major consulting companies. Instead of "telling" the client what they needed to do, Peter focused on change: rethinking the organization's *raison d'être*. Much like Socrates centuries ago, Peter would simply ask questions and listen very carefully to the responses. His philosophy to consulting was to *not* presume anything nor to have a product "on the shelf", ready to package – he just listened and probed with additional questions.

He once told our class the story of his consulting opportunity with the management team of one of the largest railway companies in the United States. When he asked the question, "What does this company do?" he received the quick response, "We move materials efficiently and cost effectively." Peter replied, "While that is the process of your actions within this business, it is not your real business." The management team was shocked and without retort. Peter continued with the information he had gained about this client prior to the meeting and was ultimately able to communicate to the managers that their company was the largest single landholder in the United States (acquired via purchases and eminent domain). It was the use of this land that allowed them to build the rail system upon which the locomotives and freight trains operated.

This shifting of focus was Peter Drucker's unique style of consulting. He "forced" the company's management team to see their business in a different light—one that entirely changed their approach to day-to-day operations and strategic planning for the future. The railroad company approached their abandoned rail lines in an entirely different light in terms of land development opportunities.

In his book, *The Five Most Important Questions You Will Ever Ask about Your Organization*, Peter Drucker's chapter pertaining to question number one, "what is our mission?" describes Peter Drucker's consulting approach to emergency-room management of a large metropolitan hospital. Experienced ER physicians and ER nurses defined their mission as, "Our mission is health care." Peter's consulting approach was to engage in a discussion that had the participants step back and think "out of the box" for a minute. With probing from Peter, the organization's professionals realized that the real purpose of the ER was, "to give assurance to the afflicted". This realignment of thinking resulted in a restructuring of the entire patient and health care professional interaction. Patients were triaged within minutes of arrival at the ER, instead of wait times of hours. In some cases, the "assurances" were that a professional communicated to patients that they simply needed to let time take care of the healing to get over the flu or illness. It was this assurance that the patient required, versus an admission to the hospital.

My personal consulting practice approaches the topic of improving quality in health care organizations much the same way that Peter Drucker approached his clients: ask instead of tell and provide meaningful assistance to the unique situation at hand versus providing an "off the shelf" document. Consulting to Peter was not a "cookie-cutter" product process; it involved thoughtful probing and serious listening to assist a company's management into rethinking what they had been doing for years, repeating ad nauseam. His approach often blended a company's social responsibilities with that of the Chinese thinking of strategies of planning for existence in 100 years.

About Eric McLaughlin

Eric McLaughlin is a management consultant and Chief Presidential Academic Advisor and former Dean at the California Institute of Advanced Management. Previously Dr McLaughlin was a senior administrator and faculty member at California State Polytechnic University, Pomona, California as well as at other universities from UCLA to Washington State University. He obtained his PhD from what is today the Peter F. Drucker and Masatoshi Ito Graduate School of Management at Claremont Graduate University in the programme established by Peter F. Drucker. He has written for more than 100 publications and given scores of presentations, as well as performed consulting engagements using Drucker's methods for organizations such as the American Red Cross, the American Dietetic Association, American Medical International, Citibank Corporation, Stanford University, and West Coast Industrial Relations Association.

My Experience as Peter Drucker's Client

By Minglo Shao

In the summer of 1999, I went to visit Peter Drucker, as I was planning to establish an institution on management training to serve Chinese managers and entrepreneurs. Peter was very enthusiastic about this idea and immediately offered to be my consultant for the rest of his life. What's more, he would do it for free. Since then, I would visit him at his home in Claremont, California almost every three months until shortly before he passed away in 2005.

According to the agreement between Peter and me, I would provide a report of a few pages updating business development since we last met and send it to him in advance for his review. The report would cover the recent changes in the environment and the market, new opportunities and challenges, as well as my questions. Every time I sat down in his living room, I would find my report marked with his notes and comments on his coffee table.

Peter usually began the meeting by confirming with me if his understanding of my report was correct. He would then answer my questions listed in the report one by one. Sometimes he would point out that a problem was not a real one, but rather the facade or result caused by the real problem and would guide me in finding the root of the facade by myself. When he finished, he always asked if I had more questions. If my answer was no, he would say, "Let me ask you a few questions."

His questions were often unexpected, but at the same time very enlightening.

Not long after I set up this new institute, a professor from a famous business school approached me and suggested that we should proceed in the direction of elite education that would cultivate potential executives for big corporations and charge expensive tuitions. She masterfully designed an international study tour and recommended herself to be the candidate for the dean of this new institute.

I almost accepted her suggestion due to my admiration for the famous school and this famous professor, but still I forwarded her proposal and résumé to Peter, hoping to get his feedback. When I met with him, Peter told me that the lady was certainly a talent and her proposal was also very creative. Nonetheless, he did not agree to this proposal nor consider her to be the right candidate for the position. Peter said to me, "China definitely needs big corporations and elite leaders. But in China, as in any other country, 90% of its organizations are small- to medium-sized local ones. This professor wishes to help establish another Harvard Business School, which is not your intention. Your goal is to foster a managerial culture that emphasizes results. China's biggest weakness is that, as a big country, there are not enough people with higher education. However, you have a large number of talented people, who have learned how to survive under extremely difficult conditions and have achieved success. They may only have a general education and might not be particularly smart or outstanding, but they know how to handle things delicately. There might be millions of them, and they can lead those small- to mid-sized local organizations. They are the ones that will build up a well-developed China. These people are your real students. They are the potential resources and the rough gems. They have enormous acceptability and a craving for learning. Therefore, do not allow anyone to alter your direction." Peter's wise advice brought me back to my original intention of establishing this institute and also reminded me of his three most important questions:

"What is your business? Who is your customer? What does the customer consider of value?" Eventually, Peter helped me avoid making a wrong decision.

Our institute was categorized in China as a "non-accredited higher education organization", i.e., we were not authorized to award degrees, while a considerable number of our students wanted to obtain a Master's Degree through our programme. In 2003, a US university was willing to partner with us to offer a joint MBA degree in China. They even agreed to my request that half of the curriculum be designed and taught by our faculties while this US university awarded the degree. I was so excited to have such a good opportunity that I rushed into negotiating specific terms of our cooperation. When Peter learned about this situation, he asked me: "Why do you need them? What do you expect them to contribute to this collaboration? Do they think they can deliver?" I answered affirmatively without hesitation. Peter went on and asked me more: "Why do they need you? Can you satisfy them? What is your contribution to the success of this collaboration? Do they value you?"

I became uncertain upon his questioning. I started to wonder if this US university was just using us to enter the China market; did they truly recognize our curriculum as they claimed, or was it just because we could recruit students for them? Or was it all of the above? While I admitted to myself that his questions were meaningful, I was too eager to accept the partnership and offer the MBA. This time Peter did not stop me from moving forward.

Three years later, at the end of our second class of the joint MBA programme, this US university, having gained a certain reputation in China from our joint programme, decided to split from us and teamed up with another Chinese state-owned university. This discontinued cooperation taught me a lesson and I always remembered that I must thoroughly think through and correctly answer those questions Peter asked prior to entering any partnership. These questions actually can diagnose if the two parties really have shared values and if their missions are compatible.

Before I met Peter, I tended to take on too many projects at one time, and Peter soon noticed my problem. I visited him one day and he said to me the moment I sat down, "My friend, you looked tired. You always kick off several different projects simultaneously. I know that you would be capable of doing most of them well, but you will not be outstanding with any of them. When was the last time you had a vacation with your wife? If you go on like this, you will be exhausted and you will upset your wife, too."

Toward the end of our conversation, Peter asked me what the most important task I had for my upcoming trip back to China. I answered that I planned to spend a week in the southern part of China to visit ten customers who had attended our courses and to get their feedback on our courses. Peter asked me to write the names of these customers on a piece of paper, then asked: "What if, after you landed, you received a phone call that you needed to shorten your trip to only four days instead of a week due to something urgent? What would you do?" I replied that I could do nothing but visit fewer customers. Peter asked me to cross out the customers that were less important. After I reduced my list per his request, Peter went on to ask, "What if you received another notice that you needed to shorten your trip further from four to two days? If you want to allow sufficient time for each customer, which customers would you visit in such a limited time?" This exercise inspired me to begin reflecting on how to cut down seemingly necessary things in order to focus on one or two of the most important projects and reserve sufficient time for those that matters.

These are just a few cases with Peter as my consultant. We can see how Peter engineered his questions in a Socratic way that guided me to discover the "real problem" behind the facade. Peter, on the other hand, could be very straightforward sometimes with powerful assertions that revealed the essence of the matter. It usually resulted in the person involved to get introspective, and eventually leads to discover the "real problem", just like what I experienced in the first case told above.

To Peter Drucker, "Asking the right question" and subsequently finding out the "real problem" are far more important than just getting the resolution. It's obvious that you would be on the wrong track and wasting your time if you institute a resolution to solve problem B when you really need to resolve problem A.

Thanks to Peter Drucker's wisdom and patience, our small institute, established 16 years ago, has become the Peter Drucker Academy in China today, providing training to more than 10,000 managers each year. Looking back, Peter's repeated question still echoes in my ears. When we bid our farewell at the end of each meeting, Peter would ask, "Was it useful to you, what I said today?" Absolutely. What Peter said was always useful, whether I then understood and accepted it or not.

About Minglo Shao

Minglo Shao is the co-founder and Chairman of the Board of Trustees of the California Institute of Advanced Management and the founder and Chairman of the Peter F. Drucker Academy and the Bright China Group in China. He was a client of Peter Drucker's from 1999 until Drucker's death in 2005. Under the personal guidance and involvement of Drucker, Minglo Shao founded the Peter F. Drucker Academy in 1999, fully committed to providing executives and entrepreneurs with practical training and education in Drucker's methods. The Academy has trained over 60,000 graduates in 33 Chinese cities plus Hong Kong. Chairman Shao has established and manages many enterprises in a number of industries. Under his leadership, the Bright China Holdings has cumulatively invested over $600 million in China.

Drucker's Consulting Goes On

By Edna Pasher, PhD

When I founded my management consulting firm in Israel, I applied Peter Drucker's principles from the very early beginning. I read all of his books and articles, and he was my source of inspiration when facing the challenges in my work. However, I never experienced his consulting directly, but I did indirectly. Through another friend, Dr Tamir Bechor, who eventually taught in the Peter F. Drucker and Masatoshi Ito Graduate School of Management, which is where Drucker taught when he was alive, I met Dr Bill Cohen, president of the California Institute of Advanced Management (CIAM). In 1979, Bill was the first graduate of the PhD programme for executives that Drucker established. Bill's new school, CIAM, not only teaches Drucker's concepts but requires all students to do pro bono consulting for real organizations, including small businesses, as well as major corporations and non-profits using Drucker's methods in every course they take for their MBA.

Two years ago, CIAM pioneered distance management consulting, and I was fortunate enough to be able to utilize this free service twice. Both engagements were with the involvement and expert help of Dr Al Randall, a former combat pilot with an MD, who received an MA from Drucker when Drucker was alive, and is also CIAM's Director of Outreach.

Of course, I had already read a lot of Drucker, and the performance and actions of the two teams that acted as our consultants confirmed important facts I had already learned about him from my reading.

1. No Retirement
Peter Drucker died at the age of 95. He worked almost to his last day. In one of his HBR articles, he explained that the concept of retiring had been created when life expectancy was less than 60 years. He saw no reason why his children should have to support him for more than 30 years! Many of my friends have already retired from work. I work as much as I have always worked and hope to work to my last day, just as Peter Drucker did.

2. Knowledge Work
Drucker is the real pioneer of Knowledge Management. I am considered the pioneer of Knowledge Management in Israel. It is from him that I gained the deep understanding of this new discipline. He coined the term "knowledge workers" and explained that they cannot be managed the way people were managed in the Industrial Age. I try to remember it as a manager and as a management consultant and try to decode the unique needs of knowledge workers as the deepest basis of my work.

3. Clear Writing Style
Peter Drucker, just as my mentor in my doctoral studies, Professor Neil Postman at NYU, wrote in a simple and clear style. They both wanted people to fully understand what they meant. I try to follow this example, avoiding unnecessary jargon and data that might make it difficult for my readers to get my main message.

4. Learning from Volunteers
Drucker understood that there is a lot to be learned from volunteer organizations for the benefit of effective management in business. I believe that good work is done with passion, just like volunteering for something you have passion for, and that the role of managers is to identify what tasks and roles their people have passion for, in order to get good results.

5. Time Management

   Drucker dealt a lot with time management, especially regarding managers. How a leader manages oneself is the toughest challenge. Effective leadership is first of all about what I do myself and how, and only then, what I delegate to others and how I do that. How I allocate my own time is more important than what I expect of others. Do I set a good example for my people? Will they like to follow me?

6. Innovation Management

   Drucker conducted research and taught, as well as consulted. These three competences are mutually beneficial. Especially in innovation management, which, following Drucker, is where my own passion lies, these core competencies are absolutely a must. Without research there is no innovation. Teaching helps one stay in touch with young people through which one understands the future. Consulting is a co-creation with people who need to solve tough problems constantly, and problem-driven innovation is the best innovation.

7. Customer focused

   Drucker wrote: "There is only one valid definition of business purpose: to create a customer." I try to remember it in everything I do. The older I get, the closer I try to get to my customers. Understanding their real needs, helping them clarify their needs, helping them design more than one solution to a problem, and analysing the benefits and disadvantages of each option are at the heart of consulting. This way my team, my business partners, including CIAM, and I see our purpose as creating customers. I am mostly proud of our loyal customers, some who have been working with us for many years, innovating and growing together.

8. The Triple Bottom Line

   Drucker said: "Although I believe in the free market, I have serious reservations about capitalism." I fully agree and have looked at the issue of "the bottom line" for a long time. In our firm we believe that organizations grow in harmony with their social and physical environments – or they die. This is why we have been involved in the challenge of sustainability and sustainable development for quite a while and focus on "Smart Cities," where we study the eco-system and help organizations engage all stakeholders for the benefit of all and not just the stockholders. We believe in commitment to the Triple Bottom Line – People, Planet, Profit – or the social, environmental, and economic bottom line. This leads to reinventing capitalism, which is a must if we want a good future for our customers and future generations!

9. Culture before Strategy

Peter Drucker said: "Culture eats strategy for breakfast." Yes! Very often strategies are not implemented because they were "eaten" by the culture of the organization. If the strategy-making process is not aligned with the culture of the organization, it will not succeed. In our work we first try to understand the organizational culture and only then identify opportunities to develop in the next strategic efforts. Sometimes we need to help our client organizations change the culture itself – which takes a long time. In this case the best way is to start with increasing the strengths of the existing culture before introducing any new ideas to adopt for more effective organizational behaviour.

All this merged into an on-going relationship with Dr Al Randall and his colleagues and classmates, during which CIAM students, acting as my consultants, helped me innovate! I was fortunate to work with Dr Randall in both cases, but the unusual thing is that Dr Randall, although he led one team and a year or so later was my prime contact on another, was not the supervising professor in either of these two engagements. The fact is, Dr Randall was also a CIAM student, completing his second master's, the MBA at CIAM, while serving as a professor and administrator. Through the engagement that he participated in with his classmates, we completed two projects together. This helped my firm penetrate the global market with online consulting and assisted our new non-profit division, The Israeli Smart Cities Institute, to penetrate a foreign market in a third country where there is a desperate need to make cities smarter.

Learning management through applying Drucker's principles, while consulting to managers of small organizations as well as giant corporations, is a unique feature of CIAM. Consulting involves research and practice – what better way to get people ready to lead in a changing environment where they have to constantly apply theory and to innovate? Now our relationship with CIAM has moved forward even another significant step. We represent CIAM in Israel, since people can now study with CIAM online in addition to in the classroom in California. Moreover, we are going to start hiring CIAM graduates, as they are already experienced consultants when they graduate, to assist us in our projects. Also, California and Israel have a lot in common – the first Silicon Valley and the second Silicon Valley and the Start-Up Nation – can thus co-create a great future inspired by and based on Peter Drucker's consulting principles. I love it!

About Edna Pasher

Edna Pasher received her PhD under world-famous Professor Neil Postman at New York University. In 1978, she founded one the leading consulting firms in Israel, Edna Pasher PhD & Associates Management Consultants, of which she remains President and CEO. In 1991, she became a Founding Partner of *Status: the Israeli Management Magazine*. Five years ago she organized the first event promoting Drucker in Israel, and Status magazine became the first major medium in Israel to devote an entire issue to Drucker. She became a "Drucker client" by proxy when two different teams of MBA students from the California Institute of Advanced Management applied Drucker's principles to two of her initiatives. Most recently she founded the non-profit International consulting firm, The Israeli Smart Cities Institute.

My Experience with the Drucker Consulting Difference

By C. William Pollard

I had the privilege of knowing Peter Drucker as an advisor, mentor, and friend. We first met in person at a Board of Directors' meeting of Herman Miller. Peter had been invited by the Chairman to come and speak to us about the growing globalization of our market and its effect on the way we should do business.

Before that time, I had read many of Peter's books and writings and we had used them extensively in our ServiceMaster training programmes for managers and leaders of the firm.

His talk to the Herman Miller Board was not in the form of a speech, but was more of a dialogue in which he sprinkled his comments with penetrating questions using the Socratic method to not only communicate knowledge, but also to test our understanding. He was a master at it. As I found out later in my one-to-one meetings with him, he would often use the same method to give advice and seek understanding with his clients.

At the end of the board meeting there was an opportunity for us to shake hands and have a personal conversation with Peter. When he discovered I was the CEO of ServiceMaster, he began asking questions about the mission of our firm. He explained that he had studied our company and also was a customer of the firm. He wanted to know more about how we as a public company implemented our unique statement of corporate objectives, "To Honour God in All We Do, To Help People Develop, To Serve with Excellence and To Grow Profitably."

He asked me if I would meet with him and (yes, he even used the word) "consult" with him about how we did it.

In our next meeting and in my many meetings with him thereafter, Peter would always reflect as a person who was as open to learning as he was teaching or advising. He never came across as one who had all the answers. I greatly benefited from his knowledge and wisdom and I brought him many challenging and difficult problems as we faced the opportunity to grow our business at a rate of 20% per year for a period of over 20 years.

As we would get deeply into issues of organizational structure, growth by acquisition into new service areas, and international expansion, he would often remind me of the importance of people development. His interest went beyond what people were doing and how they did it, it included who they were becoming. He viewed this added dimension as a primary responsibility of leadership. A favourite phrase of his was that productive people work for a cause, not just a living. His advice about people reflected his philosophy of life, which included integrating faith with learning and seeking solutions to problems.

As he provided advice and counsel, he often dealt with the specific issue at hand within a context of the broader issues of life. Yes, it was important to be effective and efficient in producing needed goods and services for the customer at a fair price and a bottom line that would create value for the shareholder. But since the success of the firm was dependent on the productivity of people, he also strongly believed that the firm should have the broader objective of becoming a moral community for the development of human character.

I found Peter to be frank and direct when he observed something that was wrong and needed correction. He was able to do this in a way that people would usually respond positively to rather than reject his advice. For me, one of these times included Peter Drucker telling our board of directors that they were all wrong when they responded to his question "what is your business?" by listing the types of services we delivered instead of recognizing the importance of the training and developing of the people delivering the service.

It also included a time he had to stop me in my tracks when I was about to make a wrong decision. He pointed out that I must be suffering from the arrogance of success with a touch of hubris if I proceeded with the decision I was proposing. He suggested my focus was on self instead of others, and it would be best for the firm and its people if I would eat some humble pie and seek a compromise that would resolve the issue. And so I did.

For me the Drucker difference in consulting included:

1. A willingness to mentor as well as consult.
2. Asking the penetrating questions that would help to clarify the issues and confirm understanding.
3. Being prepared to learn from those he advised.
4. Never ignoring the people issues and always determining whether there was a commitment to develop the whole person.
5. Encouraging a vision for the firm to be a moral community for the development of human character.
6. Seeking to develop a relationship of trust with those he advised and, when needed, to be frank about what should be changed.

Peter helped me understand that my leadership of the firm was just a means – to what end was the real question. And the end for Peter was the people that followed, the direction they were headed, and who they were becoming as they produced results for the firm.

About C. William Pollard, Esquire

Bill Pollard is Chairman of Fairwyn Investment Company and the author of two bestselling books. He served twice as Chief Executive Officer of The ServiceMaster Company, a Fortune 500 Company, and also served as chairman of the board. During his leadership of ServiceMaster, the company was recognized by *Fortune* magazine as the number-one service company among the Fortune 500 and also was included as one of its most admired companies. ServiceMaster was also identified as a "star of the future" by the *Wall Street Journal* and recognized by the *Financial Times* as "one of the most respected companies in the world". Bill Pollard is a member of the Drucker Institute Board and also CIAM's Board of Trustees.

Peter Drucker: Consulting and the Multidimensional Life

By Bruce Rosenstein

Peter Drucker was a rare individual who ranked at the top of three different professional fields: consulting, writing, and teaching. This multidimensional career was part of what he called "living in more than one world," – having a number of activities in your life so you are not over-weighted in any one area. As much success and satisfaction as he received in any one of those areas, my sense is that any one alone would not be enough for a full expression of Drucker as a person and as a professional and this clearly enhanced his role as a management consultant.

On April 11 2005, seven months to the day before he died, I interviewed him at the Drucker Archives in Claremont, California for my first book, *Living in More Than One World: How Peter Drucker's Wisdom Can Inspire and Transform Your Life.* When discussing the importance of priorities in life, he said to me, "My order of priorities is that writing comes first, teaching next, and consulting last." Yet he maintained a fluid, non-rigid way of looking at life. When I interviewed him in Los Angeles in the summer of 2002 for a feature story in *USA TODAY*, "Scandals Nothing New to Business Guru: Pioneer of Management Theory Has Seen This Cycle Before," he expressed it differently: "If you want to diagram my work, in the centre is writing, then comes consulting, then comes teaching. I've never been primarily an academic. I like to teach because that's the way I learn."

Drucker's work and learning in any of those three areas inevitably informed and strengthened the others. He built variety into his life as a whole, but also into his consulting practice. He advised business organizations, non-profits, educational institutions, and government agencies. He developed deep relationships with many of his clients. In the *USA TODAY* interview, he told me, "I keep in touch with all my clients, even if I've had no business with them for 20 years; they're still friends."

The organizations he consulted for became, in essence, laboratories for his ideas, but also laboratories to observe closely how effectively the organizations were operating, and what their potential could be. Drucker also learned a lot about the future from his interactions with clients, observing how they were creating their own futures.

Although it's true that Drucker could justify being highly selective about whom he wanted to work with, he had good reasons to turn away prospective clients. Sometimes the work did not require someone at his level. He told one company that they would be better off hiring a good accounting professor in their city. And he would not go against his principles. In the April 2005 interview, he told me that he wouldn't work with companies or organizations that wanted him "to be a hatchet man, which I refuse to do. I'm no good at it. I don't believe in it".

Because Drucker remained relevant during a very long life, people continued to want access to his thinking. Beyond that, they wanted to spend time with him, to be in his presence, trade ideas with and learn from him. During the 2002 *USA TODAY* interview, he said, "I have more consulting now than ever. I thought I had the most in non-profits. But it turned out I had an enormous amount of old, big-company clients coming back to me. European, Japanese, and American; how to reposition themselves in the world economy." With a display of subtle, sly humour, he said he enjoyed in particular working with small companies, "where you see results. My first client was General Motors; I started at the top and worked my way down". Of course he did have many large and prestigious corporate clients over the years, including General Electric and Procter and Gamble.

Yet to really get a sense of the variety of his work, it's instructive to look at the non-profit clients named in a 2013 book with a considerable amount of material about Drucker as a consultant and adviser: *Drucker: A Life in Pictures*, by Rick Wartzman, the executive director of the Drucker Institute. The clients ranged from the Girl Scouts of the USA and the American Red Cross to cultural organizations such as the Metropolitan Museum of Art and the American Symphony Orchestra League, and educational institutions like the University of Pennsylvania and the Stanford Graduate School of Business.

The variety Drucker built into his work, the attention to people, and the desire to keep achieving at an advanced age can be role-model activities for today's consultants and other knowledge workers. How can you build your brand, your body of work, and your reputation so people are willing to pay for the privilege of spending time with you? Wouldn't we all want to remain in demand for the entire span of our working lives?

About Bruce Rosenstein

Bruce Rosenstein has spent the last 20 years studying, writing and speaking about Peter Drucker, including an extensive personal interview Rosenstein conducted in Drucker's home, one of the last taped interviews Drucker granted prior to his death. Rosenstein's work has resulted in hundreds of articles, blogs, speeches, and two best-selling books: *Living in More Than One World: How Peter Drucker's Wisdom Can Inspire and Transform Your Life* and *Create Your Future the Peter Drucker Way*. Prior to this, he spent 21 years preparing for this role working for *USA Today* as a librarian researcher and writer of business and management books. In April 2011 he became the managing editor of the award-winning *Leader-to-Leader Journal* of the Frances Hesselbein Leadership Institute.

The Consultant Called Drucker

By Rick Wartzman

Bill Cohen has pointed out, quite correctly, that "despite his extraordinary success," Peter Drucker "did not establish a major consulting organization supporting or expanding his activities. There was and is no 'Drucker Consulting Group' or 'Drucker and Associates,' or 'Drucker LTD'".

That said, the entity that I have the pleasure and privilege of leading – the Drucker Institute at Claremont Graduate University – is what Drucker did leave behind to carry on his work. And, sure enough, our activities today include consulting for a variety of major companies across a range of industries: technology, retailing, manufacturing, and more.

Moving into consulting has been part of an eight-year process in which we've evolved from Drucker's dusty archives to become an active social enterprise with a mission of "strengthening organizations to strengthen society".

For us, then, figuring out what made Drucker so sought-after as an adviser to corporate, non-profit, and government executives has been more than a matter of academic interest. It has been the foundation upon which we've built a business.

What we've come to understand – and have made the core of our own consulting work – is that Drucker didn't see his job as serving up answers. "My greatest strength as a consultant," he once remarked, "is to be ignorant and ask a few questions."

In Drucker's case, as in ours, these questions are often deceptively simple: Who is your customer? What are you going to stop doing (to free up resources for more highly productive and innovative projects)? What business are you in? Or, as he urged the founders of the investment bank, Donaldson, Lufkin & Jenrette, to ask themselves in 1974, after they had enjoyed a heady period of growth: "What should your business be?"

"I shall not attempt to answer the question of what your business should be," Drucker added. "First, one should not answer such a question off the top of one's head. Secondly, one man's opinion, no matter how brilliant, is at best one man's opinion."

Other times, corporations sought Drucker's counsel to deal with narrower challenges. In 1992, for example, he wrote a 56-page analysis for Coca-Cola that explored distribution, branding, and advertising. Still, the approach was always the same: "This report raises questions," Drucker told Coke. "It does not attempt to give answers."

We've also come to appreciate the delicate personal balance that Drucker struck as a consultant. He enjoyed close relationships with many of the CEOs and other executives with whom he worked – "Whatever problem a client has is my problem," Drucker declared – but he would never be mistaken (or mistake himself) for an insider.

"The professional needs commitment to the client's cause... but he must stay free of involvement," Drucker explained in a 1981 essay titled "Why Management Consultants." "He must not himself be a part of the problem." In the end, Drucker asserted, "The management consultant brings to the practice of management what being professional requires: detachment."

Another thing that made Drucker stand apart was his integrity. He wouldn't come in, do a job, and bill a client without knowing whether he had made a real difference. "Remember," Drucker told the assistant to the chairman of Sears, as he turned in an invoice in March 1955, "that this is submitted on condition that there is no payment due unless the work satisfies you."

Indeed, Drucker knew that the test wasn't whether he had delivered some sharp insight. All that counted was whether his client could use that insight to make measurable progress on an important issue. It's the performance of others, Drucker wrote, that "determines in the last analysis whether a consultant contributes and achieves results, or whether he is … at best a court jester".

For our part, we work hard to follow up with our clients and make sure that we've delivered genuine value through our consulting practice, which we've dubbed "Drucker Un/Workshops". (They are so named because, through these engagements, we look to catalyze the understanding that will get executives unlocked on a crucial challenge or opportunity).

Finally, Drucker knew that the most dangerous thing for any consultant was to become too impressed with his own wisdom. We try to be very mindful of this and never pretend to know more about an executive's business than the executive does.

Drucker didn't like his clients getting carried away, either. "Stop talking about 'Druckerizing' your organization," he told officials at Edward Jones, the investment firm. "The job ahead of you is to 'Jonesize' your organization – and only if you accept this would I be of any help to you. Otherwise, I would rapidly become a menace – which I refuse to be."

We hew to this very same principle today. We put our clients through all sorts of exercises in which we provide Drucker-based frameworks. But we never try to "Druckerize" them. That's because we know that they'll only get results when they take our ideas – Drucker's ideas – and make them fit their own organizational culture.

For as Drucker said, "I can only ask questions. The answers have to be yours."

About Rick Wartzman

Rick Wartzman is the Executive Director of the Drucker Institute at Claremont Graduate University and the author and editor of five books, including *What Would Drucker Do Now?* and *The Drucker Lectures.* Previously Wartzman was a writer and editor at the *Wall Street Journal* and the *Los Angeles Times.* Though he continues to write periodic columns on Drucker for such magazines as *Time* and *BusinessWeek,* he himself became a business manager as well as a curator, a leader of professional researchers, a professional speaker, an educator. He is one of the few management consultants able to apply Drucker's principles – occasionally uniquely uncovered – directly from the original sources found in the extensive archives willed to the Institute by Peter Drucker and his family.

Index

Index

Index

An Introduction to
William A. Cohen

Dr William A. Cohen, was the first graduate of the doctoral programme that Peter Drucker co-founded. What Drucker taught him changed his life. Shortly after graduating, Cohen was recommissioned in the Air Force and rose to the rank of major general. Eventually he became a full professor, management consultant, and the author of more than 50 books, while maintaining a nearly lifelong friendship with his former professor. In 2009 he was named a Distinguished Alumnus by Drucker's school, Claremont Graduate University, and two years later he co-founded the non-profit California Institute of Advanced Management with the mission of offering affordable graduate degrees based on Drucker's principles. He served as its president from 2010-2016. He now serves as president of the Institute of Leader Arts, an international training and consulting company.

He can be reached at **w.cohen@stuffof heroes.com.**